• THE LORE OF
CYCLING

Gary Beneke • Mark Beneke • Tim Noakes • Mary Reynolds

with contributions by
John Stegmann and Louis Reynolds

Oxford University Press
Cape Town
1989

26/11

Oxford University Press
Walton Street, Oxford OX2 6DP, United Kingdom

OXFORD   NEW YORK   TORONTO
DELHI   BOMBAY   CALCUTTA   MADRAS   KARACHI
PETALING JAYA   SINGAPORE   HONG KONG   TOKYO
NAIROBI   DAR ES SALAAM   CAPE TOWN
MELBOURNE   AUCKLAND

AND ASSOCIATED COMPANIES IN
BERLIN   IBADAN

ISBN 0 19 570548 3

© Oxford University Press 1989

Front cover photograph: Jac de Villiers
Back cover photographs: top, Shawn Benjamin
bottom, Neil Herman
Front endpaper: *The Argus*
Back endpaper: Eugene Parsons
Design of cover and book: Su Hart

Oxford is a trademark of Oxford University Press

Published by Oxford University Press Southern Africa,
Harrington House, Barrack Street, Cape Town, 8001, South Africa

Printed and bound by Clyson Printers, Maitland, Cape.

CONTENTS

THE AUTHORS

Mark Beneke is well known as one of South Africa's top racers. He has been South African Amateur Road and Track Champion, has Springbok colours and has spent three years racing in Europe. He now rides as a professional member of the Southern Sun/M-Net cycling team. Perhaps the greatest of his many victories was when he won South Africa's major stage race, the Rapport Tour in 1985. When he is not on a bicycle, he works as a pharmacist.

Gary Beneke, Mark's younger brother, began cycling competitively when he was twelve, gave up when he was thirteen, and re-entered the fray at sixteen. He went on to become a Springbok cyclist, and he now rides as a professional in the powerful Southern Sun/M-Net team. He has won numerous major races, the most important being the 1988 Rapport Tour. He is on the coaching committee of the South African Cycling Federation and is a qualified masseur. His articles on cycling appear regularly in *The Star* newspaper and he is a consultant for *Tri-Cycling* magazine.

Tim Noakes is Liberty Life Professor of Exercise and Sport Science at Cape Town University's Medical School. He is Director of the Bioenergetics of Exercise Research Unit, funded by the Medical Research Council and the University of Cape Town. He is an active runner and cyclist, and is well known for his research into marathon running. He is the author of *The Lore of Running* (Oxford University Press).

Mary Reynolds uses her bicycle for keeping fit, for utility trips and for touring. She once ran the Pedal Power magazine, and now works as an editor.

Contributors:

John Stegmann is a founder member of the Western Province Pedal Power Association (and is now an Honorary Life Member). He helped to get the first Argus Cycle Tour off the ground. He is an architect, a designer and builder of recumbent bicycles, and a member of the International Human Powered Vehicle Association.

Louis Reynolds is a paediatrician who uses a bicycle for training and getting to work on. Though he alternates between two racing bikes, he has a special interest in the utility bike's potential as an instrument for urban change.

ACKNOWLEDGEMENTS

The authors and publishers would like to thank the numerous people who have given generously of their time and advice and helped with the writing of this book. In the space available, it would be impossible to mention all who have helped, but we would in particular like to thank the following: Louis de Waal and John Wilmot of the Pedal Power Foundation, Harry Bairstow, Bruce Pickering-Dunn, Gus Ferguson, Basil Cohen, Gotty Hansen, Gill and David Goldkorn, Alex Selkirk of Chris Willemse Cycles, Paul Vesely, Paul Krige, Bill Horne of Deale and Huth for permission to use Shimano material, Mark du Plessis of Cape Cycle Systems, Derrick Coetzer of Philamy Importers and Exporters, France, for access to Mavic and Wolber material, D.R. Maree, Ian Grayson, Thea Hughes, Steve Black, Eugene Parsons, Su Hart and Peter Hill. We are grateful to Douglas Malewicki for permission to use his performance comparisons and aerodynamic drag charts, and to Dr Chet Kyle on whose data much of the information in these charts (and other parts of the book) are based. Special thanks are due to Neil Bramwell and Louis Reynolds for their help.

Picture credits:

The unlisted line drawings are by Lawrence Bolel, Euan Waugh and Michelle Saffer.

While every effort has been made to trace and acknowledge copyright holders, this has not always been possible. The publishers would be pleased to be told of any errors and to correct them in the event of a reprinting of this book.
'SU' stands for Source Unknown.

Page 1, left, *The Argus;* right, Rob Kamhoot. Page 2, top, Shawn Benjamin; centre, Neil Herman, bottom, Ollie Hughes. Page 3, top and bottom, Mark van Aardt. Page 4, Shawn Benjamin. Page 5, Marc du Plessis/Cannondale. Page 7, Mono Pumps (Pty) Ltd. Page 9, Louis de Waal. Page 10, Ian Grayson. Page 11, W. Gronen. Pages 13 - 15, Africana Museum. Page 16, SU. Page 17, bottom, S A Museum. Page 18 & 19, Africana Museum. Page 20,top, SU. Page 21, top, Africana Museum, bottom, *The Hub*. Page 22 & 23, SU. Page 24 & 25, Raleigh, South Africa. Page 26, Africana Museum. Page 27 & 30, Jac de Villiers. Page 35, SU. Page 36, top, Mark du Plessis/Cannondale. Page 37, Francois du Toit. Photographs on pages 38, 41, 43, 44, 45, 46, 47, 48, Jac de Villiers. Page 53, top left, Mark du Plessis/Cannondale; top right, Afrapix; bottom left, *The Argus,* bottom right, Jac de Villiers (Soweto bike by Makubhela). Page 54, John Heard. Page 55, top pictures, Jac de Villiers; bottom, Ian Grayson/Bruce Steer. Page 56, Image Bank. Page 57, Jac de Villiers. Page 58, Ollie Hughes. Page 59, John Wilmot. Page 60, top, Marc du Plessis/Cannondale; bottom, Shawn Benjamin. Page 61, Jac de Villiers. Page 62, *The Argus*. Page 63, top left, *The Argus;* right, Keith and Milda Baxter. Page 64, Charles Baillie. Page 65, top and bottom, John Stegmann. Photographs, Page 67 & 68, Jac de Villiers. Page 75, Mark du Plessis/Cannondale. Page 79, *The Argus*. Page 81 & 82, Jac de Villiers. Page 87, John Heard. Page 89, Jac de Villiers. Page 99, David Kramer (photograph by Tony Meintjes). Page 108, Gary Beneke. Page 109, top, Shawn Benjamin; bottom, Mark du Plessis/Cannondale. Page 118, Derrick Coetzer/Philamy. Page 121 - 123, W. Gronen. Page 124 - 125, John Stegmann. Page 126, top, Glen Brown; bottom, IHPVA. Page 127, Coroma Doors. Page 130 - 132, John Stegmann. Page 135, C. Kyle. Page 136, Jac de Villiers. Page 137, *The Argus*. Page 169, *The Argus*. Page 170, top and bottom, Africana Museum. Page 171 & 172, Harry Bairstow. Page 175, 176, 177, *The Argus*. Page 178, Gary Beneke. Page 180, *Rapport*. Pages 181, 182, Louis Reynolds. Page 186, Gus Ferguson for poem, 'Hinault's not what he's missing'. Page 189, Gary Beneke. Page 190, 203, 205 & 209, *The Argus*. Page 210 & 11, *Beeld*. Page 214, 216 & 219, *The Argus*. Page 220 John Heard. Page 222 & 225, *Beeld*. Page 226, top, SU, bottom Gary Beneke. Page 227,228, 231, Shawn Benjamin. Page 233, left, Shawn Benjamin; right, Steve Black. Page 235, Shawn Benjamin. Page 238, Ollie Hughes. Page 239, Bruce Pickering-Dunn. Page 240, Eugene Parsons. Page 241, Steve Black. Page 242 & 243, Ollie Hughes. Page 244, top and bottom, Doug Jamieson. Page 245 Gill de Vlieg, Afrapix. Page 246, Shawn Benjamin. Page 248, Jac de Villiers. Page 250, Shawn Benjamin. Page 251, Jac de Villiers. Page 252, Ian Smith, Holdfast products. Page 253, Shawn Benjamin. Page 266, Jac de Villiers. Page 255, Derrick Coetzer/Philamy, France, and Wolber Tyres.

CHAPTER ONE

WHO RIDES BICYCLES
and why

The bicycle is a triumph of simplicity and efficiency: relative to its mass, nothing else moves further or faster for the amount of energy consumed. It is the greenest of machines, making almost no demands on the earth's resources. In the typical urban traffic scene, the bicycle is often faster than a Ferrari, yet it is as quiet as the flight of a dove. It is little wonder that more people in the world depend on bicycles than on any other form of transport.

A bicycle has been Gracious Mbina's chief means of transport for most of his working life. He commutes with considerable flair on a red supine recumbent bike, covering several thousand kilometres a year between his job and his home. As with the heavy black utility bike which he rode for many years, he has an easy-going respect for it as an invigorating, efficient and inexpensive way of getting about.

Mark Gordon is an amateur racer who sees his ultra-lightweight racing bicycle as a consummate fusion of art and high tech-

nology. He has spent a lot of money on it, and much of his life revolves around training on it, competing on it, looking after it and talking about it. He seldom risks using it for utility trips in case it gets damaged or stolen.

Andrea Maritz's bicycle is a multi-purpose touring vehicle on which she collects milk and bread from the local shop and does sociable, longish rides at week-ends. She has cycled through Greece and France with her husband and their ten and twelve-year old sons. They are all keen to do another bike tour abroad — perhaps in Asia next time — but first they plan to get mountain bikes and to explore some of the wilderness areas of southern Africa.

With such different reasons for riding bikes, it's not often that these three cyclists are likely to cross one anothers' paths. But they come close to it at the Argus/M-Net Cycle Tour, an annual celebration of bicycling that all three, along with thousands of others, ride each year.

The Argus/M-Net Cycle Tour

Said to be the biggest event of its kind in the southern hemisphere, Cape Town's Argus Tour has grown to be a major event since its modest beginnings in 1978. In that year 550 riders gathered at the starting line and waited for an improvised cannon to signal the start of the 104-kilometre ride around the Cape Peninsula. The cannon exploded and blew to pieces, but the Tour was on, and it marked the lift-off of what was to become a major bicycle boom. By 1989 the number of riders gathered at the starting line had grown to over 12 000.

The first Argus Tour was arranged by the newly-formed Pedal Power Association to popularise cycling and to show traffic authorities and road planners that bikes were a realistic means of transport that deserved proper facilities. It is now the main event (but by no means the only one) by which the popularity of recreational cycling and amateur racing in South Africa are measured.

The Tour has all the ingredients for attracting thousands of people on bikes. Its route is through the breathtaking coast and mountain scenery of the Cape Peninsula. There are almost no entry requirements — anyone on a human-powered vehicle can enter. Finally, it successfully combines the competitive elements of a hotly contested race with the easy mood of an energetic but unhurried morning's cycling; it all depends on how you choose to ride it.

In many ways the formula has worked. The Tour draws the country's top riders, who, in a special category for racers, power their way from the start in a quietly whirring, brilliantly-coloured pack of energy. In their wake comes a vast assortment of cyclists: there are the young and athletic; there are yuppies on expensive machines flashing with exotic labels, grannies with bells and baskets on their bikes, and more grannies in black lycra shorts, doing impressive justice to their lightweight racers. Children as young as six have ridden it, and a father has done the Tour on a tandem with his four-year old son as a stoker. A one-legged rider has reached the finish, and every year several blind cyclists ride it on the backs of tandems. In addition to attracting new people to the pleasures of cycling, the Tour has inspired retired riders to get back into the saddle: Ted Clayton, an Empire Games and Olympic medallist of the 1930s who had long since hung up his wheels returned to cycling with renewed zest in his seventies and ex-Scottish road racing champion, Andy Wilson, rode the Argus Tour in the incredible time of 3 hours

The Argus/M-Net Cycle Tour, when thousands of cyclists take over the Cape Peninsula's roads.

3

51 minutes when he was 80. The Tour has also been used by a designer of recumbent bicycles as a testing ground for his machines against conventional bikes; at the time of going to press, the course record is held by a streamlined recumbent.

The Tour has succeeded admirably in popularising the bicycle as sporting equipment. But, ironically, the campaign has, in a way, overshot its mark. For though the roads now teem with recreational and racing cyclists sleekly crouched over high quality bicycles, and cycling now has the status of an upmarket sport, this has only brought us a little closer to what was perhaps the main reason behind the Argus Tour — to win approval for, and get, better facilities for commuters and recreational riders. The vision was a utilitarian and aesthetic one: landscaped bikepaths in green cities where people could enjoy their sport all the way to work and back if they wanted to. Where building separate bikepaths was impractical, it was hoped that road design would be adapted in ways sympathetic to the needs of cyclists, making it safer and more convenient for them to share roads with motor traffic.

Pedal Power Associations

In the decade following the first Argus Tour, no less than eight regional Pedal Power Associations with a total of about 20 000 members have been formed in South Africa. (They are listed in the Appendix.) Most are active in encouraging cycling and have busy diaries of events. Apart from well-known one-day events like Johannesburg's Star 100 and the Eastern Cape's Herald Cycle Tour there is now an abundance of organised fun rides, weekends away and tours. The most ambitious of these is the Natal Pedal Power Association's ride across southern Africa, which starts in the humid Indian Ocean port of Durban, crosses the Drakensberg mountains and arid stretches of Namibia and ends at Port Nolloth on the Atlantic. (It is hoped that this will be an annual ride and that it will lead to the first of many mapped routes to which other cyclists will have access in future.)

The bicycle's world-wide popularity

South Africa's bike boom is only part of a far wider global surge in the demand for pedal power. Over 100 million bicycles are manufactured annually, and more people travel by bicycle than by any other form of transport.

In Third World conditions, the bicycle has long been the most practical and affordable vehicle for most people, and it is likely to remain so for a long time to come.

But interestingly, it is in developed countries that the main growth of the past two decades has occurred. This is partly because people want to be fit, whereas twenty years ago few knew (or cared) that exercise was a solution to their pent-up stress, incompetent hearts and spreading waistlines. The growth was also helped by environmentalists concerned with improving the quality of life in traffic-ravaged cities.

Another factor has been the vastly improved quality and variety of cycling equipment available: you can get anything from a smooth-moving, streamlined racer to a tough and agile mountain bike. The bike is no longer seen as a backward and painful way of getting about, but as an exhilarating, efficient product of functional design and elegant technology. (When Oxford University Press, Southern Africa, issued a book on bicycles in the 1960s, it was taken for granted that it could only be aimed at thrifty owners of utilitarian machines; the result was a suitably humble 32-page volume titled *You and your Bicycle*, published in a series with *You and your Washing* and *You and your Ironing and Mending*. This time we are writing for people who buy bicycles for adventure, for the thrill of speed, and for the sheer enjoyment of superb equipment, no less than for their amazing practicality.)

An important result of the recreational cycling boom is that enlightened transport planners in some parts of the world — particularly the more sophisticated countries in the developed world — are now sensitive to the needs of cyclists when they devise their road schemes. Though these planners are still in the minority, they have helped to demonstrate that the bike is an appropriate and efficient commuter vehicle and that, together with good public transport, it could help to counter the world's over-dependence on clogged and polluted motor transport systems. (Paradoxically, there is sometimes surprisingly little recognition of its usefulness by planners of the developing world's transport policies: to quote an article that appeared in the Friends of the Earth news magazine, 'In a major World Bank study on China's transport system, where hundreds of millions commute daily on bicycles, the word "bicycle" did not appear once.')

The versatile all-terrain bicycle (mountain bicycle) is at the forefront of the bicycle boom in many countries. Though designed primarily for off-road riding, it makes a dependable commuting and touring bike.

The bicycle's efficiency

Scientists have shown that the rider-and-bicycle combination makes more economical use of energy than any other animal or machine, and the *New Encyclopaedia Britannica* describes the bike as 'the most efficient means yet devised to convert human energy into propulsion.' A cyclist on a light bike covering about 30 kilometres in an hour uses about 2 500 kilojoules — about as much fuel as the average cheese sandwich provides. By comparison, a walker would take about five hours to cover the same distance and would burn about four times as much fuel. You can also look at the bike's efficiency as R. E. Williams did when he calculated that a cyclist can cover about 536 kilometres on the food energy equivalent of a litre of petrol.

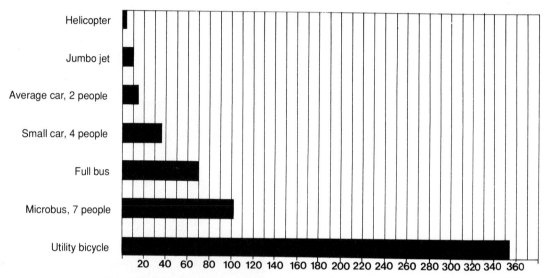

Passenger kilometres covered for the equivalent of a litre of petrol. Note that the bike here is a utility bike: depending on conditions, a cyclist on a light racer could cover over 500 kilometres on the energy equivalent of a litre of petrol.

Bicycles, ecology, cities and people

Furthermore, unlike the car, lorry and bus, the bike does not belch fumes and carcinogens into our air. It takes a tiny slice of parking and road space; both its manufacture and its running make the most modest of demands on the earth's resources; it can pay for itself in a matter of months if it is used instead of other transport; it is quiet, and for the average urban trip of up to eight kilometres, it is usually faster than cars or public transport (if you measure the trips door to door); it cruises tranquilly past the worst of traffic snarl-ups, keeping its rider fit and energized all the while.

As Stuart Wilson, Professor of Engineering at Oxford University once said at a symposium on Transport Technology and Social Change, 'The successful use of bicycle technology is easily explained:'It is because it is technology on a human scale, ergonomically sound, lightweight and efficient, both structurally and mechanically. Hence it tends to solve problems rather than create them, unlike the motor car, an example of technology on an inhuman scale, which tends to cause problems wherever it is in large scale use.'

The bike's potential importance in urban and other eco-systems becomes clear when you consider the following: 'Six million cars are scrapped in the U.S.A. alone, *every year*. How much acid rain is caused and valuable resources used in order to support such consumption? For it is consumption that is at the heart of the environmental crisis, nothing else. And the locomotive force, the prime mover in the economy which keeps consumption rising is the ever-increasing motor-ization of society — along with its multitude of by-products.' (Ian Grayson in *Freewheeling*, December 1986.)

It is the hidden costs of the world's 350 million motor vehicles that are far more horrifying than the financial costs of buying and running them: it is the contribution they make to the 'greenhouse effect' — a process that seriously threatens the future of the planet; it is the carnage on roads, the noise, the fact that between a fifth and a third of the land space in modern inner cities is given over to asphalt roads or concrete parking spaces, and that cities are shaped more by the needs of the car-owner than by ordinary people who want safe, green spaces for children to play, cheap, easy access to their places of work, and quietness. Consider this example of how distorted planning can be: at the time of writing, plans are being mooted in Cape Town to build a R12 million under-ground parking place to accomodate a mere 250 cars — in a city where tens of thousands of families are without proper housing.

It is easy to fall into a trap of thinking that it is too late and too difficult to change our present transport systems in favour of others that are more equitable and that are environmentally and ecologically less damaging. Change may be inconvenient, true. But living with the consequences of not changing may well be intolerable. For as ecologists warn with increasing seriousness, the need to change the way we live is a real, urgent issue that we have to address now if we want this fragile planet to sustain future generations.

It is not romantic or unrealistic to think that the bicycle could, along with other technology, be an important instrument for change: in some modern European and Japanese cities facilities that make bicycling safer and more convenient have resulted in 20 to 50 per cent of all trips being done on bicycles, with measurably beneficial effects on the environment.

Pedal powered technology

Pedal power doesn't stop at providing transport. It has been harnessed to provide cheap energy to perform many other tasks such as cutting wood, grinding corn, threshing rice and pumping water. With a bike fitted with a special attachment, a person can produce 100 watts of energy an hour, and operate small-scale processing machines far more cheaply than by using conventional machinery. Furthermore, the bicycle can still be used for transport.

The Mono Pedal Pump was designed at Wits University and is manufactured commercially. A person pedalling at 60 revolutions per minute can use it to pump about 2,5 to 3 cubic metres of water in an hour, which is probably less time than it takes the average rural woman to fetch a few litres of household water each day. A simple but robust chain drive in a number of ratios ensures that a variety of head conditions can be catered for.

Making room for the bicycle

Getting official approval for systems of safe urban bikeways was one of the main ambitions of some of the early Pedal Power committee members when they started promoting cycling in the late 1970s. But the authorities felt there were not enough cyclists to warrant the changes. In response, cyclists argued that the safe facilities would have to come first and that the bicyclists would follow.

Examples of transport systems which had been adapted to make room for the bicycle already existed in several countries, and there was much to learn from these. Some were impressive successes: In Stevenage, an English New Town built after World War 2, a sensitively-designed cycleway system ensured that anyone could get virtually anywhere on a bicycle without having to share a road with motor traffic; predictably, it resulted in many people using bikes for pleasure and for getting to the shops and to work. An older example is Amsterdam, where the great majority of the population own and use bicycles and are encouraged to do so by a sane system of road planning that discriminates positively in the cyclists' favour. As Nick Crane writes of the city in his book, *Cycling in Europe*, 'You only have to imagine what would happen to Amsterdam if all those cyclists changed to cars, to realise what went wrong with Europe's other cities.'

But other examples of bike planning were disappointing compromises that were all too often the results of non-cycling planners paying lip service to people's needs; many were built less with the needs of cyclists in mind than with the desire of motorists to have bicycle-free roads. One of the biggest risks of introducing bikeways is that cyclists could be banned from using the main roads, and be condemned to narrow, poorly-serviced tracks instead. Consequently cyclists have often found it easier, safer even, to go back to sharing roads with cars. In fact the trend among most bicycle activists now is towards better integration of cyclists in the general traffic scheme rather than with separate but inferior facilities.

Cyclists' facilities in South Africa

In this country, the first explorations into building bike paths were made in Cape Town; initially there were hopes that a landscaped, car-free cycleway linking the suburbs with the city would be approved. Plans were drawn up and the issue was debated at length, but eventually was blocked. Instead, some areas, notably Randburg, Cape Town's southern suburbs and Pretoria got bike lanes designed for scholars in predominantly white, high-income suburbs. Despite their lack of continuity these have done much to improve rush-hour commuter cycling in those areas, though at quiet times of day, most cyclists move back onto the roads. Along the Cape Town network, bicycle use has increased by about 25 per cent.

As part of the same project, well-made, cheaply rented lockers for bicycles were installed at some Cape Peninsula railway stations to encourage bike/train commuting. Demand is high, but the few dozen lockers available are not enough to make any significant difference to commuter patterns. (In Tokyo, by comparison, computer-operated multi-storey bicycle parking facilities at railway stations encourage 1,3 million people to cycle part of the way to work each day.)

While a very few select areas in this country are enjoying good bike facilities, and in general an awareness of cyclists' needs is beginning to influence road design, things have worsened for many of South Africa's veteran bicycle commuters. Apartheid ideology has forced working class communities (and these include many people whose only personal transport is bicycles) so far from their work places that it has become impractical for them to cycle to their jobs. These are cyclists who needed no Argus Tour to convince them of the bike's value; they know nothing of bike booms but a lot about cycling's cheapness and convenience.

Trade figures bear this out: the numbers of bikes sold in this country have, contrary to popular belief, remained fairly static over the past 20 years. (About 400 000 are sold annually.) But the proportion of roadsters to racing and other high quality bikes has changed: ten years ago, about 10 per cent of bikes sold were high quality, and 90 per cent were utility and school bikes. Now about half of bikes sold are utility bikes and half are expensive, high quality machines.

Top: An urban demonstration project in which cyclists can travel safely and conveniently, The Hague. Bottom, left: A cycleway near Haarlem. This forms part of the Netherlands' 22 000-kilometre network of urban and rural bikeways. What happens when a country is as bicycle-friendly as this? In the Netherlands, there are 13 million bicycles to a population of 14,6 million, and 11 billion kilometres a year are travelled by bike. 80 per cent of students and a third of commuters travel by bicycle, and more than half of daily shopping is done on bikes. The Dutch also use bikes for leisure, riding about 65 million kilometres a year during holidays in foreign countries. According to a recent survey, '90 per cent of Dutch people are 100 per cent in favour of bikes.'

Bottom, right: Part of Cape Town's demonstration project.

The future

A question often asked in the bike trade is 'How long will the boom last?' In the century since the bike was invented, the bike has several times risen to pinnacles of popularity only to subside back into lowly status as a workhorse for children and the poor. But if the examples of other countries which have integrated bike use into daily life are anything to go by, there is every reason to believe that this boom could be different and that bike use will go from strength to strength. That is provided that cyclists' organisations and traders and road planners put as much energy into bringing good bikes into mainstream use as they have into popularising them as exciting but exclusive sporting equipment.

A utilitarian but efficient long wheelbase bike designed to be maneoevrable and stable when carrying loads.

CHAPTER TWO

BICYCLES
and their BEGINNINGS

The invention of the bicycle in the nineteenth century had an explosive impact on society and on industry: it made independent, convenient transport available to the masses for the first time; it gave rich and poor the freedom of the countryside; adventurers circled the world on it; and it was even taken up as a symbol of liberation by Victorian feminists. The early bicycle factories became the base of a vast transport industry that was later to manufacture the automobile and the aeroplane.

The first bicycles to reach South Africa in any numbers arrived in the 1870s; they were examples of those extraordinary machines which were called ordinaries or high-wheelers in their day, but which are better known to us as penny farthings.

The ordinary was, in its time, the culmination of over half a century of fairly sporadic experimentation with human-powered transport. Though the ancestors of the bicycle probably go back to pre-Christian vehicles propelled by hand-cranks and to hobby-horses used in medieval revels, it wasn't until the early nineteenth century that the bicycle began to take shape in anything like the form in which we know it.

The draisienne.

In 1816 Karl von Drais de Sauerbrun, a German baron, produced a prototype which became known as the *draisienne*. It was an improvement on early hobby-horse designs and consisted of a steerable (but not always stoppable) wooden structure with a pivoting front wheel linked to a rear wheel by a beam with a seat on it. The rider moved by scooting along with his feet. Though Drais tried to promote his invention as a utility vehicle, the *draisienne* had little more than a frivolous appeal: for several years it was fashionable with young blades who cavorted through the streets of London and Paris on copies of it, but it was also the butt of heartless ridicule by cartoonists. The craze died. The disappointed Drais had, however, made an elementary but important point: in regularly averaging speeds of 13 kilometres an hour, he'd demonstrated that on a machine of this kind a person could, on the rare good roads that existed, move much further and faster than on foot and enjoy greater independence than the horse or any other form of transport offered at the time. In England, a copy of his machine won a London-to-Brighton race against a four-horse coach by half an hour.

About 25 years later a Scottish blacksmith, Kirkpatrick Macmillan, came nearer to building something like the bicycle we know: his *velocipede* had front-mounted cranks, which the rider swung back and forth with his feet to move a pair of treadles which turned the back wheel. He proved something that must, at the time, have seemed improbable, namely that it was possible to propel a two-wheeled contraption with both feet off the ground without falling off. Macmillan won a race against a post carriage on his invention, but, like other experimental variations that appeared over the next two decades, his velocipede wasn't practical enough to have mass appeal.

A historic breakthrough was made in 1861 in the Paris workshop of the Michaux perambulator-building company. Possibly inspired by the workings of cranks on a vertical grindstone, the Michauxs produced a velocipede driven by pedals attached to the front axle. Though built of wood and iron and weighing about 27 kilograms, their machine was, by the standards of the day, light and graceful, and when it was shown at the Paris World Exhibition in 1867, it was an instant success. By 1865 the Michauxs' annual production of *boneshakers*, as the British chose to call them, had reached 400; two years later the same factory was turning out 200 machines a day.

Bicycle racing, which proved to have spectacular advertising value for manufacturers, began in 1868; in the following year a Michaux boneshaker won the first long-distance bicycle race on record. The race drew about 200 riders — five of them women — and the winner covered the 123-kilometre Paris-Rouen course in under ten and a half hours.

Further glamour was lent to the boneshaker by the Prince Imperial who rode through Paris on a rosewood and aluminium-bronze model.

Soon several manufacturers of note were working on bicycle design. The Paris Bicycle Show of 1869 revealed several important technical advances: there were lighter all-metal bicycles with tubular frames, ball-bearings, simple freewheel devices and gears, and solid rubber tyres had replaced iron rims. In the same year, tensioned wire spokes began to replace rigid iron struts.

Interest in bicycles was spreading; by now they were being manufactured in America, and even in the Cape Colony several blacksmiths were at work building velocipedes. In 1870 a Pietermaritzburg firm imported several, which the *Natal Witness* described as 'extraordinary locomotives' calling for 'a great deal of curiosity and inspection'. The first person to regularly use a bike in Pietermaritzburg was the lamplighter, who did his rounds on a bike, but his progress along the streets was hampered by boys having rides on it. In 1871 a farmer called Manning stunned the Natal colonists by cycling from Harrismith to Pietermaritzburg.

The high-wheeler or ordinary

War in Europe interrupted the development of French bicycle design, and the 1870s saw British inventiveness (with a fair measure of eccentricity) take over. Much of the credit belonged to James Starley, who was a foreman at the Coventry Sewing Machine Company when it began making Michaux velocipedes for the British and French markets. Regarded as the father of the British bicycle industry,

Kirkpatrick Macmillan's velocipede, built in 1839, was the first rear-wheel driven bicycle. Macmillan was fined five shillings for knocking down a child on it.

Starley was one of several people who, coupling their creativity with the explosion of new manufacturing techniques and materials that the Industrial Revolution had brought about, set out to improve on the French bicycle designs. In addition to the boneshaker, the French had developed a bicycle which had a large wheel at the front and a small one at the rear. The design was based on the logic that if one turn of the pedals caused one turn of the wheel, it followed that the larger the wheel was, the faster the bicycle would be. (Before the era of the ordinary was over, front wheel diameters were to reach 60 inches and more.) Starley improved on the *high-wheeler* by developing a gear that made the wheel revolve twice for each turn of the pedals and introducing light wheels with hollow iron rims and spokes under tension. He later replaced radial spoking with tangential spoking to resist torque. These bicycles weighed about 20 kilograms, but track racing models that weighed less than half of that were also built. *Ordinaries* caused enormous excitement among those who were adventurous and acrobatic enough to ride them. By 1877 there were at least 50 000 in England. Clubs were formed in Britain and America and as far afield as China, India, Australia and South Africa, where the first club was rallied to meetings in Cape Town's Greenmarket Square by a bugler.

Top: The first practical and popular bicycle was designed in the Michaux workshop, Paris, in 1861. The English called these bicycles boneshakers, and one Frenchman described them as resembling 'the ghosts of departed spiders'. This one was photographed in St. George's Street, Cape Town in 1874.
Left: James Moore on an early, radially spoked high-wheeler in 1874. Moore had won the world's first road race on a Michaux bicycle in 1868.

13

ACROSS SOUTH AFRICA ON A BICYCLE.

It was unusual for women or children to ride high-wheelers; this family very likely earned a living as performing cyclists.

Johannesburg Amateur Bicycle Club.

By 1879 a rider of an ordinary had covered 160 kilometres in well under eight hours, and another had rolled over 406 kilometres in a day. The crowning achievement was Thomas Stevens' ride around the world on an ordinary: he pedalled eastwards out of San Francisco in 1884, and returned in 1887, via Europe, the Middle East and Asia, having covered 21 600 kilometres.

To the public, the clubs who took to their wheels at weekends were seen as a menace. Horses sometimes bolted in panic at the sight of them so vengeful carriage-drivers weren't above driving the cyclists into ditches. Bystanders amused themselves by poking sticks between the spokes of moving ordinaries or by laying stones across their paths and seeing the riders catapulted head first over the top.

Despite its imperfections, the ordinary marked a turning point in the bicycle's history. It established it as a fast and exciting sporting vehicle, and the technology that had been developed to lighten it and strengthen it for racing was ready to be used on the next stage of development — the designing of a stable and safe machine that the masses could ride.

A tricycle, 1884

The safety bicycle

During the era of the ordinary there were many experimental variations of bike design on the roads, for example tricycles had given women a limited taste of what cycling could offer. But the main direction in which designers were moving was towards a sporty, but practical and safe machine. By the early 1880s the ordinary was beginning to be replaced by a rear-wheel driven bicycle called (no doubt with huge relief) the *safety*. The Rover safety which John Kemp Starley (nephew of James) built in 1885 had wheels of nearly equal size and had a decisive influence on future design. By 1887 the safety looked very much like the utility bike we know today: it had a rear wheel driven by a chain, which allowed for gearing; the front and rear wheels were of similar size, and it had a diamond-pattern frame and direct steering. The finishing touch came in 1888 when John Dunlop invented the pneumatic tyre, initially with the aim of providing a smoother ride for his small son who tricycled to school over Belfast cobblestones. Dunlop's experiments were soon perfected by the Michelin brothers in France. The pneumatic tyre made the safety comfortable, and also greatly reduced rolling resistance, thus contributing to its swiftness as well.

The bicycle was set to become a runaway, world-wide success.

The safety and society

The safety's impact on nineteenth-century society was explosive. Before the century was over it had made independent, convenient, affordable transport available to millions; it had transformed the leisure hours of people all over the world; it had carried adventurers round the globe; and it had taken fortune hunters in Canada, South Africa and Australia across terrain where there was little alternative transport. It had even added considerable fire to the feminist movement. It had also formed the base of a vast transport industry that was later to produce the automobile and the aeroplane.

In the safety's early years, before mass-production techniques were developed, cycling remained a craze for the rich and fashionable, and they indulged in it with insatiable enthusiasm and extravagance. *The Hub*, a British cycling journal of the time, described a bicycle gathering at which 'peers and peeresses could be counted by the hundreds; millionaires were as common as blackberries, and one part of the lawn was portioned off for royalty'. Virtually every royal household in Europe had a stable of bicycles. Even the matronly Queen Victoria, impressed by the sight of a girl on a Starley tricycle outstripping her horse-drawn carriage, ordered two. Like many other theatrical personalities, Sarah Bernhardt listed cycling among her entertainments, along with tiger-shooting and hot-air ballooning. Some of the bicycles of the time were probably too magnificent to perform at all: a bride in 1896 was given one that had ivory and silver handlebars with jade knobs at the ends, a silver bell and a crystal lamp. The Queen of Italy reportedly rode a bike with gold wheels — something that must have done a lot more for glamour than speed.

When prices dropped, the bicycle really came into its own. According to a journal of the 1890s 'in America, every shop girl on four or five dollars a week, every office boy and all the other young

The Rover Safety (1885) had a decisive influence on bicycle design.

THE ROVER SAFETY
BICYCLE (PATENTED).

Not everyone took to the safety, as this extract which appeared in the 1890s in the Journal of Cape Town's City Cycling and Athletics Club shows:

"Safety". Safety! — ye gods!!! Against my better self I ascended the beast, that has no soul to be damned nor body to be kicked, and broke my own record, likewise the bicycle, likewise my cherished nose. ... The man who says bicycle to me again dies. I should like to chase him to death with wild bicycles and slabs of road metal. ... I offer the suggestion for the public safety that any bicycle going about un-muzzled be incontinently removed to Roeland Street Goal ... and there carefully and elaborately smashed by the large-booted feet of the establishment.

counter skippers must own a bicycle apiece'. People who had depended on the limited public transport of the day could now get where they wanted to, when they chose to; for the many rural people who had never been further from home than they could walk, the bicycle literally opened up new horizons. Sociable touring became so popular that soon there were hundreds of clubs; some, like the Cyclists' Touring Club in Britain and the City Cycling Club (now only a racing club) in Cape Town, still exist.

Top: When this advertisement appeared in the early 1890s, the safety bicycle had most of the features of today's utility bike. Left: The City Cycling and Athletics Club (which still exists) on the Grand Parade, Cape Town, *circa* 1893.

Before long, bikes were to be found in almost every part of the world. In 1896 *The Hub* reported that in Afghanistan the Amir of Kabul had ordered British bicycles for his harem, that Australian women were borrowing their husbands' knickerbockers to go riding in, and that 'Johannesburg has gone cycling mad'. The mining magnates Lionel Philips and Barney Barnato pedalled from their mansions to their offices, and Mrs Barnato was described as a prominent member of the cycling club at the Wanderers. The same journal reported that even Paul Kruger, who bought one on his doctor's advice, found the bicycle acceptable, 'unlike the cricket bat and other *uitlander* innovations'.

To cope with the demand, the 70-odd bicycle factories that had existed in Britain in 1886 had become 700 by 1896, and there were thousands more in other countries. In 1896 the Paris paper, *le Figaro*, estimated that there were ten million bicycles in the world.

Bicycle racing had become a major spectator sport in the days of the ordinary. Its popularity continued to grow, and in Europe and America races sometimes drew crowds of 30 to 40 000. As with any sport which involved big money, it was not always clean: in 1893 R. J. Mecredy warned in *The Art and Pastime of Cycling* that 'there are on the race path men, who for ways that are dark, rival the heathen Chinese'. Organized racing existed even in such unlikely places as Cookhouse and Queenstown in the Cape Colony. In Johannesburg, where racing had developed against the rough, raw background of a new mining town that was pouring out fabulous wealth, cyclists competed for extravagant prizes and spectators gambled heavily; it was said that the only people Johannesburgers idolized were cycle racers and the Queen.

A cycling party in the Pietersburg district, 1899.

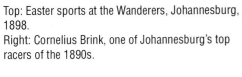

Top: Easter sports at the Wanderers, Johannesburg, 1898.
Right: Cornelius Brink, one of Johannesburg's top racers of the 1890s.

Sol Plaatje

Sol Plaatje, an intellectual and campaigner for the rights of Africans, used a bicycle to traverse South Africa in the early years of this century, while he was investigating the effects of the Native Land Act on people's lives. A founding member of the South African Native National Congress, he used the information gathered on his bicycle travels to write *Native Life in South Africa*. Later he presented his investigations to the British Prime Minister, Lloyd George, as part of a protest against the treatment of his people (to no avail).

The bicycle and bloomers

To women in the nineteenth-century Emancipation Movement, the bicycle seemed a perfect ally: it provided an exhilarating freedom and a very real mobility, and it was quickly taken up as a symbol of liberation. Female cyclists were under pressure to wear demure but hot cycling outfits, such as those prescribed by the Cyclist's Touring Club, which included a woollen garment next to the body and a long, full skirt over knickerbockers. But many women, realizing that physical comfort was just as much a right as the vote was, adopted 'rational dress', a more comfortable outfit which included bloomers and did away with the skirt. (These were named after Amelia Bloomer, a leading figure in anti-slavery causes and women's rights in America.)

Bloomers scandalized many onlookers and were the subject of heated and inordinately lengthy debate in the press for years. The Prefect of the Paris Police ordered that women walking about the boulevards in bloomers be fined unless they had a bicycle with them, and an Australian cycling club banned rationally dressed females because their bloomers 'brought to light all that is least sightly in women'.

What ho! How embarrassing!

from The Cape Cyclist of 1899

A young lady cyclist has met with an accident of a very peculiar nature. She was coasting down a hill with skirts flying in the breeze. Suddenly two gentlemen cyclists following behind the fair cyclist saw her machine waver and stagger, then it seemed as if the rider and machine got mixed in a sort of Chinese puzzle, and by the time the onlookers had arrived at the scene of disaster the lady had extricated herself and was standing minus skirt. She was blushing furiously and in pity the men betook themselves off without offering help. The accident was caused by the skirt being caught by the revolving pedals.

The start of the Mile Championship, Ladies' Jubilee Cycling Sports
at the Wanderers, 1897.

'Miss Ethel, were you ever mistaken for a man?'
'No Charlie, were you?'

From *The Hub,* 1896

21

Women sometimes put up spirited defence of their right to cycle in comfort without being harassed: *The Hub* reported in 1896 that in New York three bloomer girls 'flogged a Kodak fiend, broke his camera and gave him a lively chase for attempting to photograph their rational dress'.

Another blessing that the bike was credited with was the unlacing of corsets: when French women took to bikes, the fashion-makers in Paris 'allowed waists to increase by four or five inches'; a contemporary journalist wrote that 'the exercise of the wheel, working upon the emancipated female frame has opened the way to a novel sensation of complete and most enjoyable freedom. The increase in health and strength and the added pleasure in life is convincing ladies that it has blessings of which they had never dreamed.'

Bicycle manufacturers were quick to realize that by directing much of their advertising at women they could double their market. Posters reinforced the aspirations of a new generation of women when they showed them as not only free, but feminine as well. Some showed goddess-like girls who, bare-breasted and sweatless, stretched for the stars on their celestial bicycles, and, moreover, reached them. Others showed elegant women whose wheels remained firmly on earth, but who left male cyclists trailing in their wake.

The Women's Emancipation Movement took up bicycles as a symbol of liberation, and advertisers were quick to reflect this in posters.

The twentieth century

By the end of the nineteenth century the bicycle had made a far-reaching impact on industry and design. Bicycle factories flourished in most industrialized countries, and technology that had been developed by the early bike-builders laid the foundations for the automobile and aeroplane industries that followed. (Now that the car industry has forced the bicycle into a position of poor-relation, it's ironic to think that the first Rovers, Humbers, Peugeots and Opels were bicycles and that it was as bicycle-builders that Orville and Wilbur Wright first set up in business.) Roads, too, had benefited: in Britain, for example, government expenditure on roads almost doubled in the 1890s.

The twentieth century has seen the fortunes of the bicycle vary in different parts of the world. In the industrialized world it was pushed into a poor second place by the car; this, together with the effects of the Great Depression forced

Raleigh advertisements, *circa* 1940–1950.

American bike production in the early 1930s down to a fifth of what it had been at the turn of the century. In much of Europe and Britain the bike remained a very widely used utility and leisure vehicle until after World War II when cars became easily available. Since then there have been several booms and declines in the bike's popularity for sport and recreation. But in some parts of the world, this century has seen the bike establish itself as the backbone of transportation systems. China's 210 million bicycles (a quarter of the world's total) are the people's main way of getting about and of transporting anything from pigs to refrigerators or grandmothers. In the Netherlands, a country that is technologically so very different from China, there are 12 million bicycles to a population of 14,6 million; almost half of all trips there are made on pedal power, and traffic authorities are trying to increase that proportion. And in every part of the world, the bike has, in its quiet, efficient way, broadened the lives of millions of people.

RALEIGH

THE ALL-STEEL BICYCLE

During the Anglo-Boer War the British patrolled railway lines on an eight-man war cycle which was probably built by Donald Menzies in Cape Town. A special rim could be fitted over the pneumatic tyres so that it could run on rails, where it reportedly reached speeds of nearly 50 km/h. It could be fitted with a Maxim gun, and extra men or supplies could be carried on the coupling framework. It was mainly used to check railway lines for explosives, to transport the wounded and to carry despatches.

Bicycles in the Anglo-Boer War

The 1890s had seen bicycles become popular in southern Africa both for leisure and utility; the war of 1899–1902 saw it become a tough and practical adjunct to combat for both the Boer and British sides.

In a minor way, cycling had been an established part of British military training before the war broke out. Once in South Africa, where horses died in large numbers from horse-sickness and were scarce, the British realized that bicycles had some distinct advantages. And they were plentiful: in Johannesburg alone there were about 9 000 civilian bicycles by 1897.

Though the veld was described by a member of one grandly named cycle corps, the City of London Imperial Volunteers, as being 'just ridable' but thorny, bumpy and sandy, the British profited from having several hundred bicycle troops; like the Boer cyclists, they played an active and often hair-raising part in reconnaissance work, spying, and in carrying messages, mail and stores.

The Boers, who had easier access to horses and probably less access to bicycles, had one 108-man cycle corps, the Wielrijders Rapportgangers Corps. It was led by Danie Theron, who became legendary for his part in the war. To persuade the doubting Transvaal government to allow him to raise a cycling corps, Theron had got Koos Jooste, a cycling champion, to race (and beat) a horseman over 75 kilometres.

In Bicycles in the Anglo-Boer War of 1899–1902, D. R. Maree describes some of the extraordinary tasks that were given to cyclists:

One was to transport carrier pigeons; carrying them on horseback upset them, whereas they took more kindly to cycle transportation. Scout Callister of the Cape Cycle Corps achieved great fame by cycling 120 miles, gaining a vantage point, and then releasing birds whenever he saw Boer activity. (Presumably in the hope that they would carry a message back to base.) Major B. F. S. Baden-Powell of the First Battalion Scots Guards had a collapsible cycle which carried a kite. The kite was used at first for taking photographs of the camp by a remotely controlled camera, and later for raising an aerial for experiments in wireless telegraphy.

This war provided the first real testing ground for bikes in battle. It was probably as a result of their unobtrusive efficiency during the Boer War that the British went on to use them in small units in World War I.

CHAPTER THREE

FRAMES
and COMPONENTS

The cycling boom has brought a plethora of equipment into the shops: there are tough, precision-made all-terrain bikes, stable and reassuring touring bikes, lightweight, streamlined racers, and more. Choosing can be exciting but confusing. This chapter lists the points to consider when buying a bicycle. It discusses the cost of bikes and where to shop. It tells you what makes a bike suited for a particular purpose, and it goes on to describe frames and components, giving guidelines to assessing their function, quality and value.

There are different bikes for different purposes. At one end of the scale are sedate heavyweights which have changed little in design since the turn of the century; at the other are highly specialized, streamlined lightweights, the results of ultra-sophisticated technological inventiveness. Prices range equally widely: at the time of writing, a cheap new bike can be bought for as little as R250; a bicycle at the top of the racing range can cost R20 000 or more.

Between those extremes there's an almost endless variety of bicycles, all lending themselves to adaptations and improvements as their owners' needs and budgets change.

This chapter describes the components that make up a bike and it gives guidelines to choosing parts that will be best suited to the type of cycling you want to do. The next chapters follow on from it: Chapter 4 describes the main types of bikes available, which, for convenience, have been grouped in the following categories: utility bikes, children's bikes, tourers, racers, tandems and recumbents. Chapter 5 tells you how to choose a bike that is the right size, and how you should be positioned on it; it also tells you how to order a custom-built bike, and what to look for when buying a second-hand bike.

If you want to go more deeply into the technical aspects of bikes than we have space for here, see the list of other publications in the Appendix at the end of this book; several excellent books which concentrate on bicycle technology are available.

Buying a bicycle

Before you consider individual types of bikes, ask yourself some basic questions:

- What do you want to do on the bike? Do you want it for sociable rides at weekends, to get fit, to race, to scramble across Lesotho on, for commuting to work or for touring with a friend and a sleeping bag? Do you want to haul groceries and children on it? Do you want it for several of these purposes?
- How much are you prepared to spend? How much is it sensible to spend?

To make a reasonably informed choice you need to know what features make for quality and what makes a bike suited for a particular purpose.

Quality: what does it mean?

There are many subtle qualities you start to look for in bikes once you're familiar with them, but the main, basic ones are:

- **Strength:** A bike's slender structure may be subjected to considerable stresses of load-bearing and jolting over roads for tens of thousands of kilometres in its lifetime. A bike with a strong frame and strongly made components is safer and lasts longer.
- **Lightness:** A light bike is less tiring to propel and therefore faster than a heavy one. Light frames feel lively and full of go while heavy ones feel wooden. A bike's price goes up in more or less direct relation to its lightness.
- **Smooth operation:** The way hubs, gears, pedals and steering work all make the difference between a bike that moves fluidly and efficiently, and one that grates along, dissipating its rider's energy.
- **Safety:** Strength, lightness and smoothness will mean nothing if the bike isn't safe.

The easiest way of tracking down quality is by going to a dealer who has a good reputation with other cyclists and to rely on her or his (usually) well-informed judgement. But a better way is by learning something about bikes and components yourself.

Where to shop

New bikes in the upper-quality bracket are available only from specialist dealers. Some good models in the middle price bracket can be bought in supermarkets, often for about 15 per cent less than a bike dealer could sell them for. However, if you're buying a worthwhile bike it's better to get it from a specialist bike dealer with a good reputation among other cyclists. Here are some well-tried reasons for doing so:

- Bike dealers are nearly always cyclists themselves and can give more practical, hands-on advice than the average general dealer's assistant can. If you're new to bikes, you'll need that advice.
- Unlike most general dealers, cycle shops stock a range of bicycle parts. So if you're buying an off-the-shelf bike but you don't like the saddle, or the gearing isn't suitable for the type of riding you plan to do, or whatever, it can be changed on the spot, possibly while you wait. Apart from being convenient, this saves money: you won't be left trying to sell a slightly used piece of equipment later.

- Good dealers have their own workshops on their premises. Consequently adjustments can be made easily while you're being sized up. Also, if your bike has teething troubles as, I regret to tell you, it probably will, a bike dealer is in a better position to correct it quickly. Though bikes bought from general dealers are covered by guarantees, the fact that they have to be sent off to the manufacturer's workshop or to an approved agent can, in practice, make the whole business tedious and frustratingly impersonal.

Allow a fair amount of time to shop for a bike; try not to go on a Saturday, and give your business to a dealer who'll give your needs real and full attention.

Brand names: what do they mean?

Some brand names are deservedly synonymous with quality. Others are simply confusing. This applies particularly to bikes bearing the labels of big manufacturers: their main trade is in bottom-of-the-range lines, but they also make good middle-range bikes and bikes that rank among the best in the world; sometimes the only common feature in a range is the label, and not quality.

Distributors and manufacturers can and do lend a sense of foreign mystique to bikes by sticking on French- or Italian-sounding labels — regardless of whether the bikes were made in Taiwan or some southern African outpost. (This deference to Europe is absolutely unnecessary: some excellent bike equipment has been made locally and in Taiwan.) There's virtually no control over the use of terms such as 'lightweight' or 'racing bike' in advertising, and they're often used to describe cumbrous push-bikes. Bulk deliveries of identical machines may be distributed to several outlets, all of which stick on their own brand labels. Also, the components of a specific model that's delivered, say, in January, may be very different from the components on the 'same' bike delivered in March: the difficulty of guaranteeing supplies of equipment from overseas (all middle- to high-quality tubing and components are imported) makes this inevitable.

Price

Good bikes are expensive anywhere. In this country prices are artificially high because of the high cost of importing equipment. But for people of average means they are still a fairly easily affordable investment in years of fun, health and utility. A good bike can pay for itself many times if it's used instead of more expensive forms of transport.

The current bike boom has resulted in greatly improved ranges of equipment in our shops, but it has also brought a lot of phoney hype about unnecessarily sophisticated equipment. Professor Chester Kyle, a cyclist himself and one of the brains behind the design of the bicycles on which the American team won their recent Olympic gold medals, helps to put price into sensible perspective when he writes: 'The average cyclist has little to gain by purchasing very expensive racing equipment, though many do. If their goal is to go faster, the skill, desire and athletic ability could be far more important than equipment, which doesn't greatly affect the speed of the average cyclist.'

At the time of writing, R1 000 buys a bike with basic requirements for comfort and efficiency such as a high-carbon steel frame, wheels with aluminium alloy rims and high pressure tyres, and an 'anatomic' saddle. R1 500 will buy a bike that's got noticeably more life in it. Above about R2 000, the law of diminishing returns starts to apply: the more you pay, the less significant, proportionally, are the refinements you are getting. Above about R2 500 you will very likely be paying for quality that only an experienced enthusiast would notice or appreciate.

Bicycles and their characteristics

Even the uninitiated will know that each of the three bikes shown here will feel and perform quite differently. But what, exactly, is it that makes one bike leave the others in the dust, or that gives one the edge in comfort or that gives an ordinary-looking machine a price tag ten or twelve times higher than another?

The three main things which determine whether a bike is destined to deliver newspapers all its life or to cross the Alps or to do something between those extremes are frame geometry, materials, and the quality of components.

Frame geometry is determined by the angles and lengths of the frame tubes, and it affects efficiency and responsiveness. A tautly-designed, compact frame is rigid and transfers the rider's energy to the rear wheel very efficiently; it therefore makes a potentially fast bike. A frame that has longer tubes and relaxed, shallower angles is more comfortable and more stable but makes less efficient use of the rider's energy.

The materials that make up the frame and other components of a bike influence its weight, strength, rigidity, comfort, efficiency and price.

The quality of components determines how long they last, how easy they are to service and how smoothly they work; the more smoothly they work, the more efficiently a rider's effort is used to drive the bike forward. Suitability and compatibility of components is as important as quality: there's no point, for example, in having racers' wheels — however good they are — on a touring bike.

Before going into any more detailed description of the way bicycles are made up, you may find it useful to have a look at the diagram of a typical bicycle, and to familiarize yourself with the names of parts.

The typical bicycle: how it is made up

The frame: The frame has been called the soul, the heart, the backbone and the skeleton of the bicycle. It's all of these. This assemblage of tubes is not only the structure on which all the other components fit and work together, but it also determines the feel, the character, and the basic nature of the bicycle.

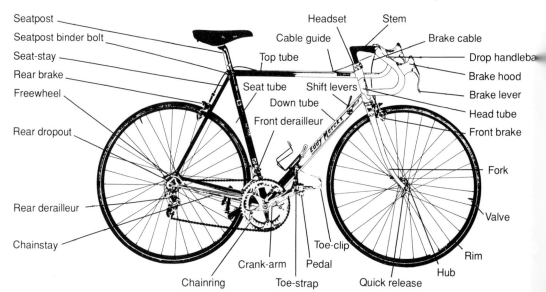

The components: The parts attached to the frame comprise the following units:

- The wheels.
- The steering system, consisting primarily of the fork and handlebars.
- The transmission or drive train, which transform the rider's energy into forward motion by making the rear wheel turn, and the gearing which regulates the rate of pedalling.
- The brakes.
- The saddle, which is attached to the frame by an adjustable saddle post.

Frame design or geometry

The most commonly-used frame design, and the one which is described here, is the diamond pattern which evolved in the 1890s. Other notable frame designs belong to the small-wheeled shopping bike which appeared in the 1960s, the tandem, which is a variation of the diamond pattern, and the recumbent. These are described in the next chapter on the pages which deal specifically with those bikes.

The geometry of a frame is a major factor in the way a bike performs. The key features in frame geometry are:

- *Frame angles:* This refers to the head-tube angle. In other words, if a frame is described as having a 68 degree angle, it means that the head-tube angle is 68 degrees. Usually the seat tube angle is the same. (See the diagram.)
- *Wheelbase length:* This is the distance between the front and rear wheel axles.
- *Seat tube height:* This is the distance between the centre of the bottom bracket and the top of the seat tube.
- *Fork rake length:* The rake is the curve at the bottom of the fork.

If a bike is compactly put together with steep frame angles, it will follow that it has a short wheelbase and a shortish seat tube; its compactness will help to make it rigid and light. (Rigidity or stiffness is a very desirable feature: it enables

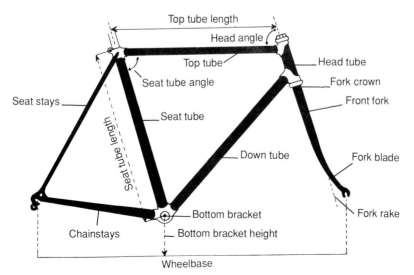

The frame and its significant measurements and angles.

Woman's frame

Mixte frame

'Women's' frames

The design that is often used for women's utility bikes was created for riders in skirts who don't want to swing their legs over the saddle to mount. While this may be useful in some circumstances, the absence of a top tube does weaken the frame and make it more flexible and therefore less efficient. This type of frame is also unstable when heavily loaded.

The *mixte* frame for women is strengthened by a low substitute for the top tube; however it still suffers from frame flex and is heavier than an equivalent standard 'man's' frame.

Most women who ride for any reasonably long distances now use standard frames.

the rider to transfer pedalling effort to the rear wheel efficiently; a flexible frame, on the other hand, 'whips' from side to side as the rider pedals, and some energy is absorbed in unproductive lateral movement.) This type of bike has a short fork rake which results in twitchy steering. Steep geometry makes a frame responsive (which means that it reacts to a burst of increased pedalling power by accelerating forward rather than by flexing sideways). Its efficiency is at the expense of some stability and comfort. It is the obvious choice for racing. Road racing bikes usually have a seat tube angle of between 73 and 76 degrees.

If, on the other hand, the frame has relaxed, stretched-out geometry with shallow angles, a long wheelbase and a long fork rake, it will produce an easy-going machine that is comfortable and stable, even when carrying extra loads. The fork rake will give it steady steering. The extra length in some of the tubes will add a little to the weight. This length will also mean that the bike will flex laterally more than a compact bike can; this, of course, dissipates some energy. (This tendency to flex laterally can be countered by using tubing with thicker walls than a racing bike would have, or by using wide-diameter tubing.) A flexible frame gives a smooth ride because it absorbs the shocks of bumping along the road, while a rigid frame tends to transmit road-shock to the rider. The geometry of a shallow-angled, long frame is the type you would find on a touring bike.

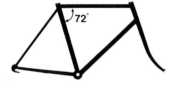

72°

Shallow angles and a long wheelbase

The height of the bottom bracket from the ground is another variable in frame design. Usually between 260 and 280 millimetres from the ground, it is higher in track bikes to allow for the steeply banked tracks. It is sometimes higher in bikes designed for sharp cornering. Bottom brackets are also higher in mountain bikes to ensure that rough ground is well cleared.

Those are the fundamentals of frame geometry. Between the racing bike and the tourer there are many intermediate designs which give a good balance of handling qualities.

75°

Steep angles and a short wheelbase

Typical angles and dimensions of different bicycles (approximate)

	Angles	Wheelbase	Fork rake	Bottom bracket height
Racing bike	73-76	98 cm-99,5 cm	3,5 cm-4,5 cm	26,5 cm-28 cm
Touring bike	72-73	101 cm-107 cm	5,5 cm-6 cm	25 cm-27 cm
All-terrain bike	70-74	104 cm-114 cm	5 cm-7 cm	29 cm-33 cm

Materials

Steel and its alloys: The base material from which most bike frames are made is steel. Steel is simply iron strengthened by the addition of carbon. Carbon steel is often referred to as 'high tensile' steel. As steel with low carbon content is not very strong, tubing made from it has to be thick, and therefore heavy, to stand up to use.

The cheapest frames are made of low-carbon tubing which starts off as a flat strip of metal and which is then rolled and welded along a seam. Cold-drawn tubes (which are drawn out of solid metal and are seamless) are generally more expensive and stronger. (Contrary to popular opinion, seamed tubing is not always inferior: some respected tubes, such as Reynolds 501, are seamed.)

Steel can be considerably strengthened when other materials are added to it to form an alloy. An example is chrome-molybdenum steel (often abbreviated to chrome-moly or chromoly), an alloy which is often used in bicycle manufacture; manganese-molybdenum steel is another popular alloy. The extra strength achieved by the alloying process means that tube walls can be thinner and lighter without loss of reliability. Controlled heat treatment and mechanical working of metal can further increase its tensile strength.

The quest for lightness can be taken further by a process called *butting*. A butted tube has a thin wall along most of its length, but at the ends, where it will be joined to other tubes, it is thickened on the inside. This is to strengthen it, firstly against the extra stresses that these parts have to bear, and secondly against the weakening heat of the frame-builder's brazing torch. Single-butted tubing is thickened at one end. Double-butted tubing is thickened at both ends. Recently triple- and quad-butted tubing has also been developed.

Some manufacturers also marry strength with lightness by using internal reinforcing ridges in lightweight tubing.

There are several brands of high quality steel tubing available, and a bike built from any of them will have a label saying so. The most famous manufacturers of lightweight steel tubing are Reynolds in England and Columbus in Italy. Other brands known for consistently high quality are Vitus, Tange, Oria and Ishiwata. These manufacturers make a wide range of tubing which varies in weight, wall thickness and, of course, price. To give you an idea of the difference between, say, a Reynolds 531 frame and a bottom-of-the-market steel frame, the former has tubes with a wall thickness as low as 0,55 millimetres and weighs 1,8 kilograms, as against the latter which has tube walls about 1,4 millimetres thick and can easily weigh 3 or 4 kilograms.

In addition to its strength and relatively low cost, steel alloy has several other important advantages:

- It is reliable, but in the unlikely event of it failing, it will bend rather than break suddenly.
- Because it is inherently stiff, the diameters of the tubes can be small; this helps to reduce wind drag.
- It is often feasible to repair steel frames, whereas with other metals it is risky or impossible. Minor kinks can often be straightened without any heating process, and brazing can be reheated if a tube needs replacing.
- Fittings for components can be brazed on; this makes them integral parts of the frame rather than fitted-on additions.

The disadvantage of steel is its tendency to rust if paintwork is not cared for. Steel or steel alloys are used for other parts of bicycles apart from the frame.

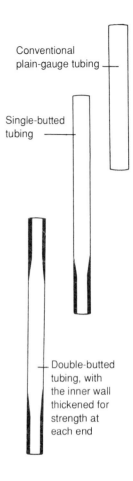

Conventional plain-gauge tubing

Single-butted tubing

Double-butted tubing, with the inner wall thickened for strength at each end

This table compares steel alloy tubing made by three well-known tube manufacturers — Reynolds, Columbus and Oria. Tube sets exclude lugs, dropouts and the bottom bracket.

Tubing	Material used	Mass (for a 56-cm frame, 11 tubes)	Variation in gauge of tubing (mm)	Use and comments
Reynolds 501	Chrome-moly, double-butted main tubes	2 025 g	0,9 mm 0,6 mm	All-purpose tubing ideal for junior riders, fun cyclists and touring. Price: medium
Reynolds 531c	Manganese-molybdenum alloy (double-butted main tubes	1 800 g	0,81 mm 0,55 mm	Road racing events Price: medium to high
Reynolds 653	Manganese-molybdenum alloy - double-butted main tubes	1 700 g	0,71 mm 0,55 mm	Recommended for road racing and time trialling events Price: high
Reynolds 753	Special manganese molybdenum alloy butted tubes	1 650 g	0,7 mm 0,55 mm	Recommended for time trial events and mountain climbing (on smooth road surfaces) Price: high
Columbus Aelle	Carbon-manganese alloy	2 345 g	0,8 mm 1,0 cm	A robust tubing, ideal for junior racers and recreational riders. Price: medium
Columbus SL	Chrome-moly CYCLE ® double-butted	1 932 g	0,9 mm 0,6 mm	Excellent for road racing, time trials — all-round road use. Price: medium to high
Columbus SLX	Super-butted CYCLEX® (chrome-moly)	1 945 g	0,9 mm 0,6 mm	Extremely rigid and reliable. Preferred by master artisans (Colnago) Price: expensive
Oria GM 0.0 (Mannesmann)	Chrome-molybdenum	2 078 g	1,0 cm 0,8 mm	Recommended for touring, amateur racing and junior riders. Price: medium to high
Oria GM 0.0 (Mannesmann)	Chrome-molybdenum	1 950 g	0,95 mm 0,5 mm	Specialized road racing and time trial events. Price: Expensive

Aluminium and its alloys: Though aluminium bicycles were being advertised at the turn of the century, it is only recently that this metal and its alloys have been widely used for frame building and for making bicycle components.

Its chief advantages are lightness and an excellent capacity to absorb road shock. Unlike steel alloys, it doesn't rust. The aluminium alloys used for bike frames are about 60 per cent lighter than steel, but because they are not as strong, manufacturers have to compensate either by making the tube walls thicker or by making the diameter of the tubes thicker. Even with this compromise, an aluminium frame is about 20 per cent lighter than an equivalent high-quality steel alloy frame.

Wide-diameter aluminium tubing produces a very rigid and efficient frame, and is being used increasingly for touring bikes and mountain bikes; it is also used for racing bikes, though racing rules prevent its use in top-level events. A steel alloy frame of the same rigidity would give a tiring ride, but with aluminium this is partly offset by the metal's shock-absorbing properties.

The 'normal'-diameter aluminium tubing is a popular material for racing bikes, particularly with lightweight riders. Under a heavy rider it tends to suffer somewhat from frame flex. A disadvantage of frames built of normal-diameter aluminium tubing is that they don't last as long as steel alloy frames because the metal is prone to fatigue. In other words, there is a limit to how much stress an aluminium frame can withstand before it starts to feel 'dead', or, in extreme cases, actually breaks. (Even if you were covering 300 kilometres a week on such a frame it would probably last you many years — but a steel frame would last longer.) On balance, however, this tubing remains popular because many riders find its advantages far outweigh its disadvantages.

Aluminium tubes can be joined together with screws or glued lugs, or by special welding techniques known as tungsten inert gas (TIG) welding.

Aluminium alloys are used to great advantage in high quality components; the lightness they can give to moving parts like wheel rims and chainwheels can significantly improve performance: by lightening the moving parts of a bike you improve its efficiency measurably more than if you lighten non-moving parts, like the frame, by the same weight.

By comparison with other high quality tubing, aluminium's price is middling to high.

Carbon fibre: The use of carbon fibre in frame building is a new development. Carbon fibre strands are woven together and moulded into tubes with the help of resin. The tubes are joined by lugs, screws or special glue. Recently, a carbon-fibre frame, the Kestrel, was built as an all-in-one moulded unit, and not from separate tubes.

Carbon fibre is rigid, light and very strong, but it is brittle. Frames made from carbon fibre are responsive, rust-free and very expensive.

Kevlar and titanium tubing: These are high-performance materials which have fairly recently started being used for bicycle frames. They are beyond the price that most people can afford, and beyond the scope of this book.

Tensile strength

Tensile strength, a term often used with reference to bicycle tubing, is determined by pulling a standard size sample of metal until it breaks. Standard chrome-moly tubing has a tensile strength of 720 mPa to 870 mPa — 100 000 to 120 000 pounds per square inch (psi). The strongest steels used in bicycle tubing have tensile strengths of over 1 100 mPa (150 000 psi), with some reaching strengths of over 1 500 mPa (200 000 psi).

Fat tubes, thin tubes, oval tubes

The rigidity of frame tubing has an important bearing on the efficiency of a bicycle: the more rigid the frame, the more responsive the bike.

The rigidity of a tube is determined partly by the thickness of the tube wall, but even more by its diameter.

If you double a tube's wall thickness, the tube's weight, strength and rigidity will also be roughly doubled. But if you double the *diameter*, you will get a very different result: weight will roughly double, strength will increase by a factor of four (the square of the diameter increase), and rigidity will increase by a factor of eight (the cube of the diameter increase).

Using this principle, the rigidity and strength of a tube can, of course, be increased without increasing its weight: by judiciously increasing the tube diameter while decreasing the wall thickness you would end up with a tube that is significantly stronger and stiffer than a narrower tube of equal weight. To take the process a step further, you could use fat tubes to **decrease** weight without sacrificing strength or stiffness.

The study of the way that the *cross-sectional shape* of a tube affects its performance is a subtle science that bicycle builders have explored with some interesting, if not always successful, results.

Frame tubes are subjected to stresses from several directions, as well as to twisting forces. In general, round tubes are well-suited to coping with these stresses. But, in some instances, oval or elliptical tubes have been used to good advantage.

Through its short axis, an elliptical tube has only about a quarter of the rigidity that a round tube with the same circumference has. But through its long axis, it is a lot stiffer than a round tube. With careful design, it is possible to take advantage of an elliptical tube's flexibility in one direction, and its rigidity in another. An elliptical top tube, for example, can minimize lateral flex in a frame, while allowing vertical flex as the bike goes over bumps. The result is efficiency coupled with comfort.

Another important feature of oval tubing is that it can help to streamline a bike: the air drag caused by an oval tube can be 25 to 30 per cent less less than that of round tubing of the same strength.

Building a frame from oval tubes is, however, far more expensive and difficult than building it from round tubes.

A frame which combines the lightness of aluminium with the strength and rigidity of wide-diameter tubes. Note that the down tube — the tube that takes the greatest stress on a frame — is the widest.

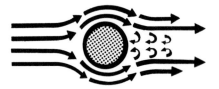 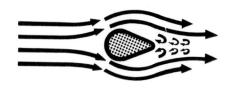

The shape and the greater frontal area of a round tube creates more wind resistance and more turbulence than an oval 'aero' tube.

The frame-builder's role

Having a good make of tubing doesn't necessarily guarantee a good frame. The skill of the frame builder also plays a critical part. Though frames in the lower and middle price ranges are almost always made in factory production lines, those made of high quality tubing require individual, skilled handling. Frame construction can be a difficult and delicate art, particularly when the tubes that are being assembled are paper-thin. It is through their ability to consistently build high quality, reliable frames that master artisans like Masi, de Rosa, Colnago and others have become household names in the cycling world.

Lugs

The process of building a frame starts with the frame builder buying a set of tubes from the manufacturer. Lugs (if they are used), dropouts and fork crowns are bought separately. The tubing is scrutinized, cut to size and then put in a jig to set up the geometry of the frame. Then the tubes are fused either with the aid of lugs, or, if the frame is to be lugless, by direct tube-on-tube brazing.

With the exception of Reynolds 531, which can withstand brazing temperatures of up to 850 degrees Celsius without being weakened, most of the strong alloys require carefully controlled temperatures: over-heating the metal can result in a frame that has a dangerously weak point in it, or that is heavier than it needs to be. Tubing that can't take great heat is soldered with silver which allows for low brazing temperatures of 550 to 650 degrees Celsius. The expensive input of skill and materials are two of the factors that add to the cost of lightweight frames.

Dropouts

Frame-builder Francois du Toit in his Bellville factory.

Components

Wheels

After the frame, the wheels are the most important parts as far as the 'feel' of the bike is concerned: there is a very distinct difference between the ride you have on a lightweight wheel shod with silk tubulars as opposed to a heavy wheel with clincher tyres made for touring.

Consisting of a hub, spokes, rim and tyre, a wheel is a fragile-looking assemblage, yet it is expected to support great weight, withstand much stress and, ideally, be light at the same time. Clearly quality is important.

There is a wide range of different wheels for different purposes: track racers, for example, use ultra-light wheels with narrow, smooth tyres and a minimum of spokes, while at the other end of the spectrum, mountain bikers depend on robust wheels bearing wide tyres with deep, knobbly tread.

When you ride, the weight of your wheels is magnified several times by the centrifugal force of rotation; the faster they spin, the more inert or 'heavy' they become. It follows that choosing the lightest that you sensibly can — taking into account the load-bearing and other demands you place on a wheel — is important. If you reduce the weight of your wheels by 500 grams, you can expect your bike's performance to improve as much as it would if you reduced the frame or some other non-moving part by a kilogram. Reducing wheel weight is a relatively inexpensive way of reducing the bike's overall weight.

If you do very different types of riding on one bike, it is wise to get a second pair of wheels: one pair, for example, might be light for fast training rides and another might be more robust for using on a loaded touring bike.

Hubs: The hub is at the centre of the wheel, and turns on ball-bearings around an axle. Hubs come in two basic styles — large-flange (also known as high-flange) and small-flange (or low-flange). Flanges are commonly drilled to accommodate 24, 28, 32, 36 or 40 spokes.

Rear and front hubs with quick-release levers.

When large-flange hubs are used, it follows that spokes will be relatively short. This results in a rigid wheel which contributes to making a bike responsive. (Sometimes spokes are bound at the cross-over points to increase rigidity.) The disadvantage of the inflexible, short-spoked wheel is that it does not absorb the bumps of the road, and gives a fairly harsh ride. Large-flange hubs are mainly used on bikes used for track and criterium racing. If you need an unusually great number of spokes to give extra strength to wheels — as you might on a tandem or a heavily-loaded touring bike — you would need large-flange hubs to accommodate them.

Because small-flange hubs take longer spokes, they allow for greater flexibility and comfort. They also facilitate a wider variety of spoke-crossing patterns.

The illustration shows a small-flange, quick-release hub for a rear wheel. The measurements shown are significant: distance a depends on the type of cluster mounted. A 7-cog cluster obviously requires a longer axle than one with five speeds. Hubs come in various lengths, and when you are buying one it is important to know what sort of cluster you will be attaching.

Most high-quality hubs are constructed of durable aluminium alloys and are fitted with a quick-release lever which you simply flick to take the wheel off the bike. This makes repairing punctures or loading a bike into a car quick and easy.

Hubs contain either sealed bearings or conventional ball-bearings. Sealed bearings need less maintenance and will almost certainly replace conventional ball-bearings in future.

Spokes: Spokes attach the rim to the hub. This sounds obvious, but is, in fact, the result of brilliant engineering — something you will appreciate if you ever have to suffer the havoc caused by broken spokes.

Spokes are made in different materials, shapes and thicknesses. This, together with the number of spokes used, influences the weight and strength of the wheel.

The materials used may be galvanized steel (which is strong, rustless and reasonably priced), chrome-plated steel (slightly less strong and prone to rust) or stainless steel, which makes the best, though the most expensive spokes. Stainless steel spokes are not as easy to replace as the other types.

The most usual spoke thickness used for training and recreational riding is 14-gauge (2 millimetres). On a wheel where strength is critical, (for example, on a tandem, or on the rear wheel of a loaded touring bike) you might use a spoke as thick as 12-gauge (2,6 millimetres). Spokes on racing bikes may go down to a slender 16-gauge (1,6 millimetres) diameter, though these will be strengthened at each end. (Note that these gauges are British measurements; the French gauge system for spokes is different.)

Spokes are available in three configurations:

- *Plain (or straight gauge):* These have a consistent diameter from spoke head to thread. They are reasonably priced and strong, and are by far the most commonly used type.

- *Double butted:* These have butted ends, which means that at the extremities — which is where spokes are most likely to break — they are thicker than in the middle part. Double-butted spoking results in weight-saving without weakening the spoke. It is often used on racing bikes where weight is critical.

- *'Aerodynamic':* Aerodynamic spokes are flattened; the benefit of this is an infinitesimal reduction in air resistance. (Air resistance is explained in Chapter 9.) They are mainly used for track or road time trials.

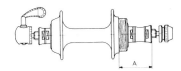

A rear hub.

Small-flange front hub.

Large-flange front hub.

Rims for wire-on tyres:

For a narrow, high pressure tyre. The reinforced eyelets are a sign of quality.

An 'aero' profile helps to reduce effects of wind resistance.

Mountain bike rim.

Rims for tubular tyres:

Road-racing rim.

Racing rim with aero profile.

Rims: The materials used to make rims vary from from mild steel to durable, anodized aluminium-magnesium alloys. All better quality bikes are fitted with aluminium alloy rims because they are lighter and usually stronger than the cheaper steel variety. Brakes work far better on aluminium than on steel; this is specially true in wet weather, when the braking distance on a bike with steel rims can be two or three times as long as that on a bike with aluminium rims.

Rims are designed to take either tyre-and-tube combinations (clincher or wired-on tyres) or tubular tyres. Rims for clinchers are sometimes known as Endrick rims. They are fairly deeply recessed and have a lip designed to prevent the inner tube from popping out from beneath the tyre. They come in a variety of widths to take different widths of tyres. It is important to match the rim width with the tyre width. Badly-matched tyres and rims will, at best, increase rolling resistance, and at worst, are dangerous.

Rims designed for tubular tyres have a shallow recess because these tyres are simply glued on.

The wide variations in the price of rims depends mainly on the materials they are made of; specialized heat treatments to strengthen rims may bump up the price, and so can anodizing — a process through which aluminium is hardened by the addition of a thin surface layer of aluminium oxide.

When buying a rim, check that it has enough holes to take the number of spokes you intend using.

Wheel construction: The way a wheel functions is strongly influenced by the way it is constructed. The factors to consider are:

- *The spoke-lacing pattern:* Wheels can be laced in various ways. On radially-spoked wheels, the spokes go directly from hub to rim. This is the lightest and most rigid arrangement, and it is possibly the most aerodynamically efficient. But it is also the weakest. Front wheels used in time trials are often spoked this way.

  Most wheels have triple-cross spoking — in other words, each spoke crosses another at three points. Two- and four-cross spoke patterns are also used. The more crossings, the more resilient and heavy the wheel.

Radially spoked. Three-cross spoking. Four-cross spoking.

- *The spoke tension:* Spokes have a hook at the end which attaches to the hub, and a thread at the rim end, which fits a nipple. Spoke tension depends on how tightly the spoke is screwed into the nipple. The greater the tension, the less flex there is in the wheel. It is important that the tension of each spoke is equal, otherwise the rim may distort.

  It is difficult to recommend an ideal tension; it depends on the type of rim used and the type of riding you want to do.

- *The dishing of the wheel:* Viewed from the back or front, the rim of the wheel should line up with the centre of the hub. This alignment is particularly important in the case of the rear wheel whose longer axle may be used to accommodate a wide cluster. If the rim is off-centre, the handling of the bike will be affected; you may find it going off course if you relax your grip on the handlebars.

Tyres: These are the pneumatic shock absorbers of the bicycle. Choosing and maintaining them well is an important part of cycling; a blowout when you're cornering or descending a hill can be disastrous.

There are two main types: the tube-and-tyre combination known as wired-ons or clinchers, and tubulars.

- *Wired-on tyres:* These are used with an inner tube and are what most cyclists are familiar with. They are available in a wide variety of widths and treads for different purposes. For fast riding on tar roads, for example, narrow, light, fairly smooth tyres are the best choice. For touring, on the other hand, you would benefit from the greater comfort, better traction and better resistance to cuts and punctures that you get from a wider high-pressure tyre with a well-defined tread pattern. But, of course, the wider tyre would have greater rolling resistance and would slow you down.

Recently there have been tremendous advances in the manufacture of wired-on tyres. They are made to withstand very high pressures, and consequently have low rolling resistance. Top manufacturers such as Michelin, Wolbe and Vittoria now produce light wired-ons giving the sort of ride which in the past was only thought possible on tubulars.

Wired-on tyres are cheaper than tubulars and last longer, and puncture repair is far simpler.

- *Tubular tyres:* These are also known as tubbies, tubs or chewbelus, and are used almost exclusively for racing. As you can see from the diagram, the tubular tyre is an all-in-one system, with an inner tube sewn into the tyre casing. They should only be used on rims designed for them and they should be carefully glued on, following the manufacturer's instructions. Tubulars are specialized: if you are buying them for track racing, see that you get track tyres and not road tyres.

Tubbies need care not only in use but also in storage: when riding, see that they are inflated to the pressure recommended by the manufacturer; when you are not using them, reduce the pressure to about 2 bars. The best way of storing them is in a clean, dry, dark place, slightly inflated on a rim.

The advantages of tubulars are their light weight and the fact that they can be pumped to high pressures (11 bars). But they are expensive. Repairing punctures is a long-drawn out business involving glue, a needle, thread, a tough thimble and a good temper.

A properly dished wheel: Viewed from the back, the rim of this wheel lines up with the centre of the hub.

Wire-on (HP).

Tubular (sprint).

Wheel and tyre size

Wheels and tyres are sometimes still measured in inches, though metric measurements are becoming standard. A 27 x 1 inch tyre is made to fit a rim with a 27 inch diameter, and it measures 1 inch over its inflated cross section. The same tyre marked according to metric measurements will have the figure 25-630 on its side, indicating that its cross section measures 25 millimetres, and that it fits a 630 millimetre rim.

Most modern road bikes have 700C wheels, a metric measurement which is very close to the 27 inch wheel. A 700C wheel measures 622 millimetres across from the inner bead of the tyre on one side to the inner bead on the other.

Mountain bikes have smaller wheels; they usually measure 26 inches, but sometimes 24 inches. (Mountain bike wheel sizes are usually given in inches.) Wheels with a small diameter are stronger and stiffer than their larger counterparts, but they have greater rolling resistance, and tend to give a less smooth ride.

Tyres and rolling resistance

The greater the area of contact between the road and the tyre, the greater the rolling resistance will be, and the more effort will be needed to propel the bike forward. The area of contact depends on the width of the tyre, the pressure it is pumped to, and the weight it is supporting.

A narrow tyre that is pumped to a high pressure and that carries a light load will have little of its surface in contact with the road; consequently its rolling resistance will be at least 30 per cent lower than that of a wide, low-pressure tyre.

Drag caused by the rolling resistance of tyres accounts for between about 0,23 of a kilogram and 1 kilogram, depending on whether lightweight tubular tyres or knobbly balloon tyres are being used.

Rolling resistance is virtually unaffected by the bicycle's speed — in other words, it is almost the same at slow speeds as it is at high speeds. At speeds of over about 15 kilometres an hour, rolling resistance accounts for less drag than air resistance does,but at higher speeds, wind resistance accounts for a far higher proportion of drag than rolling resistance does.

Apart from tyre pressure, tyre width and the weight on the tyre, factors that affect rolling resistance are:

- *The matching of the rim and tyre:* Incorrectly-matched tyres and rims have increased rolling resistance.

- *Secure adhesion:* A tubular that is not glued on properly has increased rolling resistance.

- *Wheel diameter:* The wider the diameter, the less the rolling resistance.

- *Tyre tread:* The smoother and thinner the tread, the less the rolling resistance.

Disc wheels: Instead of spokes, these have a 'disc' of material attaching the hub to the rim. The materials that have been used have included carbon fibre, Kevlar, aluminium and plastic resins.

The disc wheel is not a new invention. It was described as 'the greatest change ever affected in the modern cycle' in the British *Cycling* magazine in 1891. But it is only in the last decade that they have been widely used, particularly in individual and team time trials in road and track racing.

Their main advantage is a reduction in wind drag, especially when conditions are calm or when there is a head wind. At a speed of about 45 kilometres an hour, a disc wheel can have at least 150 grams less air drag than that of a conventional spoked racing wheel. Over a distance of 4 or 5 kilometres, this can save several seconds. Another advantage of disc wheels is that they produce a greater rolling momentum once launched.

Their disadvantages are that in high winds or cross-winds they act as sails and make handling and cornering difficult. The materials used to make them are rigid and result in an uncomfortable ride. They are usually heavier than conventional wheels. Finally, they are very expensive.

Disc wheel.

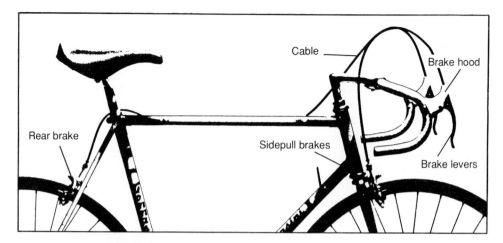

Calliper brake system.

A sidepull calliper brake. When the brake levers are operated, the callipers are forced inwards and the brake shoes are brought into contact with the rim. Cheap sidepull brakes are generally considered to be less effective than similarly-priced centrepull systems, and they are difficult to adjust, requiring mechanical expertise. However, upper quality, precision-made sidepulls outperform centrepull brakes; helped by their short, rigid calliper arms, they provide powerful, controlled braking. Sidepull calliper systems are the most widely used in racing.

A centrepull brake system. Although these have more component parts than sidepull brakes, they are easier to adjust. This is a particularly valuable feature if you happen to get a dinged rim when you are touring and are far from home. Inexpensive centrepull brakes work better than inexpensive sidepulls.

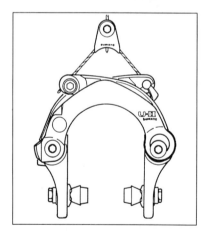

Brakes

Cycling is about movement, speed and going places. It is also about stopping. The main safety mechanism on your bike is the brake system. Brakes are made up of several component parts, each of which plays an important role in their smooth, reliable functioning. It is essential that the whole system is in harmony — your life could depend on it.

There are several brake systems. The most widely-used are calliper brakes. Other brake designs include disc brakes, drum brakes, and coaster or back brakes.

Calliper brakes: These include sidepull, centrepull and cantilever brakes. All are worked by means of levers mounted on the handlebars; cables connect the levers to brake arms which close in on the wheels when the levers are operated, pressing the brake blocks against the rims. Good calliper brakes provide excellent, graduated stopping power, but ill-judged use can lead to inexperienced riders locking their wheels and skidding or somersaulting.

A disadvantage of calliper brakes is that they are less effective in wet weather, but this can be partly countered by using aluminium rims on your wheels.

Robustness, rigidity and smooth operation are signs of quality. The less flexible the braking system, the more direct is the stopping power. Good brakes are usually made from aluminium alloys that have been anodized to increase strength.

The *levers* on calliper (and other) brakes often serve a dual purpose: with the addition of rubber hoods, they become extensions of the handlebars. Many riders prefer climbing hills out of the saddle and support themselves on the levers rather than on the bar itself. Aerodynamically-designed levers allow the brake cable to pass either through the handlebars or alongside the bars where they can be taped in. This more streamlined approach has become very popular and will probably soon be standard.

Brake cables, the lifelines between levers and callipers, are made from woven steel fibres. For brakes to operate smoothly, the cables must be free to move within the casing that protects them, and the casing itself must be flexible. Cable casings are sometimes lined with a teflon coating which helps to ensure smooth, frictionless functioning.

At one end of the cable a nipple is fused to the steel strands. This anchors the cable into the housing within the brake lever. With long use, the cable strands wear and they tend to snap at the nipple fusion point. Frayed or fraying cables prevent the smooth functioning of a brake system and should be replaced without delay. (Chapter 6 tells you how to maintain brakes.)

Cantilever brakes are a variation of the centrepull design. They are simple, efficient, and powerful. They are also steady and can prevent loaded bikes from shuddering when the brakes are applied. They are used predominantly on mountain bikes, tandems and custom-built touring bikes.

Cantilever callipers require fittings brazed to the frame, and for this reason it is difficult (but not impossible) to replace sidepull or centrepull brakes with them.

A cantilever front brake. These brakes' simplicity, power and ease of maintenance make them ideal for mountain bikes.

Drum and disc brakes: These are used mainly on bikes which take unusually heavy loads or other stresses. On tandems, for example, calliper brakes alone may not be strong enough, and they may cause over-heating of the rims and tyres, followed by blow-outs. In such cases two brake systems — calliper and drum or disc — are often necessary.

The mechanism for drum and disc brakes is similar to that used in motor cars. They are less affected by water than calliper brakes are, but their main disadvantage is that they are heavy. Also, as few bike shops stock them, buying spares can be a problem.

Coaster brake system: This system is normally used on the conventional single-speed cycle. The brake is activated by back-pedalling. The system has good stopping power, and is not affected by wet weather, as all the working parts are sealed. But they don't give the graduated braking that you get with calliper brakes.

A U-brake on the rear wheel of the same bicycle. Cantilever rear brakes have been largely replaced by U-brakes, which leave this area clear for luggage.

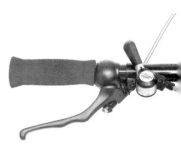

Brake levers on a mountain bike.

Handlebars

Handlebars come in a variety of materials, sizes and, of course, prices. They are made in three main designs: dropped handlebars, aerobars and flat bars.

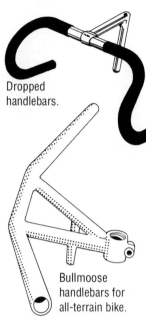

Dropped handlebars.

Bullmoose handlebars for all-terrain bike.

Aerobars

Dropped handlebars: These are the curved bars that racing bikes have and are almost standard equipment on touring and sports bikes. The reach and the extent of the drop varies, depending on what they are to be used for: touring bars are made with a fairly shallow drop, while racers' bars have a deeper drop to allow the rider to adopt a low, streamlined position.

Dropped bars have several advantages over flat bars. The forward-leaning position they put you in ensures that your weight is fairly evenly distributed over the handlebars, pedals and saddle. (If you are on a bike that puts you in an upright position, most of your weight is on your seat; on a long ride this is at best a numbing and spine-jarring experience.) With dropped bars you can put your hands in several different positions, and this helps to prevent sore hands and stiffness. Another advantage is that you are positioned to direct force to the pedals far more efficiently than you can when sitting upright. Crouching over dropped bars enables you to streamline yourself, reducing the slowing-down effects of wind drag. (It was for this advantage that those pioneers in aerodynamics, Orville and Wilbur Wright invented dropped handlebars in the last century.)

Aerobars, tribars and 'bull-horn' bars: They are variations of a fairly new development in handlebars. Aerobars have two hornlike bars facing away from the rider; they are mainly used in track pursuit events.

Tribars (which are also known under various other names) are mainly used by triathletes. These bars allow a comfortable, unconstricted, aerodynamically efficient position that has been likened to that of a downhill skier. However, it takes time to reach the brakes when using them, and they cause jumpy, unpredictable steering. They may not be used in SACF races (except in time trials), and they should not be used in traffic or when riding in groups.

Flat bars (the straight bars on utility bikes and many mountain bikes): These bars have some distinct advantages in certain circumstances, especially when speed is unimportant. Most roadster riders prefer the position they put one in because it gives a better view of the passing world. Mountain-bike riders like them for the same reason and because those designed for mountain bikes give good leverage when steering.

The ideal handlebar should be rigid, yet light and strong. Materials used vary from inexpensive, chrome-plated mild steel to very light, strong aluminium alloys. Handlebars are measured form the centre of one end to the centre of the other (see the illustration). Broad-shouldered riders should choose bars with a width of about 44 centimetres, while most small riders would be comfortable with a 38-centimetre bar.

Stems

The function of the stem is to attach the handlebar to the frame. Stems should be constructed of strong, durable materials to ensure minimum flex and maximum safety. Because the rider's weight is very often supported by the stem, it is advisable to check that the stem is never raised out of the frame beyond the maximum level. (This level is normally engraved on the stem — if not, ensure that you have at **least** a 7-centimetre extension in the frame.)

Styles and shapes do not vary to a great degree. Stems for track riding are normally made of steel and have a steeper rake. Stems for road riding are made of aluminium alloys. Lengths vary. The cyclist's height, flexibility, riding style, arm length, etc. determine what length of stem should be used.

Ensure that the expanded bolt holding the stem in position is well greased; this will prevent removal problems.

Headset

The headset is the basis of the bicycle's steering column. Made of separate sections, each with a specific function, the headset connects the frame to the fork, and ensures smooth control of the front wheel's direction.

Aluminium alloys, chromed steel and titanium are all used in the construction of headsets. The most important factor in smooth functioning is good installation and fine adjustment. (These are best left to expert mechanics.) Because the headset (along with the wheels) absorbs a tremendous amount of shock, it's advisable to have ball-bearings or needle-bearings of the highest quality. Pitting of the headset when bearings mark their casing causes rough steering and will affect a bike's handling — especially when descending and when riding without the hands on the bars.

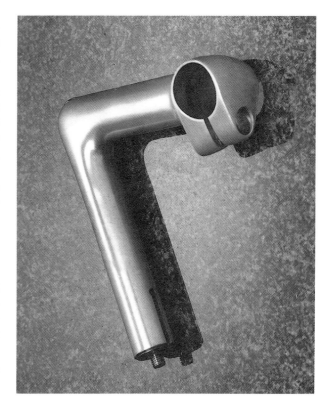

Stem

Saddles

There is a good variety available; never put up with an uncomfortable one. The cheap plastic saddles that come with low-cost bikes may be tolerable on bikes that are not ridden far, but over a distance they get sweaty and uncomfortable; many are wide and chafe the inner thigh. Mattress saddles — those broad seats set on springs — are used on roadsters and other bikes that have the rider sitting upright. The springs help to absorb the road shock that otherwise would go straight up the spine, but the bouncing about dissipates some pedalling effort.

Most touring and racing bikes are fitted with narrow, firm saddles. The most popular are the so-called 'anatomic' saddles which are narrow and have a multi-layered but firm base which cushions the body's contact points; they are covered with soft leather or a good substitute that 'breathes'. Anatomic saddles designed specially for women are broader to accommodate the wide female pelvic arch.

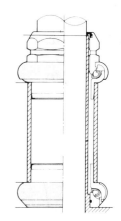

A headset.

Recently, saddles using a silicon-based hydro-elastic gel as a cushioning material have come onto the market. (The gel is widely known under the trade name 'Spenco'.) Instead of simply compressing under pressure, the gel is partly displaced, and it is said to improve comfort dramatically.

The drive train.

Pedal fitted with toe-clip.

Clipless pedal. A compatible cleat slots into the pedal, holding the foot firmly in place.

The drive train

The drive train is made up of the pedals, the cranks, the bottom bracket, the chainrings, the chain and the cluster. It is the system through which human power is translated into forward motion. The efficiency of the drive train depends on the quality and compatibility of the individual components.

Pedals: There are several types of pedal. At the bottom of the range are old-fashioned rubber pedals which don't accommodate toe-clips; these are used almost exclusively on children's and utility bikes.

Quill and rat-trap pedals and, less commonly, platform pedals are fairly standard equipment on touring and sports bikes. The performance of these is greatly improved if they are used together with toe-clips. Toe-clips attach your feet firmly to the pedal, not only preventing any slips, but also giving greater pedalling efficiency. They enable you to some extent to pull on the upstroke of a pedal rotation instead of only pushing on the downstroke. This not only puts more power into pedalling, but it also ensures that smooth momentum is maintained.

Although many riders are moving over to clipless pedals, the conventional toe-clip system is still very much in use in track racing, when you need a very secure foot/pedal fusion.

Some riders of all-terrain bikes like to be able to put their feet down onto the ground quickly, especially when doing rough off-road riding, and they prefer to ride without toe-clips

Clipless pedals are a new development which, despite their high cost, seem set to overtake the conventional pedal/toe-clip combination. They are often referred to as 'Look' pedals, though Look is simply one of several good brands on the market.

They were developed by Group Tapie Sport in conjunction with Bernard Hinault, one of the greatest cyclists France has ever produced.

These pedals have to be used together with a compatible cleat fixed to the sole of the cycling shoe; this cleat attaches itself to the pedal through a simple click-in and click-out action. On most models, a spring-mounted back-plate ensures that the feet are kept firmly in position, but at the same time, you can lift a foot off the pedals very quickly — a boon in emergencies.

Some models of clipless pedal allow a fair amount of foot movement, while others hold the foot quite rigidly in place. Choice depends largely on personal preference, but there have been claims that the types that immobilize the foot sometimes cause joint and neuro-muscular problems.

Both clipless and conventional pedals have an axle which is screwed into the cranks. The axles rotate on sealed bearings or on ordinary bearings. There should be as little tolerance or 'play' in the pedals as possible. Any lateral movement of the pedal, especially up hills, will cause havoc with pedalling action and may result in knee problems.

The crank-set: This consists of crank-arms, studs and chainrings.

Crank-arms on cheap bikes are attached to the bottom bracket axle by a cotterpin which is at right angles to the axle. Cotterpins tend to give trouble. Better bikes have cotterless crank-arms which have a tapered hole which fits over the end of the axle. The cranks are essentially levers which turn the gear, and the efficiency of the leverage is affected by their length — long cranks giving greater leverage. But long cranks can be inhibiting because they increase the risk of striking the road with the pedal at corners.

Cranks come in lengths ranging from 165 to 185 millimetres; most standard bikes are fitted with 170-millimetre cranks.

Choice of crank lengths depends on the following:

A crank-set, consisting of two chainwheels and a pair of crank-arms.

- The *type of bicycle*: Track or road.
- The *height of the rider* and the *length of the rider's legs*: Tall riders may benefit from using longer cranks.
- The *type of event* being ridden: For example, cranks of up to 180 millimetres can be used by long-limbed athletes in time-trial events where there are no sharp corners, but in road races, 175 millimetres is usually the maximum.
- The *individual pedalling style* of the rider: Francesco Moser used 172,5-millimetre cranks for his World Hour record, against the advice of experts who said he should use 177,5- to 180-millimetre cranks; conversely, Charly Mottet, wearer of the yellow jersey in the Tour de France, often uses 180-millimetre cranks despite being only 175 centimetres tall.

Chainrings: Chainrings (usually two, sometimes one or three) are, on most better bikes, attached to the right-hand crank-arm by Allen-key studs. This means that they can be exchanged for others if you want to alter your gearing or replace your chainrings with others of better quality. (On some cheaper bikes, this is not possible.)

There are two different shapes of chainring. The conventional chainring is round, while a relatively new system is egg-shaped.

The number of gear teeth on chainrings varies; it can range from 26 on the small chainring of an all-terrain bike to 60 on the large chainring of a bike made for powerful bursts of speed. Chainrings with even more than 60 teeth have been used for attempting land speed records.

The number of teeth partly determines what gear ratios you have access to: gear ratios depend on the number of teeth on the chainring and on the rear sprocket, and on the size of the wheel. The fewer the teeth on your small front chainring, the lower the gears that you have access to; the more teeth there are on the large front chainring, the higher the gears you can use.

The bottom bracket: This consists of a shell — actually a large lug — through which an axle passes. On all but the cheapest bikes this axle is squared and tapered to accommodate the crank-arms, and it rotates on bearings held in position by cups. Manufacturers conforming to British standards normally make the right-hand cup with a left-hand thread, while the cup on the left has a right-hand thread. Those conforming to French standards do it the other way

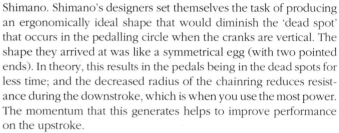

Elliptical chainrings

Chainrings are traditionally circular. Recently, however, elliptical chainrings have been marketed, the most widely used probably being the Biopace chainring made by Shimano. Shimano's designers set themselves the task of producing an ergonomically ideal shape that would diminish the 'dead spot' that occurs in the pedalling circle when the cranks are vertical. The shape they arrived at was like a symmetrical egg (with two pointed ends). In theory, this results in the pedals being in the dead spots for less time; and the decreased radius of the chainring reduces resistance during the downstroke, which is when you use the most power. The momentum that this generates helps to improve performance on the upstroke.

The Biopace is said to be especially suitable for cyclists with a slow cadence (mountain bike riders, for example), though designs for others have been developed and racers have reported good results. But some riders have dismissed elliptical chainrings as gimmicks, and it is possibly too early to know whether they have come to stay or not.

around. Find out what type you have before you remove or replace cranks, otherwise you may strip the thread.

The bottom bracket bears enormous stresses; it is important that it is strong and that there is a minimum of tolerance between the cups, the axle and the bearings. Poor adjustment will cause wear in the bearings.

Chains: The chain has to withstand tremendous forces and pressures, and it is mechanically one of the hardest-working parts on your bike. Good maintenance is essential if it is to have a long life. Keep it clean of grit and grime, well lubricated and free of tight links. (See Chapter 6 for advice on chain maintenance.)

Chains come in two widths: those for track bicycles have a width of 1/8 of an inch (3,2 millimetres) between the inside linking plates while chains for road bikes have a width of 3/32 inches (2,4 millimetres).

After about 5 000 kilometres, chains stretch and should be replaced.

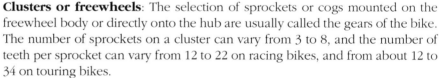

Clusters or freewheels: The selection of sprockets or cogs mounted on the freewheel body or directly onto the hub are usually called the gears of the bike. The number of sprockets on a cluster can vary from 3 to 8, and the number of teeth per sprocket can vary from 12 to 22 on racing bikes, and from about 12 to 34 on touring bikes.

In choosing the range of gears or sprockets for a bike, you should be guided by what sort of terrain you are going to tackle. (The more teeth on a sprocket, the lower the gearing can be. So, if you are going to tackle steep terrain with a heavily-loaded bike, your largest sprocket should have 32 or even 34 teeth.) Other factors to consider when you choose gears are your strength, your pedalling style, and your personal gear preference.

It is possible to get a cluster of easily interchangeable sprockets; these make it possible to alter the range of available gear ratios on a bike simply by exchanging some of the sprockets for others. In this way you can make a bike suitable for touring through steep terrain, and then by swopping some sprockets for others, give yourself the closer range of ratios that you would need for faster riding on flatter roads.

Clusters are hard-working components and are subject to metal fatigue and wear and tear through friction. Worn sprockets should be replaced because they will cause the chain to 'jump' and will dissipate your energy.

Gear systems

Three-speed gears (also called hub gears): These are simple to work, easy to maintain and fine for bikes that are only used for short trips — school bikes and shopping bikes, for example. Their main disadvantage, apart from giving a very limited range of gears, is that the gears are generally very widely-spaced. (If you are looking for a gearing system that is simple to operate but that gives a comfortable range of gear ratios, you might be better off with a 5-speed derailleur system than with a 3-speed system.)

Derailleur systems: The derailleur gear system offers from 5 to about 21 gear ratios, depending on the numbers of chainwheels and sprockets used. The system is made up of levers, cables, and the front and rear derailleurs. Commands to change the gear are directed through the levers and cables to the derailleurs, which literally 'de-rail' the chain from one sprocket to the next.

A good gear-lever system should be easily adjustable, and move firmly but fluidly with no slipping. When the gear is in the position you have chosen, it shouldn't budge, even when the bike is buffeted by the shocks of riding over rough terrain. A maladjusted gear system can be the cause of financial, mental, physical, mechanical, and even marital strain.

There are three lever systems currently in use:

- *The conventional friction lever.* The lever is tightened against a plate. The friction of the lever against the backing prevents the lever from slipping.

- *The retro-friction system.* A spring is fastened to the lever and housing. Pressure on the lever loosens the spring. More pressure is needed as the spring tightens, but this also prevents the lever from slipping.

How to calculate your gear ratios

To calculate your gear ratio in inches (which is still a commonly-used method), you multiply the number of teeth on your front chainwheel by the wheel diameter (measured in inches), and divide the answer by the number of teeth on the rear sprocket (cog). So if your chain is stretched between a front chainwheel that has, say, 42 teeth, and a rear cog with 21 teeth, and you have 27-inch wheels, you will be in a 54-inch gear.

$$\frac{42 \times 27}{21} = 54$$

This way of measuring gear ratios goes back to the days of the penny farthing: gear ratios are equivalent to the diameter of the front wheel of a penny farthing. In other words, if you are in a 54-inch gear, you will cover as much ground with one turn of the pedals as you would on a fixed-gear penny farthing with a wheel that measures 54 inches (about 137 centimetres) across. If you stretch out the circumference of the hypothetical 54-inch wheel, you can see exactly what that distance is. (It would be 4,31 metres.) A gear ratio chart appears in the Appendix.

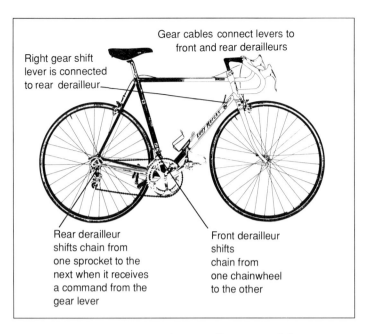

Right gear shift lever is connected to rear derailleur

Gear cables connect levers to front and rear derailleurs

Rear derailleur shifts chain from one sprocket to the next when it receives a command from the gear lever

Front derailleur shifts chain from one chainwheel to the other

■ *The index or click system:* This is an easy-to-use, precise system which, on better quality bikes, is replacing the older gear-changing systems. The click system normally only operates on the lever controlling the rear derailleur. The lever is mounted on a backing plate which has grooves into which bearings slip. With pressure, the bearing is lifted out of its housing and is brought around to the next groove. Each movement corresponds with a measured increase or release in tension of the cable, and, if the system is well adjusted, the derailleur is placed precisely over each sprocket with an audible click.

Correct adjustment of the gear system is critical to smooth working; it sometimes takes some time to get it right. It is also important to use compatible components.

The front derailleur: The sole function of this mechanically simple piece of equipment is to shift the chain from one chainring to another. The derailleur can be clamped around the down tube or attached to a brazed-on fitting on the frame. It should be adjusted carefully. (See Chapter 6.) Most good models are made of aluminium alloys, with the spring portion being made of high-tensile steel.

The rear derailleur: Tulio Campagnolo was a great racing cyclist, and through his direct participation in the sport he noted the need for a simple, lever/cable-operated system. Applying his experience and talent, he designed and produced what is perhaps Campagnolo's greatest contribution to the cycle component industry — the rear derailleur. The Campagnolo system has been copied by virtually every cycle manufacturer, and is still in use more than fifty years after its invention.

The rear derailleur's function is to shift the chain from one rear sprocket to the next, in response to the rider moving the gear lever.

The mechanism is based on a parallel movement, in which the moving cage plate with jockey wheels is in line with the cogs, ensuring responsive and smooth gear changing.

The Japanese have designed a variation on the Campagnolo system, in which the derailleur body runs parallel to the chainstay. Both systems are effective if they are correctly adjusted and maintained, and will give smooth gear changes.

Derailleurs used on touring and mountain bikes have specially adapted cage-plate derailleur wheel-mountings. The distance between the wheels is longer than normal, so the derailleur can accommodate wide sprocket variations.

Materials used in derailleur-manufacture vary. The parts receiving the toughest treatment should be specially case-hardened. Maximum rigidity and minimum tolerance in the working parts are signs of quality.

It isn't essential to buy expensive derailleurs. Many middle-of-the-range models are extremely reliable, smooth and precise.

Rear derailleur

CHAPTER FOUR

DIFFERENT BIKES
for different purposes

What do you want a bike for? For keeping fit and seeing the country? For racing? For hauling children and groceries, or for scaling the Drakensberg, or for going to work on? Do you want it for several of these purposes? This chapter describes the main types of bikes available and the features that make them suitable for the work that they are built for.

Utility bicycles

There are countless variations of the basic utility bicycle. Some are known as roadsters, some as shoppers, and others, somewhat ominously, as push-bikes. Utility bikes can in rare instances be expensive, but in the main they provide cheap, convenient transport for schoolchildren, mail and newspaper deliverers, professors, and anyone simply wanting to get from one place to another. Humble but faithful plodders, they are the mainstay of the bike trade, not only in this country, but in the world. Their versatility and appropriacy for all sorts of conditions have made them a vital part of transportation systems in many parts of the First and Third World. In the technically sophisticated Netherlands, people cover 12 billion kilometres a year on bicycles, most of them roadsters. In Beijing the streets ring daily with the bells of 5 million heavy black bicycles bearing names like Flying Pigeon, Plum Flower and Forever. And some top-level observers have claimed that roadsters played a decisive part in the defeat of the United States defence force by the largely peasant army of the Vietnamese: while American soldiers struggled to carry supplies dropped by their loud and obvious air force in the jungle, Vietnamese bicycles were quietly and invisibly trundling huge loads of equipment to their destinations.

The typical roadster has a heavy steel frame, flat handlebars, a wide saddle, mudguards, a rack for carrying loads, a chainguard and often a kickstand and a bell. Tyres are wide with deep tread. At most, it will have a 3-speed gearing system. Strength, low cost and longevity are its chief virtues.

Roadsters that have borrowed some of the lighter features of the touring bike are popular for schoolchildren.

Small-wheeled shopping and commuting bikes have been manufactured since the early 1960s. Though they're no longer as fashionable as they were (and they were very trendy in their time), they have several features to recommend

them for short neighbourhood shopping trips. They are nippy, with small turning circles, and many are designed to take awkward loads of the cornflakes-and-potatoes type more conveniently than any other bikes can. Seat height and handlebar height can be adjusted a long way up or down, so a family of tall and short people can share one as a run-around vehicle. But most are heavy and the small wheels result in a rough ride and poor braking properties.

Some are collapsible — a great advantage to someone who wants to ride to a railway station, fold the bike and put it under the seat for the journey and then get off and ride to the next destination. However, on all but the best quality bikes, the folding mechanisms tend to be troublesome and short-lived. Famous versions of folding small-wheeled bikes are the Moulton and the Bickerton, two lightweight, top-of-the-range, expensive British bicycles which are unfortunately not stocked by local dealers. But a promising Taiwanese commuting bike, the Dahon, recently came onto the local market in limited numbers. Owners have described them as practical and versatile. The Dahon weighs 12 kilograms, has a 5-speed gearing system and folds compactly. Shock absorbers prevent the jolting that many small-wheeled bikes give. Its high-pressure tyres help to offset the fact that small wheels have greater rolling resistance than large ones do. The Dahon's price is high compared with those of most utility bikes, but the components are good, and if it's used instead of a car for commuting, the savings could pay for the bike in a few months.

Long-wheelbase bikes are a variation of the utility bike which provide a stable way of hauling heavy loads. Two examples are Ian Grayson's Long Bike and his Ho Chi Min bike; both were built in response to his experiences of cycling in Asia and his native Australia, which persuaded him that First and Third World conditions call for a vehicle that carries loads with less effort, more speed and more manoeuvrability than existing pedal-powered transport could. 'People will desert their bikes if bikes do not fulfil their transport requirements', he writes. 'Many keen cyclists are reluctant car owners, because efficient load-carrying work bikes are not available. The key word here is efficient ... Bulk shopping once a week for an average family is a breeze on the Ho Chi Min, and as a workhorse on a farm, it's a virtual 10-speed wheelbarrow.' Nothing like these bikes is commercially available here, but it's high time they were.

If you're interested in designs for human powered utility vehicles (HPUVs) see the Appropriate technology section in the Appendix.

Top: The Dahon folds easily and can be wheeled along on a castor or zipped up into its own shoulder bag. Bottom: Ian Grayson's long wheelbase touring and multi-use bike is quick to load and keeps weight low, helping to ensure stability. The basket welded along it stiffens the frame.

Children's bicycles

First bikes: When buying a first bike, check that the saddle can be adjusted to a wide range of heights. Learning to balance on a two-wheeler is best done with the saddle set low, so that feet can easily reach terra firma and so that the bike can be scooted along. Once a child has learned to ride, the saddle should be raised to give a better riding position. Stabilizers or training wheels help develop confidence, but they can delay learners from getting the real feel of balancing.

Most under-sixes spend a lot of time falling off, so it's safest to have a bike that has no top tube. This lessens the risk of being knocked in the crotch — an experience which is not only common, but also very painful and can do damage.

Older children's bikes: Buying a bike for a child of about seven upwards takes some careful balancing of economic sense and care for safety. Because young bike owners not only beat their machines up but also grow out of them quickly, parents tend to think that the cheapest will do. But at this age children are starting to get onto roads, and reliable quality — especially in things like brakes — is nothing less than a life-and-death matter.

Never buy a bike that is too big in the hope the child will soon grow into it. Oversized bikes are uncomfortable and perilously hard to control. Bikes that are too small are also hard to control. It is far better to have a second-hand bike that fits than a new one that doesn't.

BMX bikes are ideal in many ways. Good quality models are stable, they have good brakes and they're tough enough to withstand cruel treatment. Off-road riding in a safe place on a BMX is more than just an exciting way of discovering

the limits of recklessness: it can develop judgement and skills such as acceleration, braking and balancing — all essential for competent town riding. That's provided that children know that stunts are safe in some places but killers in others.

BMX bikes don't have gears, so they're not a good choice for children who want to cover distances or who have hills to get over.

You're unlikely to find a child's all-purpose road bike of exciting quality locally. But with some replacement of standard parts, an ordinary bike can be upgraded to meet the ambitions of children who want to join adults on long rides. (See 'Improving an old bike' at the end of Chapter 5.) Another option is to get a child's bike made by a frame builder. If you choose sensibly-priced components, this needn't be as extravagant as it sounds. Finally, if money's no object, and if you travel, you could buy a bike overseas; the upmarket range available for children abroad matches high quality adult bikes, and includes miniature mountain bikes.

Robust wheels and tubing, wide, knobbly tyres and good brakes that are easy to manipulate, a comfortable saddle and a protected top tube and front bar make the better BMXs ideal for young riders.

In most ways, the quality of a child's bike is judged in the same way as an adult's. Here are additional points to bear in mind:

Brakes: Check that hand-operated brakes are easy to work and are strongly made. Beware of dual or so-called safety levers which sometimes come as an adjunct to standard brake levers; they may be easier for children to reach and manipulate, but most give a slower and weaker response than standard levers do.

Children whose hands are too small to manage hand brakes comfortably should have pedal-operated brakes. But these don't give graduated control and can cause skidding, so they can't be considered safe in traffic.

Wheels: Rims on children's bikes are nearly always made of steel. Think about replacing them with aluminium rims for this metal's superior braking properties. Solid, puncture-proof tyres are available, but their drawbacks are greater than their advantages: they're said to give a shatteringly rough ride, and their heavy weight adversely affects steering.

Gears: For very young riders gears are more distracting than useful. Most older children do need them. A 3-speed system is usually adequate for getting to school and around the neighbourhood. More ambitious children deserve a 10- or 12-speed system.

General: Avoid children's bikes that are fitted with nylon bearings; these wear out in no time. See that parts which may in time need replacing **can** be replaced; you may find that entire clusters of parts are manufactured all in one, and if they break, there's no easy way of replacing them.

Safety: Special attention should be paid to safe carriers for satchels and sport equipment (you can get clips for holding tennis rackets and hockey sticks), and to reflectors and other devices that make the bike conspicuous to motorists. See Chapter 16 for information on extra equipment.

Touring bicycles

A touring bike is designed for covering long distances pleasurably. It's sturdy enough to carry camping equipment without cracking up or becoming awkward to control, and it's stable enough to stay upright on rough roads. It's designed to take mudguards, and carriers for panniers (though these are often removed when they're not in use). It may have flat handlebars, but it is more likely to have the racier dropped bars. Priorities are comfort and reliability. These qualities make it dependable as a commuting bike as well. Total weight is usually 11–13,5 kilograms.

The true touring bike is less popular here than it is overseas. This is partly because the popularity of 'fun rides' (organized mass rides) has brought out competitive instincts among many recreational riders; even those who are consistent tail-enders join these rides to try and better their own previous best times (if no-one else's), and they want efficient, racy bikes. It may also be because touring in this country usually means riding far; towns and campsites are often 100 kilometres or more apart, and the benefits of a lighter, more responsive bike can make it worth sacrificing the greater comfort of a real touring bike, if one isn't carrying equipment that would negate the weight-saving. You can argue against the logic of the second point by saying that the further you ride, the more important comfort is. The choice really rests on the rider's own preferences. Nowadays many riders — even those who keep to tarred roads — see all-terrain bikes as the real touring bikes of the future. So even if your ambitions aren't to ride goat tracks through Lesotho, don't settle for a standard touring bike before reading the section on mountain bikes.

If you want to load your bike up with a tent and enjoy total independence, you should opt for the dependable qualities of the touring bike shown in the diagram. If you're keener on unencumbered, faster riding and if you have a sag-wagon carrying equipment on long rides, you'll need something like the road bike described in the 'Racing bicycles' section later in this chapter. If your needs lie somewhere between a sports and a touring bike, you should look for a bicycle that combines the features you most want.

Frame: A typical touring bike has relaxed frame angles of 72–73 degrees, and a long wheelbase, making for a stable bike that transmits a minimum of road shock to the rider. The long fork rake ensures that steering won't be jumpy — a particularly important point if you carry front panniers, as the weight of these would magnify any tendency to twitchiness. The frame dimensions have to allow clearance for wide tyres and for accessories such as mudguards.

Tubing should be reasonably light. Very light tubing would be a waste of money because the loads likely to be carried would negate some of its advantages; also, the thin walls of very light tubing would cause a lot of frame flex in a bike that has fairly long tubes, as a tourer has. Tubing such as Reynolds 501, Reynolds 531 or Columbus Aelle makes an excellent touring frame, but humbler quality can also be satisfactory.

Frame size may be up to 2 centimetres bigger than you would choose for a racing bike, if the advantages of a fairly upright position appeal more to you than the benefits of reduced wind resistance that you would enjoy on a smaller frame.

Gears: Gearing on a touring bike should enable riders of moderate fitness and strength to conquer hills without great strain, and it should put mountain passes within the abilities of riders who've done a bit of training. Ten or 12-speed gears are usual. Some touring bikes have 15, 18 or more. For a bike that's to be used in steep terrain, particularly if heavy loads are carried, the following are recommended: front chainwheels with 40 and 50 teeth (for very steep country, you might want as few as 30 teeth on the small chainwheel); a rear cluster with 28, 24, 20, 17 and 14 teeth would give a good range for typical touring needs.

Wheels: Have the best you can afford. Spokes, rims and tyres are more likely to need replacing than any other parts on a tour and should be robust. If you plan to be heavily loaded, you may need a rear wheel with more spokes than normal — 40 or 44, as against the more usual 36 or so. A four-cross pattern for lacing the rear wheel spokes will add strength (and a little weight) and cut down the possibility of spokes breaking.

Choosing between narrow, light, fast tyres and wider, more resilient, comfortable ones isn't easy. But bear in mind the fact that narrow tyres are more prone to cuts and wear and that they can be knocked sideways by small stones that a wider tyre would simply run over. The dangers of being deflected and dumped on the road are increased if you're carrying a load. Moreover, if you're somewhere between Fraauwkraal and Siberia (Cape Province) when your last spare tyre is shredded, it'll be a lot easier to replace a 28- or 32-millimetre tyre than a narrow one at a local shop. Wider tyres give you the option of exploring gravel roads. Narrow tyres don't.

Brakes: Good centrepull or sidepull brakes are fine for most touring needs. But for a heavily loaded bike on steep routes, the extra power and reliability of cantilever brakes make it worth having them mounted.

Components on a touring bike should be reasonably easy to replace, repair or find a substitute for if necessary, though if the quality's good enough, you may never need to. Quality is obviously very important, in as far as a bike that you head into the wilderness on should be reliable. You can justify spending a lot of money on a good touring bike — but you can also have a very good time on any old tourer if it's sound.

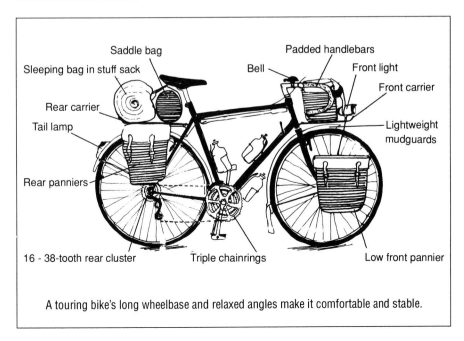

A touring bike's long wheelbase and relaxed angles make it comfortable and stable.

All-terrain bikes (ATBs) or mountain bicycles

All-terrain bikes are made for riding on gravel roads and wilderness tracks. They're characterized by agility, stability and toughness and a good model will get you through mud, beach sand, snow, and, if you wish, down a staircase. They're also at home on tar roads, where their comfort and responsiveness make them excellent for commuting and touring. They're about 20 per cent slower on open roads than most touring bikes — perhaps an advantage if you're out to enjoy scenery.

This relatively new type of bicycle has a small, but keen and rapidly growing following in this country. Overseas, all-terrain bikes account for a major part of high quality bike sales, and at recent international bike shows, as much as 75 per cent of floor space has been taken by ATB exhibits. The range of imported mountain bikes available here is limited but of high quality, and local frame builders are producing small runs as well.

One reason that mountain bikes have caused so much excitement is because they bring together the lightness and refinement of a top-class modern bicycle with the best qualities of the no-nonsense work-bike (for which people saturated with the complexities of high-tech equipment have had an aching nostalgia); the end result is a machine that's both adventurous and dependable.

Good quality and light weight (about 11 to 14 kilograms) are essential — and the rougher the riding, the more that holds true. Several low-cost imitations of mountain-bikes have come on to the market. They may make adequate commuter-bikes, but their inferior components and heavy weight make it impossible to take them seriously for off-road riding or touring.

The typical mountain bike has the following features, though there are many variations catering for the different ambitions of competitive off-road riders, tourers and those just wanting a superior *trapfiets*: a lightweight frame, flat handlebars, wide tyres, usually with a knobbly tread pattern for good traction, ultra-powerful brakes, a comfortable padded saddle and widely-ranging gear ratios.

Frames: Frame geometry varies. It may be very relaxed and stable with a long wheelbase and frame angles of about 70–72 degrees for touring and general riding. Or it may have a tighter design with steepish angles of up to 74 degrees for more responsive, agile off-road performance. The bottom bracket is usually high — 29–33 centimetres for good clearance of rough ground; this results in a smaller than usual frame, and this in turn contributes to rigidity — a very necessary feature for responsive off-road riding. Tubing is lightweight, often with a wide diameter, and is usually specially made for mountain bike use. Handlebars are straight or slightly angled, and usually wide to give good leverage for steering and to help to keep the rider stable on loose surfaces.

Wheels: These look comically solid and stout alongside standard 27-inch wheels, but new technology has made them not only robust but amazingly light. Wheel diameters range from 24 inches to the more usual 26 inches; the small size contributes to extra strength. Spokes are thick, and rims are wide (17–25 millimetres) to take balloon tyres. Rims must be made of aluminium alloy. Some cheap pseudo mountain bikes have steel rims, which are too heavy for off-road riding, and brakes don't work well on them. For really demanding riding, special high-performance rims made of hardened alloy, sometimes anodized for extra protection, are available.

Tyres for off-road riding have a deep tread pattern that reaches beyond the tyre edges, so they grip well on loose surfaces. They come in different widths — as wide as 55 millimetres for off-road riding, and narrower for hard surfaces. The knobblier the tread pattern, the better traction it will have on sandy or stony surfaces, but the more tiring it will be to ride on hard roads. Some tyres have a dual-purpose design: they're wide and knobbly enough to grip well on gravel, but they also have a raised central ridge so that (theoretically, anyway,) wheels roll easily on a hard road. ATB tyres with a relatively smooth tread have been developed for riding on tar, where they are a little faster (but more puncture-prone) than knobbly off-road tyres.

Gears: The gearing system on an ATB should be of high quality to take the severe punishing that off-road riding gives. The gearing on some models is much like that of a 10- or 12-speed touring bike; provided that it's designed to cope with steep climbs, this should be suitable for riding on tar or gravel roads. For ambitious off-road riding or for really mountainous roads, a bike with a triple chainwheel and 7-speed freewheel is a better choice.

Gear levers are mounted on the handlebars, making it easy to flick them without losing balance. Indexed gears ('click' gears) have become standard equipment.

Brakes: It's vital that these are strong, sensitive and work predictably. Most mountain bikes are fitted with cantilever brakes. Some come fitted with side- or centrepull brakes, but these are only adequate for tame riding, and it's not easy to replace them later with cantilevers, as these require special brazed-on mounting points.

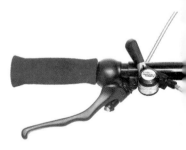

Comfortable grips, thumbshift gear levers and easily worked brake levers.

Tandems

Few things encourage companionable partnership as happily as a tandem does; moreover, it's a partnership with great practical benefits, as tandems are usually faster and more energy-efficient than single bicycles. They provide a safe way of including children on long rides, and of giving blind people a chance to enjoy exhilarating exercise. On the other hand, tandems have been known to put everlasting blight on marriages, friendships and child/parent relationships. They're not for everyone. Try out a borrowed or hired one before committing yourself to such an uncompromising alliance.

Some tandems are designed for racing (though local competition is limited to informal 'fun rides'). Some are built for touring. Recently tandems built to mountain bike specifications have appeared; however, the unwieldy length of a mountain tandem prevents riders from covering the rough terrain that a single mountain bike takes in its stride.

Tandems have the following advantages over other bicycles:

- Overall, they're faster because of the combined leg-power of two riders propelling a machine that weighs far less than two separate bicycles. Up hills, a tandem is slightly slower than a single bike, unless the two riders can work in virtually faultless unison. Down hills, the combined weight of two riders can make a tandem breathtakingly fast. In the Argus Tour, which has a special category for tandems, speeds of about 100 kilometres an hour have been recorded.
- They're more efficient. Only the pilot (the front rider) has to work against wind resistance while the stoker on the back sits in a near-perfect slipstream. (Even on a calm day, breaking wind resistance uses up about 30 percent of a cyclist's energy at average touring speeds.) This helps to make it a good vehicle for touring over long distances.
- Tandems are very stable, thanks to their uncommonly long wheelbases.
- When a strong rider and a weaker rider cycle together, a tandem helps to iron out their differences. This is specially useful when an adult and child want to ride together; at the same time, the child is far safer than he or she would be on a separate bike.

A tandem's drawbacks are that it's sometimes unwieldy and it doesn't allow the independence that separate bikes do. You can't carry as much baggage as you can on two bikes. It's difficult (and sometimes impossible) to transport by car, air or train. The unavoidable length of its tubes makes it prone to flexibility. It has to bear enormous stresses and can be a troublesome beast mechanically unless it's of high quality. Using standard bicycle

A fairing, aero helmets and the inherent efficiency of the tandem combine to make this an excitingly fast racing bike. The wheelbase on this tandem is unusually short because it is built for speed.

components — unless they're exceptionally strong — on any part that takes stress is seldom, if ever, good enough, though it's often tried. Tandem parts can be hard to find at the best of times; if they pack up in the wilderness, you won't replace them at the local store.

Frame: A tandem frame presents a major engineering challenge: firstly, the long wheelbase and the long tubes that go with it make the bike susceptible to a great deal of frame whip. On top of that, the frame has to bear the considerable torsional force that two people can generate when they pedal. And it has the weight of two people to bear, though its parts come to less than the sum of two separate bicycles. Solutions lie firstly in clever geometry: there are several frame designs that give good bracing. For obvious reasons it's a bad idea to have a frame with no top tube on the back section (the so-called woman's design). A second solution is to use wide-diameter tubing, and/or tubing with a greater wall thickness. Most good tandems are built with specialized tandem tubing. A third solution is to reinforce the joints that bear the greatest stress.

If you and your partner are of very different heights, you're unlikely to get a suitable tandem off a bike-dealer's shelf. Your dealer should be able to arrange a custom-built tandem; if not, turn to the list of frame builders in the Appendix of this book. If you do have a frame specially built, think out the whole bike carefully first: the way the frame's built will determine what wheels, brakes and other components can be used on it.

Wheels: These have to bear double the load that wheels on conventional bikes do. You have to accept that on tandem wheels strength is far more important than light weight. Ways of ensuring strength are by using 26-inch wheels instead of the less strong 27-inch type; sturdy aluminium alloy rims with 40–48 14-gauge spokes, laced in a four-cross pattern and with hubs made for tandems are basic requirements for most tandems.

Brakes: Powerful brakes are crucial. (Think about that downhill speed of 100 kilometres per hour.) It's advisable to have calliper brakes — ideally cantilevers — on both wheels plus a drum brake at the back. The pilot can control the whole lot if both calliper brakes are operated by one lever, while the drum brake is operated by the other.

Left: A tandem adapted with a raised bottom bracket attachment. Top: This couple had four tyres blow out in four hours before they replaced their steel rims with aluminium ones.

Recumbents

The loose term 'recumbent' is usually taken to mean a supine semi-recumbent bicycle — in other words, a bike on which the rider sits on a low seat with legs stretched out to the pedals in front. There are, however, other recumbents such as prone recumbents, on which the rider is face-down, and fully supine recumbents, on which the rider is flat on his back.

Several very practical recumbent bicycles have been manufactured and marketed in small numbers during the past decade, and have been successfully used for touring and commuting. Most of the activity has been in the United States and in Britain. To date recumbents aren't commercially distributed in this country, and the limited numbers on our roads have mainly been made by individuals with a special interest in designing and building bikes. Some recumbent tricycles have also been produced, but none could be considered practical for commuting or touring.

Most of the current world speed cycling records have been set using streamlined supine semi-recumbent bicycles. Some are described and illustrated in Chapter 9.

Recumbent bicycles provide a comfortable, broad seat with a backrest allowing a comfortable head position for good forward vision; and they have lower air resistance compared to a rider in the touring position on a conventional bicycle. A recumbent's advantage of having less air resistance than a conventional bicycle is felt particularly when panniers are fitted; unlike a touring bike which has panniers bulging out at the sides, a recumbent can stow luggage behind the backrest without adding to the bike's width.

The seat backrest effectively resists the reaction to pedalling — so much so that caution is needed to prevent straining untrained knee joints and muscles.

Recumbents are in many ways inherently safer than conventional bicycles: the rider's constant head position ensures good use of rear-view mirrors; the rider's low centre of gravity greatly reduces the chances of being thrown head-first over the handlebars and ensures a softer landing if one falls sideways; the lower centre of gravity also contributes to better braking force from the rear wheel, and travelling feet first is very much safer than travelling head first!

Disadvantages of recumbents include the long wheelbase (resulting in a large turning circle), lack of certain accessories and spare parts, and the transfer of grease from the chain to the rider's clothing. The lowness of a recumbent can

Easy Racer. (Rear tyre 25-630, 25-622 or 28 inch tubular; front tyre 32-419 or 20 inch tubular.) The most popular long-wheelbase recumbent ever produced, designed by Gardner Martin, 1978. The seat, handlebars and backrest are adjustable. Available from Easy Racers Inc. with a chrome-moly or aluminium frame in various sizes, with optional extras such as front and rear fairings, wheel covers and rear panniers. The company has an impressive race history: their Gold Rush, (based on Easy Racer) won the du Pont prize in 1986 by averaging 105,36 km/h over 200m. The Bat Glider on which Lloyd Wright won the 1984 Argus Tour was also based on the Easy Racer. The Gold Rush is now in the Smithsonian Institute and The Glider is part of the Rupert International Collection of bicycles in the Heidelberg Transport Museum near Johannesburg.

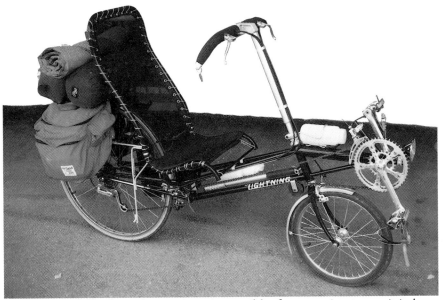

Lightning P-38. (Rear tyre 25-630, 25-622 or 28 inch tubular; front tyre 32-369.) A medium-wheelbase recumbent designed by Tim Brummer. The bottom bracket shell and handlebars are adjustable. The crank axle is high to reduce air resistance. Streamlined panniers, a front nosecone and Spandex fairing are available as well as discs to cover the wheel spokes. Brummer's Lightning X-2 holds an unofficial low-altitude speed record. Lloyd Wright rode the F-40 Tomahawk (a Lightning P-38 in tracing trim) to win the 1988 and 1989 Argus Tours.

also make it difficult, and sometimes impossible, for motorists to see it in busy traffic; recumbent riders must therefore take extra care to position themselves where they can be sure of being visible to motorists. On some recumbent designs it's difficult to set off without some slight initial wobbling, but this stops as soon as the rider has gathered a bit of momentum.

There are three basic types of recumbent, the position of the cranks in relation to the front wheel determining the type. The first type, the *long-wheelbase recumbent*, has the front wheel ahead of the cranks. The *medium-wheelbase* version has the front wheel below the cranks, and the *short-wheelbase* has the front wheel behind the cranks. Designers invariably find that a small front wheel is required and avoid the short-wheelbase because it places the rider's centre of gravity too far forward. (Most world record holders, however, have small front wheels with large rear wheels to take standard cogs.)

If you want a recumbent yourself, you will probably have to build it; instruction packages are available from several designers. We suggest you write to John Stegmann at 1 Heath St, Newlands 7700, South Africa, or to Easy Racers Inc., Box 25, Freedom, California 95019, or to the International Human Powered Vehicle Association (IHPVA), Box 51255, Indianapolis 46251, USA.

Manuped. (Front and rear tyres 25-622 or 28 inch tubular.) A medium wheelbase front-wheel-drive recumbent, made and raced between 1979 and 1983 by Fred Tatch and others, Oregon. This version is both hand and foot cranked and was used with a crude fairing to beat the USA national tandem team in a 30 km road race. Several enthusiasts are working on fwd recumbents, but neither the Manuped nor any other fwd machine is currently manufactured.

Racing bicycles

Because there are many types of competition, racing bicycles have become increasingly specialized to meet the demands of different events. What they all have in common, however, is that they are designed primarily for speed and responsiveness; frames are compact and rigid, typically with head and seat tube angles of 73–76 degrees and with seat tubes tending towards the vertical. Wheelbases are short — about 98 to 100 centimetres. Handlebars are positioned low in relation to the saddle to allow the rider to tuck up into an aerodynamically efficient position.

Lightness is another prerequisite: a kilogramme off the weight of a bicycle can save you several seconds over a race as short as 3 kilometres. Consequently sophisticated technology has been used to manufacture tubing for racing that is feather-light, unyieldingly rigid and supremely strong.

Rims are usually shod with tubular tyres for their lightness and low rolling resistance, though improved quality in wire-on tyres has made them worthy of use in races.

Specialization of bikes for particular events follows these principles:

- The shorter and faster the race, the steeper, stronger and more compact the frame. Longer events ideally require shallower angles and a bit more flexibility in the frame.
- Sometimes crank lengths are changed for different events - longer cranks allow for smoother pedalling action while shorter cranks favour acceleration.
- For sprinting events, handlebars with deeper drops are used while in road racing shallower and squarer bars prevail.

For a long time racing bicycle technology has been at the centre of a conflict of interests. On the one hand there are designers and scientists who are continually researching and developing equipment that takes cyclists further, faster, for less effort. On the other hand there are race authorities who ensure that competition is between athletes rather than between machines by imposing restrictions on the design and dimensions of bicycles that may be used in official races. (These restrictions are shown in the diagram.) One result of this is that many modifications that could reduce the effects of wind resistance are not allowed, unless they

Bicycles used for racing must conform to these measurements:
Maximum length: 2m
Maximum width: 70cm
Distance from ground to bottom bracket (bb): 24 - 30cm
Maximum distance between top of saddle and bb axis:
  12cm
Distance between bb axis and front wheel axis: 58 - 75cm
Maximum distance between bb axis and rear wheel axis:
  55cm.

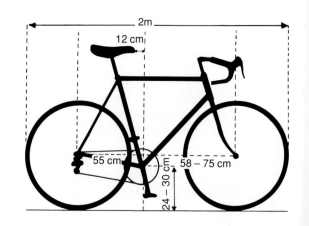

can be proved to exist for structural reasons. To give an example, you are not allowed to race on a bicycle that has spoked wheels overlaid with discs to reduce wind drag; you can, however, race using spokeless disc wheels because on these, the sides of the disc exist for structural purposes. (See Chapter 9 for details of time savings made by using 'aero' equipment; much of the equipment listed there is permissible in races.) Needless to say, the distinction between structural function and aerodynamic design are often blurred and contentious.

One can understand the reasoning behind the controls on bicycle design, but there is no doubt that it has inhibited the advance of bicycle technology.

Road racing bicycles

A road racing bicycle must not only be efficient but also strong enough to survive the rigours of long distance events. And it must handle predictably, allowing the fine control needed to ride safely in a tight bunch of fast-moving cyclists. In addition, some concessions must be made to comfort, otherwise, on long races, the rider's fatigue will outweigh the benefits of a rigid, compact frame.

Competitors in stage races often have specialized bikes for different stages. A good hill-climbing bike, for example, will be ultra-light with a very short wheelbase to minimize mass and inertia. A bike used for criterium racing, which demands quick and continuous reactions to corners, and frequent speed variations, should have a compact frame with angles of 74 - 75 degrees. It should be able to lean to an angle of 35 degrees before the pedal hits the road (the usual lean angle is about 30 degrees). Short cranks and a high bottom bracket will give a bike a greater lean angle. Because criteriums are usually ridden with the hands on the drops of the bars, the handlebars often have a softer curve than that of most road bikes, to prevent them from interfering with the wrists.

Road racing bicycle

A small front wheel radially spoked and with an aero-profile rim, a rear disc wheel, and bullhorn handlebars contribute to reducing the effects of wind drag on this time trial bike.

Time trial bicycles

The design of bikes used for time trials and triathlons is dictated by the fact that cyclists ride these events alone, without the benefits of drafting behind other riders. And the distances they cover are generally short; 40 kilometres is typical, though they can cover as much as 120 kilometres. Consequently time trial bikes are built to give as much aerodynamic advantage as competition rules will allow, even though this may impair steering accuracy. 'Aero' or bullhorn handlebars, disc wheels (more often the rear one, though sometimes both), aero tubing and components, and a front wheel smaller than the rear one all contribute to making the lone rider's race against the clock faster.

Track racing bicycles

Brakeless and limited to one fixed gear, the track bike is the ultimate in stripped-down simplicity. It is rigid and short for maximum acceleration in sprints, with frame angles of about 75–76 degrees, and has handlebars set low to enable the rider to use arm and back muscles to pull on them and deliver extra power to the pedals. The front forks are often circular in cross-section (unlike the forks of road bikes, which have an oval cross-section). This is to give the forks the extra lateral strength needed to overcome stresses that come from riding on banking. The bottom bracket is usually high (about 280 millimetres) off the ground to ensure clearance of banked tracks.

Gear ratios on a track bike are altered by changing the chainwheel blade or the rear sprocket. Race rules restrict young riders to fairly low gear ratios to prevent muscle or joint damage.

CHAPTER FIVE

CHOOSING A BIKE:
size and position

For the casual rider who is not overly concerned with details, there are simple rules of thumb for choosing a bike that's about the right size. But the better your bicycle fits you, the more comfortable you will be and the more efficiently you will ride. This chapter tells you how to judge what size of road or mountain bike you should ride, and how you should be positioned on it; it also discusses buying a bike, ordering a custom-built bike, assessing a second-hand bike and improving an old bike.

The simplest method for choosing a bicycle that fits you well enough to be safe and comfortable for short rides is as follows: Straddle the frame, putting your two bare feet on either side of it; there should be 4–5 centimetres between your crotch and the top tube. Next, sit on the bike (with someone holding it up), put your *heels* on the pedals, and rotate them backwards; at the bottom of the downstroke, your leg should be almost straight. Don't be tempted to over-adjust the saddle height in order to achieve this: between 5 and 10 centimetres of the seat post should be showing. Once you're riding on the bike, you should not feel that you are having to stretch uncomfortably, and brakes should be easy to to reach and manipulate. Nor should there be any feeling of being cramped.

Of course, if you're buying a quality bicycle, you will want a more accurate way of judging whether a bicycle fits you, as careful attention to measurements can result in subtle but significant improvements in performance.

Though detailed theories exist on frame size selection, there is no universal agreement on what is right; many knowledgeable cyclists hold different opinions. But the guidelines given here are based on widely accepted theories, and they have worked for me. The following section deals mainly with selecting the right size of bicycle for racing, fast recreational riding and touring; mountain bike sizes are discussed later in the chapter.

Leg straight

Heel on pedal

How to measure a frame

The seat tube measurement: The correct size of frame is determined mainly by the length of the rider's legs. Consequently, frame measurements are based on the length of the seat tube. So when people talk about a 54-centimetre frame,

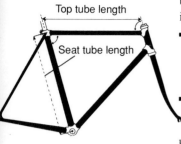

Top tube length

Seat tube length

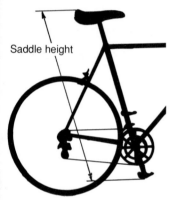

Saddle height

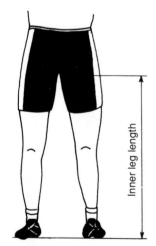

Inner leg length

Scientists have calculated that the cyclist is most efficient when the saddle height is 109 per cent of the inner leg measurement.

they mean a frame with a 54-centimetre seat tube. The seat tube can be measured in one of two ways:

- The *centre to centre* method involves measuring from the centre of the bottom bracket to the centre of the seat tube lug. This is the most commonly used method in the industry. Some frame builders stamp this measurement on the underside of the bottom bracket shell.
- The *centre to top* measurement: this measurement is taken from the centre of the bottom bracket to the top of the seat tube lug.

It's important to be clear about which measurement is used, as the difference between them is about a centimetre — enough to be noticeable.

The top tube measurement is the next important dimension. It is made from the centre of the seat tube lug to the centre of the top tube lug (or the equivalent spot if the frame is lugless). This measurement is normally the same as the seat tube when measured by the centre to centre method; this configuration suits cyclists with physiques of average proportions.

If you have unusual proportions, it may be worth getting a frame builder to construct a frame with top tube and seat tube measurements that match your measurements.

You can get a preliminary idea of what your frame size should be by taking your inside leg measurement and subtracting a third from it. So if your inner leg measures 80 centimetres, a 53–54 centimetre frame will probably fit you, though you should also do the checks described later in this chapter. (The leg measurement should be made from crotch to floor, when you are standing barefoot.)

Frame size and seat post length: The length of the seat post that shows between the seat tube and the saddle varies, depending on the frame size. Generally, the larger the frame size, the further out the seat post should be. As a rough guide, a 57-centimetre frame (measured centre to centre) should have approximately 10 centimetres of seat post exposed, while a 52-centimetre frame should not have more than 9 centimetres showing. There should always be an adequate length of seat post within the seat tube: it is dangerous to extend the seat post beyond the maximum mark which is marked on it.

Determining the correct saddle height

Saddle height is taken to be the distance between the top of the saddle and the centre of the pedal axle, measured when the pedal is down, and the crank arm is in line with the seat tube. The most common way of determining the optimum saddle height is by measuring the length of the rider's inner leg (floor to crotch) and multiplying it by 109 per cent. Alternatively, multiply the distance from the top of the femur to the floor by 96 per cent. Both these methods will, theoretically, give you the correct height.

To ensure that the measurement is as accurate as possible, wear cycling shorts or skants to prevent interference from clothes; stand barefoot and erect against a wall, with your feet about 18 centimetres apart; take three measurements, and use the average. Once you have calculated the measurement, the following factors must be taken into account:

- Foot size: People with small feet might require a lower saddle and vice versa.
- Individual pedalling style.
- The thickness of the sole of the cycling shoe and cleats. (The measurements

of the sole and cleat thickness should be added to the saddle height measurement.)
- The thickness of the cycling shorts' chamois.
- The amount of give in the saddle.
- The cyclist's legs: some cyclists have a natural tendency to ride knock-kneed or bow-legged, or one leg may be longer than the other.

All these factors may affect saddle height by up to 2 centimetres.

Good positioning

Correct foot position

Before you can judge what the right position for your feet is, you should see that your cycling shoes fit like the proverbial gloves: any slipping within the shoes can cause chafing.

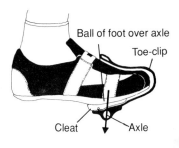

Correct foot position.

The ball of the foot must be over the pedal axle. The foot should be parallel to the crank arm, when it is lying parallel to the long axis of the cycle. (The 3 o'clock position.) In general, toes pointed in or out should be considered out of alignment, as they can cause knee problems. However, the cyclist who congenitally has pigeon-toes or feet that stick out should never try to force them into a straight line as this will probably also result in knee or ankle problems.

The toe-clip size, for those who use them, is also important. The foot should not push up against the clip: I recommend a gap of 0,5 to 1 millimetre between the shoe and the clip. A rough guide to the toe-clip size is:
- Shoe size 1–5 = small toe-clip
- Shoe size 6–8 = medium toe-clip
- Shoe size 9 up = large toe-clip

Before purchasing the clips, make sure that your cleats — the devices that are screwed on the soles of racing shoes, and which slot securely into the pedal — are correctly positioned on your shoes. You can do this by putting on your cycling shoes (without the cleats) and then riding with your foot correctly positioned on the pedals; the pedals should mark the soles of your shoes, showing where the cleats should be fitted. When you attach the cleats, make sure that the groove is aligned with the back edge of the pedal. The new cleat system that slots into clipless pedals (see Chapter 3) is easily set up. Clear instructions usually come with the pedals and cleats.

Saddle position

The saddle should ideally be set in the middle of the seat post: a hypothetical vertical line drawn through the middle of the saddle should bisect the post.

It's important that the saddle should be at the right angle — either parallel to the ground or tilted up to a maximum of 2 millimetres. You can check it by placing a spirit level along the top of the saddle. An incorrectly tilted saddle, with the nose pointed down or too far up can cause back problems, and pins and needles or numbness in the crotch and hands.

Many women seem to find it difficult to arrive at a comfortable saddle angle. The best solution is usually to get a saddle specifically designed for women, and to position it parallel to the ground.

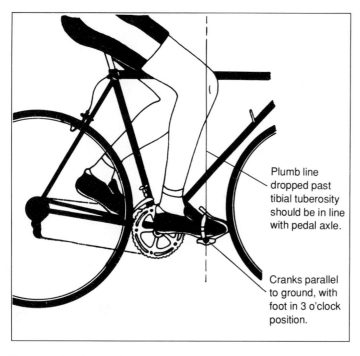

Plumb line dropped past tibial tuberosity should be in line with pedal axle.

Cranks parallel to ground, with foot in 3 o'clock position.

The correct seated position.

Positioning yourself

Once you have set the height and position of the saddle correctly, and have positioned your cleats, you should check that your body is correctly positioned in relation to the bottom bracket.

Get someone to hold you up while you are seated on the bicycle in the position you usually sit in, and then pedal backwards. Stop at the position illustrated here. Drop a plumb line from the centre of the tibial tuberosity (the little bump that is about a centimetre behind the patella and above the shin). This line should bisect the centre of the pedal axle. If you are too far back or forward, you can move the saddle accordingly. I have found this position ideal for racing, though some riders find that moving the saddle forward slightly puts them in a more effective racing position.

Shallower-angled frames (as you would find on a touring bike) allow the rider to sit further back, which tends to be more comfortable.

You may find that factors such as your pedalling action, the length of your femur and the size of your feet make it necessary to deviate slightly from the ideal position described here, but you should not deviate from it by more than 1,5 centimetres either way.

The length of the handlebar stem

There are many factors involved in choosing the right stem length; you will find the advice of a good dealer valuable here. The main factors to consider are the length of the upper body in proportion to the legs, arm length, suppleness of the spine, the type of cycling you intend doing, fitness, body fat and, of course, personal experience and preference. Use these guidelines to determine the correct stem length:

- Stand next to the cycle; place an elbow joint against the front of the saddle, and hold the arm parallel to the top tube with fingers outstretched. The fingertips should be about 1 to 2 centimetres short of the handlebars.
- Get on the bicycle and get someone to hold you up; assume a racing position with your hands on the drops of the bars. When you look down, your front hub should ideally be obscured by the handlebars. If you can see the hub, it should only just be visible on the inside of the handlebar. If it is visible beyond the bar, your stem is too short.

Height between saddle and stem

The difference in height between the saddle and the stem is critical to comfort and performance. Before measuring it, check that the frame size/seat post proportion is correct. To determine the difference in height, you have to project a horizontal line from the top of the saddle and measure the distance between

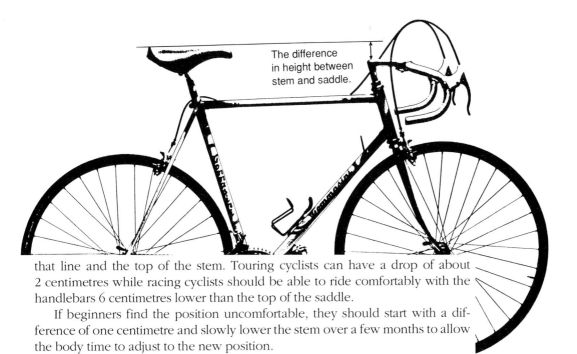

The difference in height between stem and saddle.

that line and the top of the stem. Touring cyclists can have a drop of about 2 centimetres while racing cyclists should be able to ride comfortably with the handlebars 6 centimetres lower than the top of the saddle.

If beginners find the position uncomfortable, they should start with a difference of one centimetre and slowly lower the stem over a few months to allow the body time to adjust to the new position.

Handlebars

Your choice of bars depends on what you intend to use them for and the width of your shoulders. In general, racers tend to use narrower bars than tourers because they enable one to tuck into a neat, aerodynamically efficient position. A rough guide to bar width for racing is to correlate it to shirt size. If you wear a large shirt, try a 44-centimetre bar (measured centre to centre), and if a medium shirt, go for a 42-centimetre bar.

The handlebar should be adjusted so that the upper part of the bar is parallel to the ground. Bars should never be pointed upwards towards the rider as this is dangerous and uncomfortable. Handlebar plugs are essential; they keep your handlebar tape in place and make the bars safer in case of an accident.

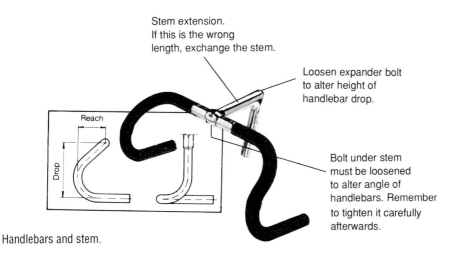

Stem extension. If this is the wrong length, exchange the stem.

Loosen expander bolt to alter height of handlebar drop.

Reach

Drop

Bolt under stem must be loosened to alter angle of handlebars. Remember to tighten it carefully afterwards.

Handlebars and stem.

Women and frame sizes

Women often find it difficult to find high quality frames that fit, because most are made with men's proportions in mind. The average woman has a longer torso and longer arms in proportion to her legs than men have. Some overseas frame builders produce frames especially for women; here, you may have to get a frame custom made if you can't find a well-fitting standard frame.

Size and position: a summing up

If you re-set your bicycle to accord with the measurements recommended here, you may find there is a vast difference between your old and new positions. Give yourself time to get used to the change; if you find it difficult, adjust your bike towards the ideal position gradually.

Novices tend to feel more comfortable on bikes that are larger than the sizes recommended here; again, give yourself time to get used to what experts have found to be optimum measurements. For racing in particular, it is generally better to opt for a frame on the small side; for touring, many people find that a frame up to 2 centimetres bigger than they would choose for racing is comfortable.

A racing position should be sleek, neat, streamlined and comfortable. Your back should be as flat as possible and not humped, with your arms slightly bent. For touring, you will probably be more concerned with comfort and with seeing the scenery than with speed and aerodynamic efficiency, and a more upright position will suit most riders.

Sizing an all-terrain bike

Frame size

Because the bottom bracket of an all-terrain bike is usually 4–9 centimetres higher off the ground than that of a conventional road bike, the seat tube is correspondingly shorter. So if a road bike with a frame of, say 54 centimetres fits you, a 46-centimetre ATB frame should be about right for you. Another way of calculating the right frame size is by taking two thirds of your inside leg measurement (crotch to floor) and subtracting 5–9 centimetres.

And don't rely only on the calculation: it's important to straddle the bike as well, with your feet flat on the ground on either side and check that there is a good 5–9 centimetres of clearance between your body and the top tube. (Clearance on an ATB with a sloping top tube may be greater.)

Saddle height

For riding on well-surfaced roads, your saddle height should be as it is on a conventional road bike, or slightly lower. Saddle height on an ATB can quickly be altered: the saddle post is extra-long and can, with the flick of a quick-release lever be extended or shortened. This feature enables riders to enjoy the stability of a low centre of gravity on steep and bumpy descents. Make sure there is never less than 7 centimetres of saddle post in the seat tube, otherwise you risk it breaking.

Handlebar position

Most novices feel most comfortable with the handlebars positioned high, with the stem about level with the saddle height. More experienced riders prefer handlebars set about 5 centimetres lower than this. This allows a more stream-lined riding position; it also helps to centre your weight, making it possible to shift weight forwards or backwards more easily, and thus to have firmer control over the bike. If you do raise the handlebars, see that at least 5 centimetres of the stem remains in the head tube; if you pull it out too far it may break.

Check that the handlebars are at a comfortable distance from the saddle, otherwise you may find that riding jars the joints and stresses the back and shoulder muscles. (Use the same checking method described for road bikes.) You should be able to grip the bars without bending the wrists. Bars that force your wrists into an uncomfortable position should be exchanged for others that are angled differently. (ATB bars can be quite sharply angled or almost straight; racers tend to prefer the latter shape.)

Wide handlebars give good leverage when you steer, but they slow reaction times. Most ATB bars are made about 63 centimetres wide, but experienced riders frequently saw them down to about 58 centimetres.

When you try an ATB out in a shop, it's not always easy to predict whether it'll still be comfortable after a day of bouncing over rocks. For this reason the advice of a dealer who rides an ATB can be invaluable.

Experienced off-road riders find that handlebars placed low in relation to the saddle help to centre the rider's weight and makes it easier to shift weight backwards or forwards quickly — a necessary strategy when coping with sudden drops or rises in terrain.

New, old or custom-built?

When you buy a bike, you have basically three choices: a new bike off the shelf, a bike built to your specifications and lastly, a second-hand bike.

Buying a bike off the shelf

A good dealer's advice on the advantages of each option is well worth seeking. Before deciding on a particular bike, ensure that you can change components that may not be suitable. This goes particularly for the stem, handlebar and gears. If you can, buy a cycle which has a groupset of components made by one manufacturer; this will help to ensure that the bike works smoothly, and it will enhance resale value. (A groupset comprises hubs, a brake set, a headset, a bottom bracket, gear levers and cables, a chainwheel set, front and rear derailleurs, a chain and cluster, and sometimes pedals.) Some dealers build up bikes from parts made by a wide range of manufacturers. This presents no problems if they are chosen for their compatibility. But be warned that some parts are incompatible with others, and matching them up is not something that a novice is likely to get right.

Buying components and frame separately

With this option you can get exactly what you require. Again I advise a groupset made by one manufacturer. There are many options available, and you should base your choice on the following:

- Availability of spares and an adequate dealer network.
- The reputation of the components among other cyclists.
- Are they right for your particular purposes? Buying a top-of-the-range groupset designed for racing won't help you if you're going to be touring.

Buying or ordering a frame: Today's top bike shops are so well stocked with good frames that most buyers can get what they want off the shelf. Or for a slightly higher cost, you can have a custom-built frame and have the luxuries of choosing tubing, colour, fittings, size and geometry.

Most custom-built frames are made for racing. Good tandems usually have to be custom made as the choice in shops is limited. And many women and unusually built men find it difficult to get a well-fitting frame off the shelf.

A frame can either be ordered through a good bike shop or directly through the frame builder, who will take your body measurements and discuss the details of what you want. (Frame builders are listed in the Appendix.) It is important to think out those details in advance because your choice of components will affect the way the frame is built; if, for example, you want to mount cantilever brakes, the frame builder must know in advance so that he can braze on the mounting points.

Buying a second-hand bike

Be sceptical. Don't believe the seller, necessarily, when you are told that a 73-year-old granny bought the bike in Sicily last year and only used it to go to the shops.

- Check the components and see if they are still being produced. Some makes show the date of manufacture.
- Check the frame for rust.
- Check the transfers to see what sort of tubing has been used. If the bike has been resprayed, try and ascertain tubing quality.

The chart shown here lists the main parts of a bicycle, typical problems that you may encounter in a second-hand bike, and what you can or can't do about them.

Part	Problem	What to do
Frame	Bent or cracked.	Don't buy. Though kinks can be straightened, this may weaken the frame.
Wheels	Rims dented or bulging.	Should be replaced as this interferes with braking. Fairly expensive.
	Rims buckled.	Minor damage is repaired fairly cheaply. (May be caused by a damaged spoke.) Badly buckled rims must be replaced.
	Hubs loose with play.	May only need adjustment. Replacement may be necessary: fairly expensive.
Headset	Steering doesn't turn smoothly all the way and may have play. Check by seeing if forks wobble when you apply front brake and rock bike back and forth.	May simply need tightening, but if in doubt check with a mechanic. Replacement may be necessary: expensive.
Drive train	Bottom bracket loose.	May need adjustment or replacement. Check if in doubt. This is a heavily stressed part which must be well maintained.
	Chainwheels don't run true when turned.	May be possible to straighten; if badly bent, replace. Fairly expensive.
	Teeth of chainwheel damaged.	Chainwheel must be replaced. Fairly expensive.
	Cogs worn	Must be replaced. Not very expensive.
	Chain stretched. Test by lifting it away from chain wheel at its foremost point. If there's a gap of more than 4 millimetres, it has stretched.	Must be replaced. Cheap and simple.
Gears	Chain falls off or gears slip during changes.	Usually simple for mechanic to correct. If problem seems serious, get a quote.
Brakes	Levers move too stiffly or too loosely. Worn brake blocks.	Levers are usually simple to adjust. Worn blocks are cheap and easy to replace.
Pedals	Too stiff or too loose.	Fairly simple mechanical adjustment.

- Examine the crank set and drive chain for excessive wear; in particular, look for chain stretch and sprocket wear.
- Examine the rims and spokes. When you spin the wheels, they must run true; they should be correctly dished and be free of dents.
- Remove the chain and spin the cranks around. The movement should be smooth and friction-free. Check for lateral movement in the cranks.
- Check the reliability of both components and frame with dealers and try to ascertain their current selling price. Try to get a dealer's guidance on the fairness of the asking price.
- Take the bike for a ride and don't get taken for one. Base your decision on logic and on your passion to own it.

Improving an old bike

You may have an old bike lurking in some corner, that is worth reviving. For starters, it will probably need servicing. (See Chapter 6.) You can vastly improve an old bike by replacing poor parts with better ones. But first check with a reliable dealer that the frame is good enough to warrant the changes. The following is a list of what are frequently worthwhile improvements:

- Replacing the gearing system with one better suited to climbing hills (assuming you want to climb hills).
- Replacing steel rims with alloy ones, fitted with high pressure tyres.
- Replacing cheap, wobbly pedals with a good pair.
- If your cranks have cotterpins, replace them with a cotterless set; cotterpins are notorious for giving trouble.

MAINTENANCE and REPAIRS

Apart from its amazing efficiency as a mode of transport, one of the most wonderful things about the bicycle is the simplicity of its working parts. There is nothing that ordinary people will find mysterious about them. And this is one of the many liberating virtues of the bike: the more you understand it and the more maintenance and repair jobs you do yourself, the more control you have and the less you need experts and mechanics in your life.

A well-maintained bike goes better and lasts longer than a neglected one. This chapter tells you how to do the ordinary day-to-day maintenance and repair jobs that will keep your bike in shape. With a basic, inexpensive set of tools virtually anyone should be able to do them. There are other more intricate jobs that need to be done occasionally. These need

special, sometimes expensive tools and many people take their bikes to good bike shops for complicated repairs, but there is nothing to stop you from getting the tools and doing them yourself. Ultimately, investing in a good set of tools will save you money. The Appendix refers you to specialized books that describe in detail how to do even the most complicated jobs.

Basic maintenance jobs

The essential jobs are listed here under the different components of the bike. The number of asterisks given to each job shows how difficult it is, how often it needs to be done, and how expensive the necessary tools are:

* Easy; frequently done, virtually routine; simple tools needed.

** More complex; some special tools needed, but these are not too expensive; done at infrequent intervals.

*** More complex still; specialized tools needed; should be done at least annually.

Frame:	Cleaning and touching up *	
Wheels:	Repairing punctures *	
	Correcting slight to moderate buckling *	
	Replacing broken spokes *(**)	
	Servicing hubs **	
Brakes:	Replacing worn brake blocks *	
	Centering and adjusting *	
	Replacing cables. *	
Handlebars and steering mechanism:	Replacing handlebar tape *	
	Servicing the headset ***	
Gears:	Servicing *	
	Adjusting derailleurs *	
	Replacing broken cables *	
Drive train:	*Chain:*	Cleaning and lubricating*
		Removing and replacing **
	Freewheel:	Removing ***
		Changing sprockets **(*)
	Bottom bracket:	Servicing ***
	Pedals:	Servicing **

Recommended tool kit

Basic *

- Puncture kit and tyre levers, preferably plastic. For tubulars you will need contact glue, rim cement, a stitch cutter and strong needle and thread (dental floss will do).
- Spoke key.
- Set of Allen keys: you need at least 4, 5 and 6 millimetre sizes. Other sizes may also be necessary.

- A Y-socket tool, with 8, 9 and 10 millimetre hexagonal sockets.
- Screwdrivers: one with a flat blade and a Philips type.
- Touch-up paint, thinners and a small paint brush.
- Molybdenum grease and dry molybdenum or oil containing teflon. Don't use aerosol sprays unless they are ozone safe. Central to the philosophy of cycling is a sensitivity and concern for our environment, and the use of aerosols containing chlorofluorocarbons is a serious threat to our future because these substances damage the ozone layer of the atmosphere.
- A cable cutter that can cut cables without causing them to fray.
- Hand cleaner, old rags, old toothbrushes or nailbrushes.
- A good quality monkey wrench.

Basic tools, *clockwise from top:* puncture kit, tyre leavers, monkey wrench, cable cutter, Y-socket tool, spoke key, combination tool with Allen keys and screwdrivers.

More advanced **

- Cone spanners
- Chain-removing tool
- Sprocket remover (for cassette hubs)

More advanced tools, *left to right:* cone spanners, sprocket-removing tools (chain whips) for cassete hubs, and a chain rivet extractor for removing the chain.

Specialized ***

Most of these tools fit specific brand names and are not interchangeable. Check before you buy.

- Freewheel remover
- Bench vise
- Crank extractor
- Bottom bracket spanners
- Pedal dust cap remover
- Flat 15 millimetre spanner for pedals
- Headset spanners

Specialized tools, *left to right:* crank extractor, freewheel remover, bottom bracket lockring and headset tool, bottom bracket right hand cup and pedal axle tool, bottom bracket left hand and headset cup tool, crank bolt spanner.

Luxuries

A proper bike maintenance stand and a floor pump may seem extravagant, but they are extremely useful.

Floor pump

Maintenance stand.

General principles: prevention is better than cure

Left- and right-handed threads

Most components and nuts have ordinary right-handed thread: you tighten them by turning clockwise. The left pedal (where it screws onto the crank), and the fixed cup of the bottom bracket on most bikes, tighten anticlockwise: they have left-handed threads. To see whether a thread is right- or left-handed, hold the part vertically in front of you: if the ridges run upward to the right, it is right-handed, if upwards to the left, it is left-handed.

Left-hand thread   Right-hand thread

Rules for using tools

Set aside enough time to finish the job: Don't leave a complicated job half done to return to later. You may forget where you left off and omit an important step.

Use the correct tool for the job: A spanner that is too big for the nut will round the corners. A screwdriver that doesn't fit will destroy the groove on the screw.

Work carefully and never use excessive force: The light aluminium alloy most components are made of is relatively soft and threads are delicate and precise. If you tighten something without lining it up properly (or overtighten it), you will strip the thread and ruin the component.

Never do big jobs immediately before big rides: Allow time to test your bike fully after working on it. It is a real nuisance if you're somewhere in the bundu and your crank comes loose or a pedal comes off or your rear derailleur gets tangled up in the spokes because you forgot to adjust it properly.

Rules for riding

Before every ride: Check your wheels, chain and brakes.

- *Wheels:* Inflate tyres to the recommended pressure. For narrow high pressure tyres and tubulars this means as hard as you can pump them by hand, but it is better to use a pressure gauge. Check that the quick-release mechanisms on your hubs are tightened correctly, especially if there are inquisitive children around the house.
- *Chain:* Make sure it is properly lubricated.
- *Brakes:* Pull levers hard. Badly worn cables will break — better that it should happen at home than when you're riding down a steep hill in a race, or worse, in traffic. Check that the callipers are properly adjusted and centered.

On the ride: Be sensitive to any strange noises your bike makes and to any signs of malfunction.

After the ride: Check the tyres and spokes, rub the chain clean, and clean the bike.

- *Tyres:* Look for and remove any bits of glass, stone or thorns that you may have picked up. These often don't cause punctures the first time round but stick in your tyre and work their way in slowly towards the tube as you ride.
- *Spokes:* Spin the wheels and check for broken spokes. These usually make the wheel wobble.
- *Chain:* If you wipe the dirt off the chain after each ride and lubricate it when necessary, it will last longer and so will your chainwheel and freewheel sprockets.

- *Bike in general:* Sweat is very corrosive. It drops off your head while you ride and collects on the top tube under the brake cable and on the down tube in the region of the gear-levers, where it eats away at the paint and eventually causes rust. Wipe it off and protect the paint with a moisture repellent.

Bearings, cups and cones

The basic principles outlined in this section apply to a number of components. The fine details of their servicing are beyond the scope of this book; the Appendix refers you to other books with the necessary details.

The hubs, pedals, bottom bracket and headset turn very freely because they have ball- or roller-bearings inside them. In all cases the principle is the same. There is an *outer cup*, an *inner axle with cones*, and these are separated by a ring of steel *bearings*, allowing them to run freely on one another. The bearings are packed in grease to prevent wear, and the cones and cups have to be adjusted very accurately. In the hubs you can adjust both cones; in the pedals, the outside cone only. In the bottom bracket it is the left cup which is adjustable, and in the headset the upper cup. Once the adjustments are made they are locked in place with locknuts. Many modern components have sealed bearings. These do not normally need maintenance.

Cups, bearings and cones.

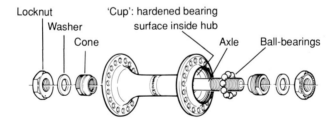

A hub. The bearings run on hardened surfaces inside the hub shell 'cups' and on the cones.

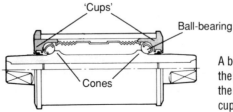

A bottom bracket. Here the axle is known as the spindle. Hardened bearing surfaces on the spindle function as cones. The left-hand cup is adjustable.

Servicing bearings, cups and cones

In principle you service these components as follows: Carefully dismantle by unscrewing the locknut, removing the washer (hub, pedal, headset), and then unscrewing the cone (hub, pedal) or cup (bottom bracket, headset). If the ball-bearings are mounted in a cage, take note of which way round it goes.

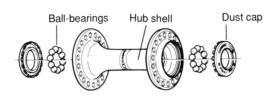

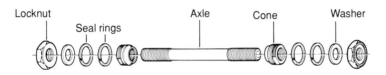

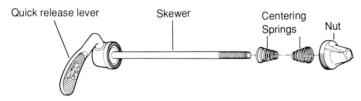

A modern hub and all its parts. To service, remove locknut, washer and cone from one side. Some models do not have seal rings.

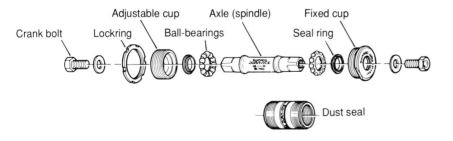

Exploded view of a bottom bracket. The 'cones' are bearing surfaces, integral to the spindle. Some models don't have seal rings. Ball bearings in this model are held together for convenience; in some, they are loose. The adjustable cup and lockring are on the left side of the bike and must be removed for servicing. Only tackle this job if you have the correct tools, including a crank extractor.

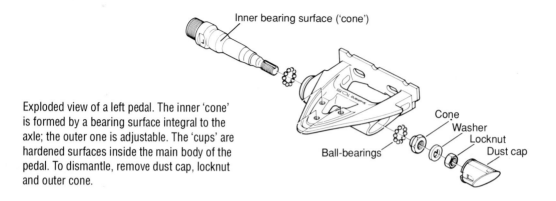

Inner bearing surface ('cone')

Cone
Washer
Locknut
Dust cap

Ball-bearings

Exploded view of a left pedal. The inner 'cone' is formed by a bearing surface integral to the axle; the outer one is adjustable. The 'cups' are hardened surfaces inside the main body of the pedal. To dismantle, remove dust cap, locknut and outer cone.

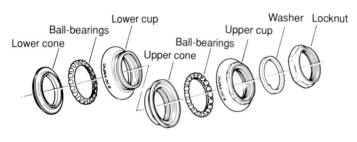

Lower cup
Ball-bearings
Lower cone
Upper cone
Ball-bearings
Upper cup
Washer Locknut

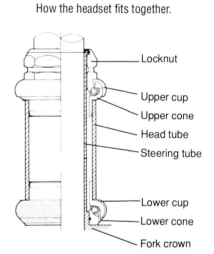

How the headset fits together.

Locknut
Upper cup
Upper cone
Head tube
Steering tube
Lower cup
Lower cone
Fork crown

Exploded view of headset. The lower cone is fitted to the steering tube above the fork crown. The lower cup is fitted to the head tube. The opposite applies at the top end: the cone is fitted to the head tube, the cup screws onto the steering tube and is adjustable. To service, remove the locknut and upper cup. The entire assembly will come apart: remove fork, clean bearings, grease and reassemble carefully.

If they are loose, don't lose any. Clean the cones, cups and the bearings with a solvent or penetrating thin oil, and check all the bearing surfaces carefully for wear. Pack the cups with a good quality waterproof grease, and carefully reassemble. The best way of adjusting them correctly is to tighten the adjustable bit hand tight and then to hold it there while you tighten the locknut onto it. Usually there is a washer that cannot turn between the adjustable bit and the locknut which makes things easier. Then turn the axle: it should turn easily and smoothly, and there should be no play. If it feels gritty, it is too tight and must be loosened; if there is any play, it is too loose. Keep working at it till you get it just right and *be patient*. The job is only done when the adjustment is correct and the locknut tight.

Changing tyres and tubes and repairing punctures

High pressure tyres

It is a good idea to carry a spare tube, tyre levers and a puncture kit on all rides. If you have a puncture, you simply replace the tube and repair the puncture when you get home — the repaired tube then becomes your spare. You may, of course, have more than one puncture, so you will need the repair kit anyway.

Removing the wheel: With quick-release hubs this is easy — just remember to move the chain to the outside (smallest) sprocket on the back wheel first by alternately moving the gear-lever and turning the pedals with the wheel off the ground. If you don't have quick-release hubs, try prising off just the part of the tyre around the puncture so that you can reach the tube and repair it without removing the wheel.

Removing the tube: Let all the air out. If there is a nut around the base of the valve, remove it. Hook the flat end of a tyre lever under the bead of the tyre and, taking great care not to pinch the tube, prise it out over the rim. Some levers can be hooked onto a spoke in this position. Repeat this procedure with a second lever about 10 centimetres away. You may need to repeat it a third time. When the tyre no longer wants to pop back, simply slide the lever all the way round between the tyre and rim till the whole bead is off. You will now be able to pull out the tube to repair a puncture, or remove the tyre as well by simply pulling it off.

Removing the cause of the puncture: Carefully inspect the tyre to find the piece of glass, thorn, wire, or whatever it was that punctured it. There may be more than one puncture.

Finding and repairing the puncture: Inflate the tube to about twice its usual size. The hole may be obvious, but if it isn't, go carefully round the tube from the valve and back, using your fingers, eyes and ears to find it. Roughen an area larger than the patch around the hole with sandpaper. Spread a thin layer of rubber

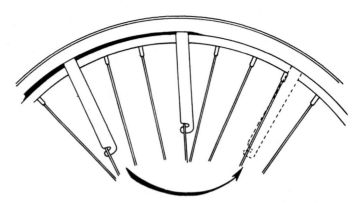

solution on the roughened area, and allow it to dry — *this is important. Once the solution is dry* remove the backing from the patch and apply it with pressure, making sure the middle of the patch is over the hole. Apply pressure for about two minutes, and then test your repair by inflating the tube and checking for leaks. Dust the area with French chalk or talcum powder before replacing the tube, otherwise the glue will stick to the tyre.

Replacing the tube: Locate the valve in the valve hole, and then insert the tube into the space between the tyre and the rim all the way round, taking care not to get it folded — the simplest way is to inflate it slightly once it is in place.

Replacing the tyre: *Do this by hand.* Start at the point on the rim furthest away from the valve, and push the bead of the tyre over and into the rim with your thumbs, working around in both directions. As you approach the valve it will get more difficult, but *do not use tyre levers.* If you do you are almost certain to pinch the tube and create another puncture. Even a difficult tyre will eventually go on. Now take the valve and push it into the tyre through the rim as far as you can to free the tube from the bead of the tyre. Inflate slowly, checking that the tyre is properly seated in the rim all the way round, before replacing the wheel.

Tubulars

Unlike wire-ons, tubulars (tubbies) have to be glued onto the rim. If this is not done properly they may come off, especially on corners or when braking, and this is extremely dangerous. Even if your bike is new, don't assume that your tyres are correctly mounted — rather take them off and re-install them.

Always carry at least one pre-glued spare when riding on tubbies.

Installing new tubulars: Use proper rim cement. If the rim is new, roughen its outer surface a little with sandpaper to ensure that the cement works properly. Inflate the tyre. Spread a thin coat of cement on the inner surface of the tyre and the outer surface of the rim. It should cover the entire contact surface of both so that there are no areas where friction can occur between them and damage the casing. Leave it for an hour or so to dry. Deflate the tyre. Put the wheel on a firm surface with the valve hole up, and insert the valve. Use your weight to mount the tyre on the rim slowly, working and stretching it in both directions around the

Use your weight to mount a tubular tyre.

Ease the last bit over the rim and centre it.

wheel. When it is on, inflate the tyre moderately, spin the wheel, and check that the tyre runs true on the rim. Adjust where necessary. Now pump the tyre hard and leave it overnight.

Removing a flat tubby: Start at the point opposite the valve and simply force it off by pushing it with your thumbs. Then pull it off around the rim to the valve and remove it.

Repairing a punctured tubular:

- *Find the puncture:* This is usually easy; inflate the tyre and find the hole through which the air is leaking. You may occasionally have to put it under water to find the leak by spotting the bubbles. Sometimes finding the puncture can be very difficult. Air leaks from the tube and tracks along under the casing before oozing through the sidewalls or the stitch holes.

- *Remove the tape:* Use a table knife or blunt screwdriver to prise the cloth tape off for a distance of about 5 centimeters on either side of the puncture. Be patient; take your time and don't damage it.

- *Cut and remove the stitches:* As you cut and remove the stitches along this length of tyre, take great care not to cut the tube. Open up the tyre and pull out the bit of tube underneath. Carefully inflate the tube until it bulges enough for you to find the hole. *Don't forget to remove the sharp object that caused the puncture from the casing!*

- *Repair the puncture:* The tube is repaired with a patch as has been described. Re-inflate the tube to make sure that the repair is sound. After dusting with French chalk, return the tube to the casing and reverse the process.

- *Re-stitch the tyre:* Use thread made for the purpose, or strong dental floss. Start about three stitches away from the opening, and insert the needle through the original holes. *Be careful not to puncture the tube again!* Carefully carry on, pulling each stitch snug, but not too tight, until the opening is closed, and then for three more stitches. Finish off by tying a knot. Pump up the tyre again to check that the stitches are going to hold and are not too tight or too loose.

Replace the tape: Use a good quality contact glue.

Removing the tape.

Cut stitches carefully, avoiding the casing and tube.

Don't puncture the tube when you stitch!

Repairing a tubular tyre.

89

Correcting a buckled wheel

Minor buckles can be straightened easily using a spoke key. If the buckle is to the *right*, you must tighten the spokes to the *left* side of the hub (and vice versa) to pull the buckled part of the rim back into line.

Using the brake blocks as a reference point, spin the wheel and decide to which side the rim wobbles. Find the highest point of the wobble by seeing where the rim comes closest to the brake block as the wheel turns. Starting with the spokes nearest this point, tighten the ones to the opposite side of the hub by a quarter to half a turn. Tighten two or three spokes on either side. To *tighten* a spoke you turn the nipple *clockwise*, looking along the spoke in a line from the rim to the hub; to *loosen* it, turn *anticlockwise*. (Some people recommend that you loosen the spokes in between — those that go to the same side of the hub, but it is usually not necessary — they are not likely to have worked themselves tight!)

Now spin the wheel again, and repeat the procedure. Your wheel should become straighter and the spokes should all have more or less equal tension. This takes practice. If you get into trouble or the spokes are stuck, take the wheel to a bike shop.

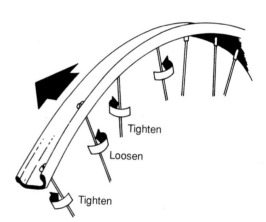

Tighten

Loosen

Tighten

Correcting a wheel that is buckled to the right. This section of rim will be pulled in the direction of the arrow (i.e. to the left) if the spokes that attach it to the left side of the hub are tightened. Turning the nipples as shown will alternately tighten or loosen the spokes.

Broken spokes

Occasional broken spokes are inevitable. Most can be replaced fairly easily, but if they are on the right-hand side of the back wheel you have to remove the cluster first. Take the wheel off the bike. Remove the tyre, tube and rim tape. Remove the broken spoke. Make sure that the new spoke is the same length as the old one, and thread it through the hole in the hub, *making sure it goes through from the correct side* — look carefully at the other spokes to see how it should be threaded. You will probably have to bend it to thread it correctly, but if you take care not to kink it, it will straighten when you tighten it. Insert the nipple into the hole in the rim, and thread the spoke towards it. *Take care to thread it correctly* and screw the nipple onto it. Then use the spoke key to tighten it and true the wheel. Now make doubly sure that the spoke isn't too long. If it is, it will puncture the tube from the inside. Check that it doesn't stick too far through the rim, and cut it shorter if it does.

Lastly, replace the rim tape, tube and tyre, pump it up, and replace the wheel.

Hubs

Once a year, with average to heavy use, you should dismantle your hubs, clean them, re-pack the bearings with grease, and reassemble them. You will need a set of cone spanners. You will probably also have to remove the freewheel, or cluster, from the back wheel. The tricky part is to get the cones just right when you reassemble — see the section 'Bearings, cups and cones'. You should also end up with equal lengths of axle protruding on both sides, though this shouldn't be a problem if you unscrew one cone only.

Brakes

Replacing broken cables

When buying new cables, try and get good quality, low friction ones, preferably the same brand as the original ones. Remove the broken cable by undoing the cable anchor bolt and pulling it out of the cable housing (outer). If the housing is in good condition, leave it in place, otherwise replace it too. When cutting the housing to the right length make a clean cut between the metal coils to avoid squashing them flat. The new cable may have two different ends for different brake systems. Decide which one you need and cut the other one off. This is tricky — it is very difficult to cut a cable cleanly without getting the ends frayed unless you have a very good cable cutter (not easy to come by). Rub the new cable with an oily rag to lubricate it (if possible use an oil that contains Teflon), and pass it through the brake-lever and the housing. When it emerges through the other end, thread it through the adjusting bolt on the brake arm (sidepull brakes) or attached to a cable hanger on the frame (centrepull or cantilever brakes). Pull it tight, forcing the ends of the cable housing into the cable stops at both ends. Turn the adjusting bolt all the way down. Hold the brake blocks against the rim, pull the end of the cable through the cable anchor bolt and tighten it. Now pull the brake-lever hard, and let go. With luck the cable will stretch a little, the housing will be pulled tightly into the cable stops, and when you let go, the blocks will be just the right distance (about 2 to 3 millimetres) away from the rim on either side.

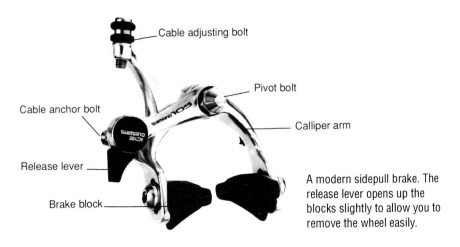

Cable adjusting bolt

Pivot bolt

Cable anchor bolt

Calliper arm

Release lever

Brake block

A modern sidepull brake. The release lever opens up the blocks slightly to allow you to remove the wheel easily.

91

Centering and adjusting

The brake blocks should be positioned in the brake arms to contact the middle of the braking surface of the rim for maximum efficiency. If they are too high, wear will eventually cause them to hit the sidewall of the tyre — a sure way of destroying it beyond repair. Positioned too low, they will wear around the inside of the rim and eventually come up against the spoke nipples. The blocks must be at equal distances from the rim so that when you brake, both hit the rim at the same time. To center them, loosen the pivot bolt and then re-tighten it, holding the brakes in place. Some makes have a nut you can hold with a spanner while tightening the pivot bolt.

The adjusting bolt is used to compensate for wear on the blocks. Periodically set these so that the tips of the brake-levers move 3 to 4 centimetres when you apply brakes. There should be at least 2 centimetres between the lever and the handlebar when the brakes are applied tightly.

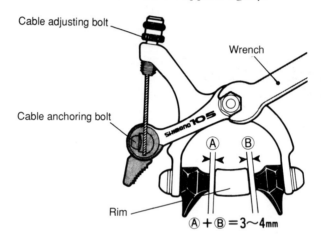

Adjusting and centering a brake.

Brake blocks positioned too high.

Too low.

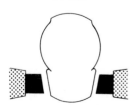

Correctly positioned.

Positioning of brake blocks.

Replacing worn brake blocks

Don't wait until they are worn through before you replace them. Some makes (like Campagnolo, Shimano) are slotted; replace them when the slots are no longer there. To replace, simply remove the worn ones, install the new ones, and adjust them as described.

Squealing brakes

New brake blocks squeal and judder when the rear end of the block contacts the rim before the front end does. To correct this you need to adjust them so that the front ends are about one millimetre closer to the rims than the rear ends are (toe in). If this can't be achieved by re-installing them, you have to twist the brake arms a little. Remove the brake blocks and apply a monkey wrench as shown. Gently twist the brake arm into the toe-in position. In this position they will work quietly and more efficiently, as the drag of the rim pulls them forward, bringing their entire length into contact.

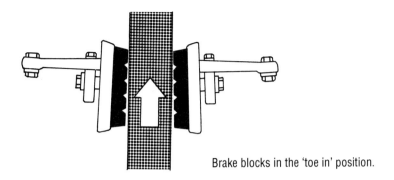

Brake blocks in the 'toe in' position.

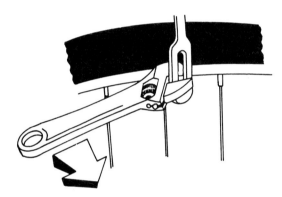

Twist the brake arms gently into the 'toe in' position.

Gears

Adjusting derailleurs

The initial adjustments of new derailleurs are best made before the chain is installed. The front derailleur must be mounted at the correct height on the seat tube and correctly lined up with the chainwheels. The limiting screws (look for them — they are usually marked H and L) on both derailleurs must be set so that all available gears can be used without throwing off the chain. The gear cables should not be slack when the levers are in their most forward positions, and the chain must be the correct length (see the section 'Chain'). Finally, there may be other adjustments that apply to your particular brand of gears, for example, if you have an indexing system. Try and get a set of instructions for your system from the shop where you bought your bike.

93

Front derailleur

Position: The derailleur is at the correct height when the outer plate of the cage is between 3 and 1 millimetres above the large chainwheel when viewed from the side; it is correctly lined up if the cage is parallel to the plane of the chainwheels when viewed from above.

Setting the limits: Move the left gear-lever all the way forward so that the front derailleur moves inwards as far as it will go. Check that the cage (chainguide) is centered above the inside chainwheel (diagram). If it isn't, adjust the L screw to center it: *loosen* it if the cage is too close to the large chainwheel; *tighten* it if it is too close the frame. You may need to loosen the cable anchor bolt and allow some slack in the cable to make this adjustment. Don't forget to re-tighten it.

Now use the H screw to center the cage above the large chainwheel when the gear-lever is moved all the way back: *tighten* if the cage moves too far, *loosen* if it doesn't move far enough. Turn the pedals and make sure the outer plate doesn't foul the crank when it is in this position.

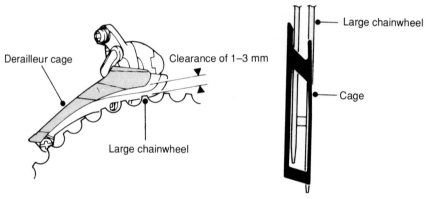

Front derailleur position.

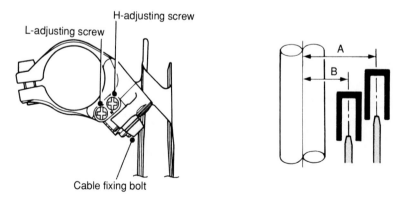

Front derailleur: setting the limits. The derailleur cage should be in position A when the gear lever is pushed forward. Adjust position with the L adjusting screw. Pulling the gear lever back should move the cage to position B; adjust the limits with the H screw.

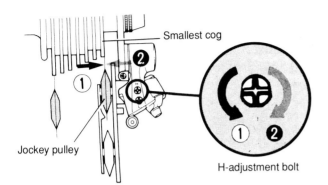

Rear derailleur: setting the limits.

Rear derailleur

Setting the limits: Push the right gear-lever all the way forward. The rear derailleur should now be positioned so that the jockey pulleys are directly under and in line with the smallest cog on the freewheel. *Tighten* the H screw if the jockey is too far out, *loosen* it if it is too close. You may have to reset the tension on the cable to make this adjustment. Make sure there is no slack in the cable when the gear-lever is pushed all the way forward and the jockey is in position below the outer cog.

Now set the L screw so that when you move the right gear-lever back as far as it will go, the jockey pulleys are directly below and in line with the inside (largest) cog. *Tighten* if it moves inwards too close to the spokes, *loosen* if it doesn't move far enough.

Once you have adjusted your gears as described, ride the bike around the block a few times, using all the gears. You may have to make fine adjustments, particularly to the front derailleur. Remember that not all the chainwheel/cog combinations are usable: don't use the outer two cogs if the chain is on the small chainwheel or the inner two cogs with the chain on the large chainwheel. If you do, the chain runs diagonally — this is inefficient and it tends to rub on the front derailleur cage.

Servicing

Once a month or so, depending on use, lubricate the derailleurs. Keep them clean.

Replacing cables

When removing a broken cable, carefully note how it is threaded into the derailleur and how the cable anchor bolt clamps it. Install the new cable in the same way, starting by inserting it from above into the hole in the gear-lever, which should be in the forwardmost position. Once it is installed and clamped by the cable anchor bolt, take hold of it about half way along the down tube and give it a good pull. Then re-tighten it to take out all slack.

Drive train

Chain

How long a chain lasts obviously depends on how much you ride and how well you care for it. Minute wear on all the bushes (pins) results in the chain gradually getting longer (stretching), so that the links no longer match the spacing on the chainwheel teeth and cogs. This accelerates the wear on these components, which can be very expensive indeed. Replace the chain before this happens. Test the chain for 'stretch' by pulling it at the foremost part of the front chainwheel. If it lifts by 3 millimetres or more, it has stretched and should be replaced.

Cleaning and lubricating

Lubricate your chain frequently by applying a dry lubricant containing teflon or molybdenum disulphide to each link. Avoid aerosols — they damage the ozone layer and our future.

If you rub the chain down after each ride it probably won't need much other cleaning. If it does get dirty it is best, but not essential, to take it off to clean. Simply rub it down well with a solvent and lubricate it.

Replacing

The new chain will be too long and you will have to discard a few links to make it the same length as the old one. You need a chain rivet extractor. These come with instructions which should be followed carefully. In particular, don't push the pin all the way out, and don't forget to spread the link at the end of the procedure.

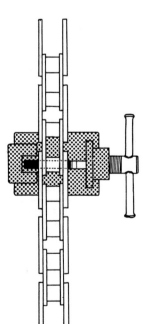

Using a chain rivet extractor.

Freewheel

Removal

You will need to remove the freewheel to replace spokes on the right-hand side of the back wheel. For this you need the correct freewheel-removing tool and a bench vise (though a large monkey wrench will do the trick). Remove the skewer from the axle. Insert the freewheel-removing tool into the splines in the freewheel. Pass the skewer through the axle and the hole in the freewheel-removing tool, and loosely tighten it to hold the tool in place. Now grip the tool in the vise and turn the wheel anticlockwise to **just** loosen the freewheel — if you loosen it too much you may snap the skewer. Remove the skewer and unscrew the freewheel. When you replace it, generously grease the threads on the hub.

Cassette hubs

To remove the outer cog you need a pair of chain whips. Apply the one tool to one of the inside cogs and the other to the outer cog. Hold the inner cog while you unscrew the outer one. All the cogs and spacers can now be removed.

Servicing the bottom bracket and cranks

The bottom bracket is subject to exceptionally heavy wear as it transmits all your weight and power to the chain. Once or twice a year, depending on use, it should be taken apart and serviced. You need a special spanner to remove the crank fixing bolt, a crank extractor and a set of bottom bracket spanners. To remove a crank, first remove the dust cap over the crank fixing bolt and the bolt itself. Screw the outer bolt of the crank extractor all the way into the crank. Then screw in the inner part. It will push up against the crank axle and pull the crank off the taper. To replace it, gently tap it on with a hammer (protect it with a piece of wood), replace and tighten the bolt. *Don't grease the taper.*

Servicing the pedals

No special tools are needed for the pedals — you can remove the dust cap and the outer cone with a pair of long-nosed pliers. For the basic principles see 'Bearings, cups and cones'.

Handlebars and steering

Handlebars

Position: The handlebars are attached to the bike by the stem, or extension. The stem must be inserted into the steering tube to the correct depth (at least 65 millimetres), usually indicated by a mark. It is held in place by an expander

bolt which fastens from above. The other bolt on the stem is the binder bolt, which allows you to adjust the angle of the handlebars. The correct position is when the drops point slightly downwards. Handlebars need little maintenance apart from replacing the tape when it is worn and making sure the bar-end plugs are in place. This is important because the ends of the handlebars are sharp and can be very dangerous in a fall.

Replacing handlebar tape: Remove the old tape and clean the handlebars with thinners. There is some controversy about whether you should start applying the new tape from the middle, near the stem, or from the bar ends — both have pros and cons. If you start from the middle you will be able to finish the job very neatly by tucking the ends of the tape into the bar ends and holding them there with the plugs. But when you ride with your hands on the tops you will tend to separate the layers of tape (which overlap with the exposed edge *towards* you) along the curve immediately above the brakes. This problem doesn't arise when you start applying tape from the ends, but you end up finishing the job off in the middle, wondering what to do with the tape ends. Some makes are supplied with a bit of fancy plastic tape that is meant to cover the ends, but they tend to come off and start flapping in the breeze. We recommend starting in the middle with cloth tape, and at the ends if you are using padded plastic or cork tape.

Headset

A detailed description of how to service the headset is beyond the scope of this book, but the basic principles are described in the section 'Bearings, cups and cones'. You need a set of headset spanners.

Frame

Cleaning

Clean your frame with a good car wax-wash. Greasy dirt can be easily removed with a powerful detergent like *Clean Green*. Polish it with a car wax made for new cars — one that doesn't contain an abrasive.

Touching up

Get a paint shop or panel beater to mix some touch-up paint to match your bike. Don't leave chips in the paintwork too long or rust will strike. If the frame is already rusted in spots, rub off the rust and a bit of the surrounding paint to bare metal, apply a rust inhibitor like *Rusist*, and then a zinc chromate undercoat before you touch it up. Use several coats of thin paint.

CHAPTER SEVEN

RIDING:
comfort and technique

Comfort is the basic starting point for enjoyment of cycling. It's also linked to good riding technique. Good technique is mainly about efficiency: it makes cycling easier, giving you greater mileage for less sweat. The initial trouble taken to get it right is amply rewarded by the sense of fluid ease you get when you ride, and because it enables you to transform your energy into forward movement with as little wasted effort as possible.

Comfort

Y ou can expect cycling to hurt a little if you're new to it or if you're covering great distances. Those circumstances aside, it shouldn't cause discomfort or pain. If it does, track down the cause and deal with it quickly or it may get worse. A list of the most common problems follows, together with a brief description of their likely causes; as you'll see, the causes and cures are dealt with in greater detail in other parts of this book. Most causes of pain are also linked to inefficient (energy wasting) riding — so you have two good reasons for ensuring that you are comfortable. It makes sense to prevent rather than cure cycling pains.

The most common problems are:

- **A sore seat**: An uncomfortable saddle or a saddle at the wrong height or angle are possible causes of this problem; see 'Saddles' in Chapter 3 and the sections in Chapter 5 which deal with saddle height and position. Your faithful old jeans, or any pants with a raised or tight seam may strangle you in the crotch if you subject them to a bike ride; most cyclists find proper cyclists' shorts (described in Chapter 16) are the most comfortable to ride in. Cyclists who ride hard and far may suffer from *perineal nodules* (hard, inflamed lumps). (See Chapter 11 for advice on what to do about those unattractive afflictions; see also the section on skin conditions that follows it.) Some women suffer from irritation caused by minute amounts of soap residue in sensitive genital tissues or in their shorts; the solution is to wash only with water or with a mild baby soap, and to rinse very well.

- **Sore hands:** Pressure on the handlebars over a long time can leave your hands blistered or numb. Changing your hand position often and using good cloth or leather (or simulated leather) handlebar tape helps; padded handlebar covers are also available. A pair of cyclist's gloves, padded at the palm helps even more. (These are discussed in Chapter 16; see also 'Feet, shoes and pedals' in Chapter 11.) A poorly fitting bike can cause hand-pain; check the information in Chapter 5.
- **Sore feet:** Riding in soft-soled shoes can make feet hurt; see 'Cycling shoes' in Chapter 16 and the section, 'Feet, shoes and pedals' in Chapter 11. Over-tight toe-straps can be a cause of pain; see that they are comfortable or think about using clipless pedals such as the Look type instead.
- **Inflamed tendons and knees:** These are fairly uncommon problems, but if they are unchecked they can become serious. They're discussed in Chapter 11.
- **General, hard-to-define aches and pains:** Most can be traced to a bike that doesn't fit you or to one that's poorly adjusted. Don't imagine that you can just get used to a frame that has you stretching or feeling cramped, or that in some way doesn't feel quite right: the longer you stay on it, the more harm it's likely to do you, and the less efficient your riding will be. Check the information in Chapter 5 thoroughly. If you can't get to the root of the problem, ask an experienced cyclist to look at your riding technique and at the way you are positioned on your bike.

Basic technique and efficiency

This section deals with the basic techniques needed for competent commuting and touring. Chapter 14 tells you about racing technique.

It's already been said that good technique is mainly about efficiency. An efficient rider channels his or her effort into driving the bicycle forward, and gets further faster, and with less effort than the rider who allows energy to be dissipated unproductively.

Good technique also puts you in better control of your bike: it makes you safer; it makes you more comfortable; and it helps to prevent injuries and strains to muscles and joints.

The basic skills aren't difficult to get right, and they come fairly easily with practice, even if you've started cycling late in life. They make as much difference to your cycling as fitness or strength do: this is why so many old riders who've spent years refining and practising their technique continue to perform well against far younger, stronger cyclists.

It's helpful to approach the subject of technique by visualizing yourself and your bicycle as a single object rolling along a road, gathering momentum as you go. Much of the momentum is generated by your leg-power. When you roll downhill, much of your momentum comes from the force of gravity; the momentum gathered from going down a hill may even be enough to get you over the next rise without requiring any pedalling effort. *Momentum, in other words, gives you something for nothing. The aim of an efficient cyclist is to conserve that momentum, to interrupt it as little as possible and to use it to the best advantage.*

But although you have the benefits of momentum when cycling, you also have to pit your efforts against several forces:

- **Wind resistance** and even still air are barriers to get through. On a still day, a cyclist riding at about 15 kilometres an hour is putting most of his or her energy into overcoming air-drag, and the higher the speed, the higher the proportion of energy required. To some degree, well-designed equipment can help to reduce the effects of wind resistance, but it is mostly riding techniques (described later in this chapter and in Chapter 9) that help to defeat the effects of wind.

- Tyres have **rolling resistance**: A wheel resists rolling in proportion to how much of its surface is in contact with the road. A narrow tyre inflated to a high pressure has very little of its surface in contact with the road and it therefore rolls with little resistance. The wider and softer the tyre, the more contact it has with the road and the more it resists rolling. The section on wheels in Chapter 3 tells you more about this.

- **Mass** is another force working against you. For one thing, the mass of the rider and bike influences rolling resistance. (The heavier you are, the more squashed-out the wheel will be where it's in contact with the road.) And the more you and your bike weigh, the more leg-power will be needed to resist the forces of gravity — particularly up hills. Down hills, mass, of course, makes you faster; however, because on average you spend far longer going up hills than you do going down them, the light rider and bike have the overall advantage. (Turn to Chapter 9 if you want to go into the relationship of mass and efficiency in more detail, and to Chapter 3 for information on lightness in bicycles.)

- **Friction** between the surfaces of components on your bike can dissipate roughly 5 to 15 per cent of a cyclist's energy. If, for example, your chain's dry, friction between it and the chainwheels will soak up much of the effort that should be driving your bike forward. In general, the better the quality of components and the better they are maintained and adjusted, the less friction there is.

As you can see, you can to some extent reduce the effect of mass, air-drag, rolling resistance and friction by choosing good equipment. But good riding technique is at least as important. And an essential aspect of good technique is to avoid interruptions in momentum: clumsy gear changes, awkward pedalling, badly-timed braking and a fizzling-out of effort before the crest of a hill will all result in extra effort being needed to get you going again.

Techniques that result in comfortable riding and in efficient use of your effort are now discussed under the headings position, pedalling, using gears, braking and defeating the wind.

Position

Most of the things you should know about position have been covered in Chapter 5. If your bike fits you, your position on it is likely to be right. But if it doesn't fit, there's no way you can ride comfortably or efficiently.

Relax. Tensing any of the muscles that you aren't using wastes energy and tires you. Also, stiff shoulders and arms will transmit shocks and vibrations from the road to your body.

For comfort and efficient pedalling, the balls of the feet — never the arches — should be on the pedals; if you use toe-straps, your feet are held in the right position (with a little leeway for the pigeon-toed or duck-footed). Alternatively, clipless pedals (such as Look) keep feet in the right position, provided that the cleats have been correctly placed.

On a bike with dropped handlebars you should be able to feel that your weight is distributed fairly evenly between the pedals, the handlebars and the saddle. This distribution of weight prevents excessive pressure being put on any part of you. Most people are comfortable riding with their hands on the tops of the bars for most of the time, and changing position from time to time to prevent numbness. You may want to move your hands to the drops for a more streamlined position on downhill slopes.

Pedalling

Pedals are the vital link between your body and your bicycle, and the way you turn them determines to a very great degree the efficiency with which you ride.

Efficient pedalling is a smooth, rotary action — never a broken, up-and-down movement. Either toe-clips or clipless pedals are virtually essential for this: they enable you to take weight off the pedals on the upstroke of the pedalling circle, and to some extent to *pull them up* instead of simply pushing on the downstroke. If toe-clips are new to you, get used to them in a traffic-free area, and ride with at least one of the straps loose so that you can get your foot out easily if you have to stop quickly.

A bonus of smooth pedalling is that it reduces the likelihood of saddle soreness; (watch a rough pedaller to see how much he shifts in the saddle). It also helps to prevent general body fatigue.

Achieving good cadence is another important aspect of pedalling. In cycling, cadence refers to the speed with which the pedals are turned. For recreational riders, a comfortable and efficient cadence is between about 60 and 85 revolutions per minute (rpm). Count your rpm when you're riding on the level and out of the wind; if it's lower than 60, you will almost certainly benefit from training yourself to get it up to a higher level.

On steep climbs or descents, you can't, of course, maintain the same cadence that you do on the flat, but the aim should be to keep as close to it as you can. This is done by changing into a gear that's appropriate for the slope. (If you've been cycling for some time but still find that hills are a serious strain to get over, your gearing is probably inappropriate for the terrain you're covering.) Knowing how to use gears well is crucial to good cadence.

Using gears

A good way of understanding how gears work before using them on the road is by looking at how they work while you're off the bike. To do this, put your bike on a maintenance stand, if you have one, or get someone to hold the bike up for you with the rear wheel off the ground. Now, using your hand, turn a pedal in the same direction as it would go if you were riding. Move the left gear-lever backwards or forwards; you'll see the chain move from the large front chainwheel to the smaller one (or vice versa); you'll also find that the force needed to keep the pedal turning changes. Notice how rapidly the rear wheel turns for each pedal revolution: the rate changes, depending on which chainwheel the chain is on. Now move the right gear-lever (this one is attached to the rear derailleur by a cable). By moving the shifting lever you cause the chain to be de-railed from one rear cog to the next. Again, notice the variances in the amount of pressure needed to keep the pedals turning, and how fast or how slowly the rear wheel turns.

Move the right gear-lever while you have the chain on the big front chainwheel and again while it's on the small one. See what happens when the chain is on the big front chainwheel and the biggest rear cog. Then try shifting it onto the small front chainwheel and the smallest rear cog. In both cases you'll notice that the chain is at an awkward diagonal angle and that it rubs against the derailleur cages. If you rode with the chain at this angle, it might fall off. The friction would certainly cause inefficiency and wear on the chainwheel and the chain.

This exercise will have shown you that you have a number of combinations of chainwheel and cog, giving you a range of (usually) fairly closely-spaced gears. If the rear cluster has five cogs on it, you have, in theory ten gears (five rear cogs × two front chainwheels) and the bike will be called a 10-speed bike; but in practice, as you've already found out, only eight are usable. Similarly a 12-speed bike will give you a choice of ten gears.

When you're out on the road on your bike, gears help you to keep to a comfortable, fairly constant cadence, regardless of whether the road goes uphill or downhill and regardless of changes in your speed. What happens when you're in a low gear (when the chain's on the small front chainwheel and a large rear cog) is that the back wheel revolves more often for each pedal rotation than it does in a high gear; this eases the work of climbing or of riding into a head wind because, although the wheel is turning slowly, your pedalling pace remains at a comfortable, fairly rapid cadence. If you're in a high gear (when the chain's on a big front chainwheel and a small rear cog) you're able to pedal comfortably downhill. If you have a good selection of gears and if you use them correctly, your legs are seldom, if ever, expected to push uncomfortably hard or to whizz round impossibly fast.

Climbs that would be unthinkable without gears can be conquered by very ordinary riders. Of course, the total sum of energy used to get a single-speed bike up a hill is the same as that used to ride a multi-speed bike up it; but on the latter, the whole task is made more pleasant and more feasible because you can control the rate at which you expend your energy.

Rules of thumb for using derailleur gears

- Keep pedalling while you're changing gears — otherwise the gears won't engage and your chain may fall off.
- If you have an index or *click* system of gears (and most good new bikes do) the lever simply clicks from one stop to the next; if you have an older system, you'll need to move the lever subtly, feeling for when the chain has engaged with the cog you're moving it to. It's easy to move it over several gears at once if you're careless.
- Try to predict when gear changes will be needed, and make them at the right time — just before a rise or dip in the road causes a change in your cadence. Aim to use your gears in such a way that your cadence alters as little and as smoothly as possible when the gradient of the road changes. Bad timing of gear-changes interrupts your momentum and is a prime cause of wasted effort.

■ Train yourself to keep up a fairly rapid cadence by favouring low gears. Slow cadence is often the result of riding in too high a gear; it's common in beginners who mistakenly believe that they're not really riding unless they can feel some meaningful agony in the legs. The opposite is true: light, steady cadence with smooth gear changes not only improves overall fitness but also prevents muscle stress and enables a rider to keep going far further than one who pounds away in high gears. Riding in high gears can cause potentially serious knee and tendon problems. It should be added that most racers do include high-gear riding in balanced training programmes to build up strength.

Braking

Walk a few steps, wheeling your bike along next to you. Apply the front brake hard. Release it, keep walking and then apply just the back brake hard. You'll notice that the front brake is by far the more powerful one (it has about three times the strength of the rear one), but that applying it hard makes the back wheel lift. Out on the road that lift can turn into a somersault. You may also have noticed that applying the rear wheel makes it lock; on the road, that can send you skidding.

To achieve controlled braking, you should use both the front and back brakes, and sit well down on the saddle, putting your weight over the back wheel to stabilize the bike. If you feel the bicycle skidding, release the brakes a little before re-applying them.

Practise *feathering*, a technique of lightly and rapidly alternating pressure and release of the brakes; this prevents brakes from locking onto the wheel. Feathering is also useful on long descents when continual pressure can cause wheel rims to overheat, glue on tubular tyres to soften and tyres to burst. On wet roads, feathering helps to dry wheel rims.

Avoid cornering and braking simultaneously. If there's an emergency and you really must brake in a corner, put the pressure on the back brake; skidding is preferable to going over the top.

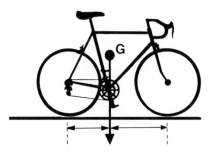

At steady speeds, wheels are firmly on the road, with the centre of gravity mid-way between them.

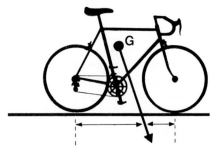

When you brake, your centre of gravity shifts forward, and the back wheel can lose traction.

This advice on dealing with brake failure on a penny farthing comes from Mecredy's *The Art and Pastime of Cycling*: (1983):

... If you find you are unable to dismount, owing to the pace and steepness of the gradient, go for the nearest hedge or hawthorn bush, and, just as you approach, throw your legs over the handles. You are sure to be hurt, but you may escape with a few scrapes and bruises, whereas to hold on means more serious, perhaps even fatal injury. If no hedge or hawthorn bush is near, throw your legs over the handles and put the brake suddenly hard on, and you will shoot forward and alight on your feet, when you must make every effort to run as hard as you can, for your bicycle is in eager pursuit, and a stroke from it may place you *hors de combat.*

Different makes and types of brake respond differently; the way they work can be influenced by, among other things, the type of rim on the wheel, wet weather, the load on the bike, the speed you're moving at and the gradient of the road. Familiarize yourself with the way your brakes work under different conditions; try to judge how long it takes and how much ground you cover before coming to a standstill from different speeds, and visualize using your brakes in an emergency situation. If you have children who ride in the rain, get them to measure the different stopping distances for a bike with dry rims and one with wet rims; they'll grasp the implications of this far better than if you simply tell them that brakes work slowly in the wet.

Important things to know about braking are:
- Bicycles take longer to stop than cars do.
- Bike brakes take longer to work when the wheel rim is wet. This is especially true of steel rims; in any conditions, but particularly in the wet, brakes work far better on aluminium alloy rims. The best brake blocks to use in wet and dry weather are synthetic. Though rubber blocks have a fair grip on aluminium, they skate over wet steel and result in stopping distances that can be four or five times as long as you'd expect in dry weather. If you get oil on the rims, you should get off and remove it before going on. (See the section 'Brakes' in Chapter 3.)

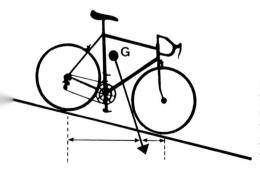

Braking when you are riding downhill shifts weight to the front wheel and can tip you over the top. Prevent this by keeping your weight towards the back of the bike; if you are carrying extra loads, keep them low on the bike.

■ Braking has the effect of throwing weight forwards and destabilizing the bicycle. In a sudden stop, and particularly if you're going downhill, this can catapult you over the front wheel; this is more likely to happen if it's the powerful front brake that is applied abruptly. Abrupt braking on the back wheel can make the bike skid out from under you.

Defeating the wind

The aerodynamics of cycling is covered in detail in Chapter 9; this is a lightweight introduction to the subject.

Just as geese get mutual benefit from flying in formation, with the leader breaking the worst of the air resistance while the others more or less cruise in the wake, so cyclists can work together in groups, sheltering each other from wind and conserving energy.

On a calm day, a cyclist riding on a flat road at a leisurely speed of 15 kilometres an hour is putting most of his or her effort into breaking through air resistance. As the cyclist's speed increases, the percentage rises: at a speed of 40 kilometres an hour, an astonishing 90 per cent of energy output is used to overcome wind resistance. In windy conditions, the effort required can make strong men cry: it takes *nine times as much effort* to pedal a bicycle at 20 kilometres an hour into a head wind blowing at 10 kilometres per hour as it does to pedal with that wind blowing from behind.

The greater a cyclist's frontal area is, the more energy is required to break through wind resistance. In other words, if you are broad-chested and you ride upright, wearing a jacket that flaps like a sail, it will take far more effort to cut through the air than it would if you were weasel-shaped and you crouched over your handlebars in leanly-cut, slinky clothes. Scientists have been fascinated by the challenge of reducing wind resistance since the bike's earliest days, and though their research has produced some impressive machines with remarkable aerodynamic properties, none have yet proved to be entirely satisfactory alterna-

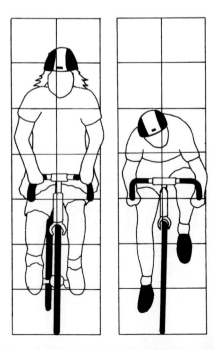

The larger your frontal area, the greater will be the effects of wind resistance, and the harder you will have to work.

tives to the conventional bicycle. Aerodynamically-designed tubing, spokes, water-bottles and other components have helped to streamline conventional bikes. (Manufacturers have even come up with aerodynamic saddles; I have yet to work out how a saddle can be aerodynamic when it has a pair of buttocks spread over it most of the time!) It's the human body on the bike that is the main cause of wind-drag, and defeating the wind remains, therefore, very much a matter of riding technique.

You can reduce your frontal area appreciably by tucking up into an aerodynamic riding position: with your hands on the drops or gripping the bars near the stem, with your chin just above the stem, and elbows kept well in, your frontal area will shrink and you will cause less resistance. The technique works best on downhill slopes because your speed is higher there. Up hills, it serves no purpose. You can test how well this technique works by trying it in reverse: start off on a descent in an aerodynamic position, and then slow yourself down by sitting up and bending your arms out sideways to cause as much air-drag as you can.

When two or more cyclists are riding together, slipstreaming or drafting is an even more effective way of beating the wind. This is a racers' technique, but it's one that every right-thinking casual cyclist should learn to use. It's not only a useful way of sharing the workload, but is also a good way of 'pulling' along a child or any weaker rider.

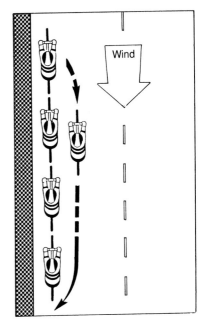

At 40 kilometres an hour on a calm day, drafting can result in a saving of about 30 per cent of effort for those in the slipstream. In windy conditions, the saving is far greater.

For novices, a good place to practise this technique is on the level, riding into a head wind, where the benefits will be most obvious. To begin with, it's safer to work with only one partner, one of you riding behind the other. If the wind comes directly from the front, the slipstream will be right behind the front rider; if it's blowing at an angle, the still air will be somewhere behind and to the side. You'll soon learn to feel around and find it.

At a metre apart, you can feel the benefits of slipstreaming, but the closer you get, the better the results. Close riding, of course, requires skill: you have to ride smoothly and predictably, and the front rider must indicate before rounding a bump or slowing down. The following rider should keep an eye constantly on the rear wheel ahead, but should take care not to be mesmerized by it. Don't allow wheels to overlap closely; in a turn, they are likely to touch and bring the riders down in a pile on the road.

The bigger the group of cyclists, the less often each person has to work in front. For a group of four riding in single file, this is the basic pattern to follow: the front rider keeps up a steady pace for a certain distance, and then indicates and moves out slightly to the right, slowing down so that the others can pass; the front rider then tucks in at the back of the line, and the procedure is repeated.

A staggered formation is best for beating cross-winds, but this isn't always possible or wise in traffic.

Cornering

Turning corners is mostly a matter of leaning into the corner and letting the bike steer itself; you'll probably find that you do that instictively anyway. At high speeds and especially on descents, cornering becomes a fairly subtle skill, but for casual riding these are the main points you need to think about:

- Make sure your speed's under control before you reach the corner. Don't brake on the corner: tyres may lose traction and skid if they have to cope with the stresses of turning and braking at once.
- Don't pedal through a sharp corner. Keep the inside pedal up — otherwise it may hit the road surface; apart from feeling like an electric shock blazing through you, this can lift the rear wheel and destabilize the bike, causing loss of control.
- Bend your inside knee away from the bike to reduce the weight over the pedal.

Techniques on all-terrain bikes

The majority of all-terrain bikes do most of their mileage on tarred roads, where their comfort and easy control make them good touring or commuting bikes. Under those circumstances techniques are not very different from those that riders of conventional road bikes use. Overcoming wind resistance is somewhat less of a factor than on road bikes because of the slower speeds of ATBs.

But for off-road riding (which Max Glaskin, author of *Mountain Biking*, has described as 'a cross between skiing, cycling, botany, bird-watching and weight-training') there are many new techniques to become mistress or master of.

Before you get out into the mud and the grit and start barreling down mountain slopes or scrambling up them, check that your position on the bike is right and that your weight is placed centrally so that you can shift weight forwards or backwards easily. (See the section on sizing and setting up ATBs in Chapter 5.) For most riding, you will need to keep weight back for stability. But you will find that shifting your weight (sometimes subtly, sometimes very assertively) to stabilize and help control the bike is fundamental to skilful off-road riding.

Climbing

Before you get to an ascent, try to judge what gear you will need to be in to climb it, and change down to it early; on steep climbs it's difficult, if not impossible, to change gears without losing momentum and traction.

Try to develop a cat-like agility, balancing your weight on the pedals, and keeping a sensitive hold on the bars. Keep enough weight forward to hold the front wheel down and to prevent your bike from doing an un-asked-for wheelie. But don't put all your weight forward, otherwise your rear wheel will lose its grip.

Learn to balance like a cat on the pedals, keeping a sensitive hold on the bars.

Descending

The important thing is to get your weight well back. For covering tricky ground, and when it is too steep to pedal, it helps to have your bum a couple of centimetres above the saddle and to grip the seat between the thighs. This helps you to control the bike's stability. It also makes it possible to steer by moving your legs in parallel in the way that snow skiers do.

If the ground is rough, keep the pedals parallel to the ground so that you clear stones and tussocks.

On steep, rough descents, keep your weight well back and your feet parallel to the ground.

Braking

The front brake is the stronger one, but beware of its power, especially on loose surfaces. Use both brakes, and use the feathering technique described earlier. In an emergency, lock the back brake and never the front one, but try to avoid this because it destroys not only the rear tyre but the trail as well. If the emergency gets really serious and you find you are heading for the edge of a krans and can't stop, put your feet down and let the bike run out under you and do its lemming act without you.

Humps and bumps

You can negotiate the average tree root or ridge across the track quite easily by approaching it at a right angle. If you go for it obliquely it may deflect the tyre and dump you.

Once your ambitions go to jumping over obstacles, there are many manoeuvres to learn, most of which are beyond the scope of this book. To do a straightforward wheelie over an obstacle, you approach it at right angles if you can, in a low gear, leaning forward. Practise it over imaginary obstacles to start with. Lift the bike by pulling on the bars while you straighten yourself up and put power into the pedals. Once the front wheel is off the ground, keep your weight off it, but watch your balance — too much weight on the back wheel will tip you over. You can bring the front wheel down by shifting your weight forward; with practice, this will also enable you to get the rear wheel to hop up over obstacles.

A word about tyre pressures

Manuacturers usually recommend pressures or between 40 and 80 psi. These pressures will help to protect tyres from wear and damage, but for riding on loose soil, a pressure of about 30 – 40 psi will improve traction.

Finally, remember to keep an eye on the track four or five metres ahead of you, and to watch out for hikers sharing the same trail.

CHAPTER EIGHT

SAFETY

It's impossible to overstress how much your life is in your own hands on a bicycle. Most cycling accidents — even those that are technically the fault of motorists — could be prevented if cyclists used enough foresight and skill, and rode defensively.

This chapter deals mainly with safe riding techniques. But safety also depends on a lot of other things, such as keeping your bicycle properly serviced and seeing that children don't ride bikes that are the wrong size for them. Other sections of this book that have a direct bearing on safety are Chapter 6 ('Bicycle maintenance'), the section on technique in Chapter 7 and 'Helmets', and 'Lights and reflectors' in Chapter 16.

For every cyclist there are probably a dozen people who'd like to ride bikes but who are deterred by their fear of sharing roads with vastly heavier and faster motor vehicles, many of which are driven by people who are unlicensed,

---

Accident statistics

The following figures have been taken from separate surveys and they apply to particular places, but they are listed here because they illustrate important points that appear (sometimes with different emphasis) in most studies of bicycle accidents:

- Most cycling accidents don't involve cars and aren't reported to the police.

- About 70 per cent of car/bicycle accidents involve cyclists between the ages of seven and seventeen years, and are the result of cyclists' lack of training and their poor road behaviour. Cycling awareness and traffic skills improve after the mid-teens.

- Though only 3 per cent of riding is done after dusk, that is when 50 to 60 per cent of fatalities occur. Most after-dark accidents happen to cyclists who have inadequate lights or reflectors, or none at all.

- 70 to 80 per cent or more of fatalities in cycling accidents result from head injuries. Most fatalities due to head injuries happen to people who were not wearing helmets at the time of the accident. There's evidence that wearing protective helmets reduces the risk of brain injury by about 88 per cent.

---

poor-sighted, stoned, drunk, juvenile, senile, aggressive, selfish or just incompetent. Much of the blame for cyclists' problems does lie with motorists and with road planners who are insensitive to cyclists' needs. But it's also true that the great majority of accidents which have happened — even those which were technically the fault of motorists — could have been prevented or avoided if the cyclists involved had used more skill and foresight, and had ridden defensively. As Richard Ballantine says in his famous *Bicycle Book*, 'The cyclist is a guerrilla; maintaining a clear escape route is always paramount.'

Many surveys and statistics have been drawn up on cycling accidents. Some have calculated the risk of injury for each kilometre travelled on a bike to be ten times that for motorists. However, for every hour of travelling time by bike or car, the accident figure has been calculated to be about the same for each. But in many ways statistics like these fail to give a true or useful picture: for example, the figure for cyclists includes children and this obviously pushes the figures far above what it would be if only adults and responsible adolescents were considered.

Faulty bicycles, poor road surfaces and lack of training have all been blamed for accidents; alcohol and prescription drugs, including minor tranquillizers and antihistamines have also been implicated. But the overwhelming impression got from statistics is that accidents have a multiplicity of very different and often overlapping causes, and that your most important weapon is a constant, sharp awareness of safety and all that it entails.

The dangers

The greatest danger of all is failure by the cyclist to concentrate and to think ahead. It's impossible to stress enough how much your life is in your own hands when you're on a bike.

In traffic you need to be defensive — constantly alert and ready to handle the unexpected effectively. Keep your fingertips on the brake-levers and one toe-strap loose so that you can slide your foot out quickly if you have to stop. Stay in a gear which allows you to maintain a good pace and to accelerate easily out of tricky situations. Train yourself to be super-observant: for example, if you're turning your head to see what's thundering behind you, observe, as you turn, what the road surface and traffic conditions in front and alongside you are. The thundering thing may be about to force you off your route. And learn to recognize the obvious: if a bus has halted at the kerb ahead, expect it to rumble out into your path. The driver's simply doing his job. Where cars are parked outside shops, know that doors will swing open into the road.

At the same time, you need to be as assertive as you can be within your rights and without taking stupid risks. You have the same right to the road as motorists. Exercise it by using your legitimate space.

Though some motorists are incorrigibly dangerous to cyclists, most respond well to a cyclist whose intentions are clear and who rides predictably.

Most road rules are designed for motorists and not cyclists, and quite often they seem to be unnecessary formalities to the person on a bicycle. (Stopping at a red traffic light when there's clearly no cross-traffic is an example. In fact, in these instances the cyclist often feels it's safer to cross against a red light and get a head start on traffic building up behind.) But, for public-relations reasons (amongst others), it's important to obey the rules of the road. Lawless cyclists antagonize the general body of motorists and this damages the chances of getting public sympathy (and ultimately official approval) for better facilities and rights for cyclists. The regular stream of vitriolic letters to the press shows that many motorists see cyclists as arrogant, dangerous, law-breaking nuisances, and some would, if they could, have them banned from the roads.

Experience teaches you what the main external dangers to cyclists are, but it's more comfortable to encounter them in a book before you meet them in real life.

Motor vehicle drivers

Many motorists are oblivious to cyclists: they simply 'don't see' them. Others see them, but don't register that cyclists have the same rights as themselves. This is borne out by one Toronto survey which showed that motorists' failure to yield to cyclists who had the right of way accounted for about three times as many accidents as any other single cause. Subconsciously, motorists expect the cyclist to stop for them; the keeping-the-underdog-in-his-place mentality is particularly rife on roads, and the lowliest of underdogs is, in the eyes of many drivers, the cyclist.

- At intersections, watch out for cars turning left across your path. Habit makes many cyclists ride on the left of the road, even when it puts them into the wrong lane for the direction they want to ride in. Even if you **are** in the correct lane, watch out for motorists overtaking and then cutting left across your path to enter a side-street or to park. Drivers often do this, mistakenly thinking that cyclists are far slower than they really are.

  The only defence against this is to be aware that it happens and to be ready to react quickly. Make your objections clear in the hope that the motorist will be more careful in future. But be very wary of firing four-letter words or rude signs at motorists: there are dozens of true stories about motorists who've responded with dangerous anger.

- At intersections try to make eye contact with motorists: it's a tactic that measurably improves communication lines.

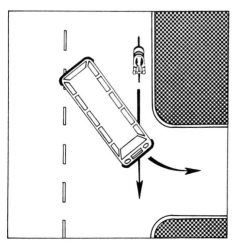

Cyclists must be alert to vehicles turning left across their paths.

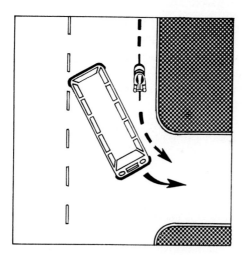

If a driver of a turning vehicle is unaware of the cyclist, or is unwilling to slow down and follow the cyclist round the corner, the cyclist may be forced against the kerb.

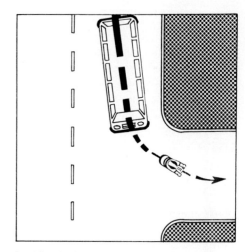

By riding in the centre of the lane, the cyclist forces the motor vehicle to follow behind.

- A car's accelerating and stopping times are much faster than those of a bike. Never follow close on a car's tail; if it stops suddenly, you're almost certain to find yourself landing face-first in metal. Never 'dice' with a car which is crossing your path at an intersection; remember that in this country it's unofficially accepted practice for drivers to jump the amber light. And it's almost normal to jump the red light.

- Some motor-vehicle routes are never worth risking. The worst are the minibus taxi routes. Heavily loaded and difficult to control, these vehicles are often driven by unlicensed men in a deadly race for passengers.

- An overtaking vehicle — especially a long one like a bus or lorry — on a corner can cut off a cyclist without the driver being aware of it. The diagram shows what typically happens. Cyclists tend to squeeze themselves against the kerb on corners, but it's usually more effective to move out assertively to the right, forcing the motorist to notice you and give you a wide enough berth. Always check what's behind you before reaching corners, and if it seems more sensible, wait for traffic to pass first.

- Trailers, boats or caravans pulled by cars should also be treated with caution because of their extra width and because they sway from side to side — something drivers seem oblivious of.

- Be very careful of the slipstream caused by fast, large vehicles overtaking you: you can be sucked in towards the vehicle and then (if you're lucky) blasted out to the rough road-edge when it's passed. Out on an open road it helps to move out towards the middle of the road while the oncoming vehicle's still a reasonable distance away and to indicate that you'd like them to slow down or give you a good berth. It usually works. It's a specially useful tactic when you have young children with you whose lightness makes them more likely to be dragged or blown off course by the slipstream.

- Deliberate harassment — especially of female cyclists — by other road users is nothing new. In the last century the Countess of Salisbury noted that London cab drivers 'had a fondness for chasing lady bicycle riders and running them down'. More recently, a Cape Town cyclist smashed in the headlights of a bus because he felt that the driver had severely harassed him, but this isn't an advisable solution.

Road surfaces

Road-edges, where cyclists are meant to ride, are often rough and potholed, littered with glass and interrupted by grids covering storm drains. The latter can trap a narrow tyre and throw a bicycle into a somersault. A layer of sand on a tar road, especially at corners, is bad news too. Where the edge is poor, it's fair to move further into the road, but make your intentions clear to motorists first and use discretion about how safe it is.

Oily patches and painted areas like zebra crossings are slippery, especially when they're wet. Cornering and braking should be done with extra care here.

Weather

If you're riding in wet or foggy weather, remember that you and the motorists around you can't see far. Bikes and cars take longer to brake in the wet. And there's a greater risk of slipping and falling.

Not being seen

In a high proportion of bike/car accidents, drivers have claimed that they didn't see the cyclist. There are many aids to visibility which are described later in this section, but the best way of making sure drivers see you is by riding where you'll be obvious to them. The apologetic cyclist who clings to the edges, appearing every now and then to pass a parked car, is a danger to himself and an irritation to motorists. Think consciously about whether you're visible or not. Along tree-lined avenues of flickering light and shade, the shadowy cyclist is hard to spot. In the glare of sunrise or late afternoon, you and your bicycle can, in the eyes of the motorist, virtually disappear in the dazzle. A bicycle is, after all, an almost transparent structure viewed from the side. And remember that you're narrow enough to fit into a driver's blind spot; even the driver who has checked in a rear-view mirror for traffic may not see you unless you position yourself intelligently.

There are two aspects to the cyclist's 'invisibility'. One is *psychological* in that motorists overlook cyclists because they don't see them as important or as a threat. The other is *physical*: bikes really can be hard to spot in a fast-moving traffic scene. With this in mind, several organizations, notably the Dutch Cyclists' Union and the US Department of Transportation, have done research into bicycle visibility and shown that the important thing, especially at night, is to see that you're unambiguously recognizable to drivers as *a person on a bicycle that's moving*. If that sounds staggeringly simplistic, remember that motorists are constantly faced with different objects moving in and out of their vision and that it's easy to mistake a cyclist's reflectors for a stationary car, a road sign or whatever, and consequently to react inappropriately. But if you make it quite clear that what's ahead is a human on a bike, you're far more likely to trigger a reaction from motorists that takes into account the cyclist's vulnerability, the fact that the vehicle ahead is slower than a car and that it may wobble slightly into the road.

The following are ways of drawing attention to your human form, and at night in particular, your bicycle and its movement:

- Light-coloured clothes help to make you visible in daylight and at night. (Statistics show that fewer light-coloured cars are in accidents than dark ones.) Dark clothes and colours like denim-blue can camouflage you on roads.

- It also helps to create the optical illusion that your bike's bigger than it is by attaching a reflector on a hinged stick that protrudes to the right. A bike wand is another device that may be useful for short children and riders of recumbents: it's a one-metre tall acrylic stick that attaches to the back of a bike and bears a flamboyant flag; at night a battery lights it up.

- Good lights and reflectors are essential after dusk. Here it's worth repeating a statistic from Florida: *50 to 60 per cent of cycling fatalities occur at night, though only 3 per cent of cycling is done then.* But it should be added that the well-lit cyclist is probably just as safe, if not safer, at night as the daylight rider.

  Where there are street lights, cyclists often fall into a trap of false security: if they can see where they're going, they feel safe, and therefore don't bother to use reflectors or lights. But to the driver, who is often blinded by the alternation of darkness and light that's part of urban driving at night, the cyclist may be invisible until he's fatally close. *The sole purpose of reflectors, and the main purpose of lights, is so that motorists can see cyclists.*

  South African law only requires a cyclist to have a front light (at night) and front and rear reflectors (at all times). But these are only visible from certain angles and at certain distances. (When close to a bike, for example, the motorist's observation angle cuts a reflector's luminosity to very little.) Lights and reflectors should be used with other aids and you should aim to be visible from all directions, all the time, from a distance of at least 120 metres.

Reflectors: Even if you never intend to ride at night, it's important to have reflectors: you can't know when a puncture or other unforeseen delay will force you to ride in the dark. In this country cyclists are required by law to have a red retro-reflector attached to the back of the bike and a white one in front. Look for good ones that comply with standards set by a reputable standards institute. The section 'Lights and reflectors' in Chapter 16 tells you what qualities to look for. Reflectors should be positioned as low as possible — on the rear mudguard, if you use one, and low on a front fork — or, even better, on both forks. This is because the angle of light cast by motor vehicles enables drivers to see low objects sooner than high objects.

Front and rear reflectors only reflect light from sources behind or in front of them. At intersections, where you should be visible to drivers approaching from the side or at an angle, it helps to have reflectors attached to spokes (close to the rims) or, if you can find them, buy tyres with retro-reflective side-walls. Both measures are eye-catching because they draw attention to the circular movement of the wheels and emphasize the fact that there's a bicycle ahead. However, the usefulness of side reflectors is limited by the fact that they're only visible to the motorist for a short distance while the bike is actually crossing the car's path: never rely on them alone. Reflectors fixed to pedals are, for their size, surprisingly effective; because of the way they move, they clearly identify the cyclist ahead.

Reflectors need a bit of care; they can't reflect light if they're dirty, if the surface gets badly scratched or if water gets into them.

Sam Browne sashes made of retro-reflective material and fitting across the body from shoulder to hip are effective. So are reflective vests, rucksack patches and strips on helmets. You can also get reflective wrist straps which are supposed to ensure that hand signals can be seen at night, but they're probably too high to be of real use; tiny wrist lights are a better bet if you want arm movements to be seen.

Lights: A cyclist riding after dark is legally bound to carry a white light in front. Several types are available and they vary a great deal in what they offer. It's important that your front light is as bright as possible, and that it's mounted high and is unobstructed.

There are two main types of lights: *battery lights* and *dynamo lights*. Both have pros and cons which are described in the section headed 'Reflectors and lights' in Chapter 16.

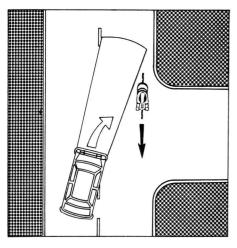

A motor vehicle about to turn right across a cyclist's path at night. In this situation, reflectors are unlikely to show up, and unless the cyclist has a front light, he will be hard to spot.

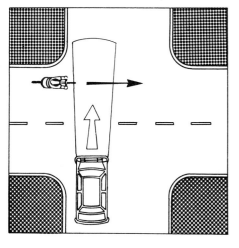

A motor vehicle and a cyclist crossing paths. Front and rear reflectors won't show up. Side reflectors will, but only when the car and bicycle are perilously close to one another. Again, a front light is essential.

To summarize the subject of visibility and its relation to accidents in night- riding, here's a list of the main types of after-dark cycling accidents:

- **An overtaking vehicle hitting a cyclist from behind:** This happens most commonly on unlit roads and when cyclists don't have adequate rear reflectors. (South African statistics show this to be a major killer on our rural roads.)

- **A vehicle travelling in the opposite direction to a bicycle turning right across the cyclist's path and hitting him:** Vigilance on the part of the cyclist and using a powerful headlamp should cut out the risk. Here a front reflector on its own might be ineffective: it might not be visible from a safe distance in the oblique angle of light coming from the car.

- **A vehicle hitting a crossing cyclist from the side at an intersection or when entering the cyclist's road from a side-street:** Again, a very conspicuous headlight is the best way of reducing the risk. Side reflectors (on spokes or tyres) will give limited additional protection.

Safety equipment

An overview of safety equipment available is given in this section. The topic is covered in more detail in Chapter 16 with guidelines to the features to look for.

Good maintenance of all your equipment is as important as having extra safety equipment. Even a softish tyre can be dangerous if it stops you accelerating away from a pantechnicon that's bearing down on you.

Rear-view mirrors are under-used, but are very useful in traffic. **Bells** are viewed by the cycling elite as the lowest sign of plebeianism, but they do work; unlike yelling, they warn unambiguously of a cyclist's approach.

Using a high-quality protective helmet significantly reduces the risk of injury.

Helmets: Reliable surveys show that 70 to 80 per cent of deaths from cycling accidents have been caused by head injuries. The cyclists who suffer the greatest number of head injuries are children. Recent Canadian and Australian studies have shown cycling accidents to be among the two most common causes of all head injuries among children admitted to hospitals there. Yet significantly far fewer children, in comparison with adults, wear helmets. And few schools encourage helmet use.

In a lifetime of cycling your chances of falling on your head at least once are fairly high. It may only take one fall to leave you either dead or not your old quick-minded self.

But fortunately the great strides that have been made in helmet research over the last decade have made comfortable, well-ventilated, lightweight head protection widely available. Superficially one brand can look pretty much like another, though they may vary enormously in effectiveness. For this reason you should choose one that carries the label of a reputable standards institute.

Children and safety

The patterns that emerge from most cycling accident statistics show that riders under the age of about fifteen years have far more accidents than adults do. This gives rise to two questions: firstly, how much can you fairly expect of children in traffic, and what inherent limitations do they have; and secondly, how far can you improve their ability to survive in traffic through training, and how do you go about doing it?

Most children under the age of nine can't assess the complexities of traffic situations well enough to make reliable decisions. They can't judge the speed, distance or direction of traffic around them accurately. They simply aren't mentally equipped to do it. Nor do most have the physical skill to react correctly in a tricky traffic situation. In training schemes for young cyclists, it's been found that under-nines don't respond to teaching nearly as well as older children do. Among experts there's consensus that they shouldn't ride in traffic unless they have the undivided attention of an adult riding with them.

From the age of nine most children have the skills needed to cope with quiet traffic. But it's madness to let them do so without proper guidance. Even with guidance, it's been found that they can't handle all the tests well in formal training schemes until they're about thirteen years old.

The most pleasant way of learning to cycle safely is by riding with a parent or other adult who's prepared to point out traffic rules, idiosyncrasies of drivers, specific dangers and so on. Not all children have access to that kind of adult, and they need some other form of training. In many developed countries there are well-established school-based training schemes for young cyclists, offering very thorough theoretical and on-road training which leads up to a proficiency test. By contrast, some South African schoolchildren have occasional training sessions from the National Road Safety Council, who also show films and distribute booklets and posters on safe cycling; some local traffic authorities also have training schemes. Recently moves were made to introduce a Cycle Proficiency Test across the country; it was initiated by a Cape Town primary school, where pupils are given a booklet which they're expected to study with their parents' help before doing a theory test which leads to a certificate — without which they can't ride to school.

Helpful as these measures may be, they fall far short of the comprehensive and practical courses such as the Cycling Proficiency Scheme in Britain and Bike-Ed in Victoria, Australia. Hopefully ours will develop to match the standard offered to children elsewhere. But in the meantime, it's worth taking note of the way courses like Bike-Ed are structured, especially if you're training your own children or running courses for other people's children.

Bike-Ed is aimed at nine- to thirteen-year-olds, and schools allow about twenty hours per course (spread over one-hour sessions over two terms). Teaching materials come in an extremely thorough and well-designed package comprising posters, question sheets, test cards, teacher support material, slides and so on, fitting into a clearly programmed course. Here are some of the findings of research relating to the course:

- A few sporadic sessions don't work. Bike-Ed organizers found that it takes at least twenty hours (spread over one-hour sessions over two terms) to complete a course effectively. They argue forcefully that inadequate training is worse than no training because it gives parents and children a false sense of security.

- Practical skills training is every bit as important as learning road safety theory. It should include emergency strategies and some of it should be carried out in traffic. In control tests, children who've had practical as well as theoretical training have improved their cycling skills far more than those who've only done the theory.

- Teachers should be confident cyclists themselves. No one may teach the Bike-Ed course before doing a two-day intensive training programme first.

Is all the effort worth it? Management problems in a scheme like this are immense. It calls on energy, commitment and time from teachers as well as material resources. But pupils and teachers in this and other schemes have reported very positive responses, and accident figures have dropped. Measuring the worth of a programme like Bike-Ed in cash terms has a very questionable usefulness, but for those who want the figures, here they are: in Bike-Ed's first three years of existence, the accident rate for young cyclists dropped by 20 per cent, and the resultant savings in accident costs outweighed the cost of researching and introducing Bike-Ed by about 180 000 Australian dollars. Put differently, it was cost-effective with a ratio of benefits to costs of over 4:1.

CHAPTER NINE

AERODYNAMICS

All cyclists know the difference between a head wind and a tail wind, but even on a calm day at high altitude the cyclist has to work at ploughing through air. With an understanding of the behaviour of air in motion — aerodynamics — all cyclists can use techniques to minimize wasted effort. This chapter looks at how cyclists have dealt with the problem during the past century, from first perceptions to the latest record-holding streamliners. Suggestions for drag reduction techniques used by riders of standard bicycles are summarized later in the chapter. Scientific and technical information is given in the Appendix for those interested in experimentation.

Introduction and early history

Charles Minthorne Murphy was born in October 1870. He learned to ride the popular boneshaker at the age of fourteen and soon became an excellent racer with an incredible pedalling technique. In 1886 he 'rode' a stationary bicycle for 79 seconds, spinning the cranks at 240 rpm; equivalent to taking two minutes off the record for the mile! When asked why he could not do that on the track, Murphy replied that there would be no limit to his speed if wind resistance could be overcome. He was unusually perceptive of the forces involved, and yet made himself a laughing stock by adding: 'Were it not for wind resistance there is not a locomotive built that could get away from me.' Thirteen years later, on 30 June 1899, Murphy did what he had claimed he could do: he bicycled behind a locomotive for more than a mile, at an average speed of over 100 kilometres an hour! The sporting world went wild and his feat was front-page news in almost every newspaper in the United States.

When Murphy made his claim, bicycles were second only to steam-powered locomotives as the fastest mode of transport, and had largely replaced horses for personal mobility. As late as August 1894 the German Joseph Fischer rode an ordinary (fixed front-wheel-drive high-wheeler or penny farthing) to soundly beat the American horseman William Cody Junior, son of Buffalo Bill, in a series of endurance races. Murphy had used a rear-driven safety bicycle, but the ordinary and other front-wheel drive machines remained in use until about 1900.

Charles Murphy going 100 kilometres an hour in the wake of a locomotive (1899).

Endurance racing: Joseph Fischer on an ordinary and William Cody Junior (son of Buffalo Bill) on a horse (1894).

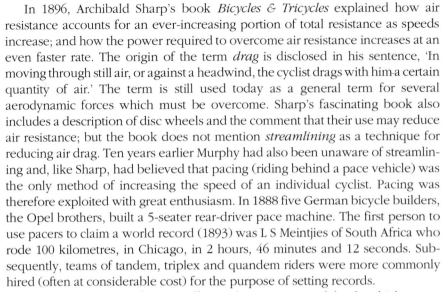

In 1896, Archibald Sharp's book *Bicycles & Tricycles* explained how air resistance accounts for an ever-increasing portion of total resistance as speeds increase; and how the power required to overcome air resistance increases at an even faster rate. The origin of the term *drag* is disclosed in his sentence, 'In moving through still air, or against a headwind, the cyclist drags with him a certain quantity of air.' The term is still used today as a general term for several aerodynamic forces which must be overcome. Sharp's fascinating book also includes a description of disc wheels and the comment that their use may reduce air resistance; but the book does not mention *streamlining* as a technique for reducing air drag. Ten years earlier Murphy had also been unaware of streamlining and, like Sharp, had believed that pacing (riding behind a pace vehicle) was the only method of increasing the speed of an individual cyclist. Pacing was therefore exploited with great enthusiasm. In 1888 five German bicycle builders, the Opel brothers, built a 5-seater rear-driver pace machine. The first person to use pacers to claim a world record (1893) was L S Meintjies of South Africa who rode 100 kilometres, in Chicago, in 2 hours, 46 minutes and 12 seconds. Subsequently, teams of tandem, triplex and quandem riders were more commonly hired (often at considerable cost) for the purpose of setting records.

The development of more efficient human-powered land vehicles was, however, about to be sidelined for many decades by several events or factors, of which four are particularly significant:

Laurens Meintjies

- The first was the development of *internal combustion engines.* By 1898 the multiple-rider pace machines were assisted by electric motors, and a year later by primitive internal combustion engines. Pioneering bicyclists were clearly showing that in order to move fast through air one had to produce a lot more power than was available from humans; but they were also being enticed away from bicycle engineering to automobile engineering.
- The second was the equally exciting discovery of *flight.* While it had been known for centuries that kites and hot-air balloons produced lift, controlled free flight was a dream until 1891 when Otto Lilienthal began hang gliding. This feat was noted by a pair of North Carolina bicycle builders, Orville and Wilbur Wright, who began an ordered series of experiments in 1899 to discover techniques for controlling flight. Only after the Wrights had achieved powered flight in 1903 did inventors begin to explore streamlining as a means of reducing air drag.
- At about this time the third event occurred: streamlined bicycles were *outlawed by competition rules*! Bicycle racing was big business a hundred years ago and the organizers of these events found that strict rules were essential for several reasons. One reason was that a variety of different machines were available — including experimental recumbents and the dangerous high-wheelers — so race organizers decided to confine the contests to athletes rather than machines. They therefore selected the safety bicycle with a diamond frame as the only acceptable machine, and carefully described it in the rules in such a way that high-wheelers and recumbents would be excluded. Later, following the same reasoning, they eliminated streamliners by stipulating that nothing could be added to a bicycle which was intended to reduce air resistance. There is, however, a strange relationship between organized competition and product development: Competitions stimulate development, but competitions must have rules, and rules

inhibit development! Unfortunately, no meaningful competitions for riders of unconventional machines were instituted until 1974. Therefore, since the turn of the century we have seen the diamond frame bicycle develop to its maximum level of efficiency within the limitations of competition rules, and to the exclusion of other types of machines.

- The fourth significant event — or rather factor — is that *designing and building* useful streamlined human-powered land vehicles is not easy. Aerodynamic theory was, understandably, very much in its infancy in 1900. This aspect, together with the exciting discovery of motor-driven land vehicles and aircraft, and the restrictions placed on racing bicycles, combined to effectively suppress development. Had the theory been more simple and solutions more obvious, competitions for streamlined vehicles would have been viable much earlier and the world's bicyclists might have become accustomed to a different standard.

Francis Faure (1933).

Enter the streamliners

In the early part of this century aircraft pioneers were using 'aero'-shaped struts instead of circular rods for their biplanes. Airships, in particular dirigibles (guided or steerable airships), such as the one Alberto Santos-Dumont flew around the Eiffel Tower in 1901, were sausages with sharp points at either end. By 1910 the dirigibles had rounded noses, and in 1914 Brennabor and Goricke raced fully streamlined bicycles which looked like mini-dirigibles with disc wheels! One crashed, but the winner averaged a remarkable 55 kilometres an hour over 5 000 metres. The previous year pioneer Frenchman Marcel Berthet had raced his streamlined bicycle at a meeting of the Manchester Wheelers in England, and the year before that E Brunau Varilla had begun filing patents in England, France and the USA for a bicycle fairing.

In the years preceding World War II a Swiss called Oscar Egg challenged Marcel Berthet on a streamlined bicycle. Egg and Berthet were old rivals and excellent cyclists; each had held the world record for the Hour on standard bicycles. Long distance races were popular at the time and both Egg and Berthet could travel 3 kilometres further in an hour on streamlined bicycles than cyclists on ordinary machines could. The UCI and bicycling public were unimpressed, possibly because of the impending world war and the factors mentioned earlier.

Marcel Berthet at a meeting of the Manchester Wheelers (1913/14).

In 1933 a German inventor, Franzosc Mochet, built a supine recumbent bicycle which was ridden by a French rider, Francis Faure, in track events, frequently outclassing teams of three and four riders on conventional bicycles. On 15 July 1933 Faure set a world record for the Hour of 45,055 kilometres. The following month the famous M Richard broke Egg's 17-year-old standard bicycle record of 42,742 kilometres by going 44,777 kilometres in an hour. The aging Berthet tried desperately to break the 50-kilometre mark on his fully streamlined 'Velodyne' and thought he had for a short while, until the track officials reduced his distance to 49,950 kilometres because the circumference of the oval differed for 4-wheeled and 2-wheeled vehicles. Late in 1937 Archi Archambaud raised the standard bicycle record for the Hour to 45,840 kilometres and early in 1938 Faure used a fully streamlined 'Velocar' to go 50,527 kilometres. But the only concession

Sid Rose and an experimental front-wheel-drive recumbent designed by Len Kirby, *circa* 1935, which he found to be unridable. However, an acrobat from the Boswell circus, while recovering from an injury in Cape Town, not only rode the experimental recumbent, but was able to do figures of eight in Rouwkoop Road.

by the UCI was the recognition of a separate set of *Records Libres* for unconventional machines.

One person who was intrigued was Sid Rose in Cape Town. Sid had joined the City Cycling & Athletic Club in 1930 at the age of nineteen to ride with people like Harry Bairstow, Ted Clayton and Hennie Binneman. In 1934 Sid read in the British monthly *Cycling* of Berthet's and Faure's achievements, but in those days no photographs were published. Sid and his inventor friend, Len Kirby, decided to build a Velodyne (fairing) and challenge Faure's 1 000- and 2 000-metre records. Sid wrote to the UCI, informing them of his intention and asking for a list of all current records. Sid and Len cycled to Youngsfield Aerodrome to study things aeronautical, took measurements of a wheelshroud and set to work on the 8-kilogram fairing nicknamed Hurry Bug. The Hurry Bug went on board the *Warwick Castle* for a tickey bound for the SA Championships meeting at the Westbourne Oval in Port Elizabeth. At the championships Sid took the 5- and 10-mile titles on his standard bicycle, and then, with a full compliment of officials present, used the Hurry Bug to clock 2 minutes, 23,7 seconds for the 2 000-metre standing start event. This was 13,3 seconds better than the existing world record for standard bicycles and 7,7 seconds better than Faure's 'free' record!

Sadly, the UCI cold-shouldered Sid who, being a very modest person, did not protest. Forty years later he said, 'This achievement did not prove that I was a world class sprinter, for I was not, but it did demonstrate the enormous advantage of streamlining'. Needless to say, these events were soon forgotten, and only enjoyed a brief revival in the late fifties when Oscar Egg produced his Sputnik.

Len Kirby (left), Sid Rose (right) and the Hurry Bug, Westbourne Oval (1935).

1974 and the IHPVA

In 1973 the Engineering Professor at California's State University at Long Beach (CASLB), Dr Chester R Kyle, knew very little about the UCI and nothing about the long history of bicycle aerodynamics. But he knew a lot about fluid dynamics and had a personality which made him intensely interested in getting his sums right; he was a keen traveller and an active, almost hyperactive, sportsman. A knee injury had made him give up basketball and take up veteran bicycle racing. While he was out training one morning a group of young students on fat-takkie bombers remarked on Kyle's slender tubbies. 'How much do tubulars help?' they wanted to know. Soon they were riding their bicycles in the faculty corridor with the professor doing coast-down tests to determine the coefficients of rolling resistance of the various tyres. The students were amazed to see how low the drag is for any bicycle tyre: 'So, what stops us from going 100 miles an hour?'

When Kyle explained that the principal villain is air drag, they wanted to know what could be done to reduce air drag. Intrigued, Kyle began testing shapes and human power output. A short while later Kyle met hang glider/microlite pioneer and aerodynamicist Jack Lambie at a conference and talked to him about streamlining bicycles. Lambie was also a keen cyclist (he and his wife cycle-toured South Africa in 1976) and, by coincidence, had been contemplating streamlining a bicycle. Lambie had calculated that the machine might go 80 kilometres an hour. They decided to test their machines in the CASLB hallway, and following the success of that meeting Kyle designed and built a full fairing for Olympic cyclist Ron Skarin's standard racing bicycle. In November 1974, on the airstrip at Los Alamitos Naval Air Station, Skarin took the existing 200-metre world record from 67,9 kilometres an hour to 69,2 kilometres an hour, and the Mile from 53,3 kilometres an hour to 65,4 kilometres an hour. Kyle wrote to the UCI to offer to have it done again for their verification. It was then that he learned about UCI restrictions on streamlining and the form of the bicycle.

A standard bicycle and full fairing — designed and built by Chester Kyle (left). John Stegmann is on the bicycle and Giles Pearson lends a hand.

Gold Rush: winner of the du Pont prize; first single-rider machine to exceed 104 km/h; seen here with Gardner Martin at the high altitude location. Photo by the consulting aerodynamicist, Glen Brown.

As at October 1989, the IHPVA World Records for land vehicles are:

200-metre flying start, single-rider

Fred Markham in Gold Rush	high altitude	105,34 km/h	May 1986
Rachel Hall in Allegro	high altitude	82,99 km/h	August 1985
Fred Markham in Gold Rush	low altitude	92,66 km/h	August 1986
Unofficial:			
Carl Sundquist in Lightning X-2	low altitude	103,29 km/h	Nov. 1986

200-metre flying start, multiple-rider

Barczewski and Grylls in Vector	101,26 km/h	4 May 1980

1-hour standing start, multiple-rider

Markham and Howard in Gold Rush Tandem	low altitude	97,434 km	Sept. 1989

1-hour standing start, single-rider

Markham in Gold Rush	72,95 km	Sept. 1989

(more than R3 million was spent on Francisco Moser's UCI record of 50,809 km, Jan 1984)

4 000-metre track pursuit

Markham in Gold Rush	3 min 43:79	August 1986
(Olympic record, Steve Hegg, USA – UCI rules	4 min 25 sec	July 1984)

Kyle and Lambie decided that in order to explore the potential of human-powered vehicles they would found the International Human Powered Vehicle Association (IHPVA) and arrange competitions with as few rules as possible. The first International Human Powered Speed Championships (IHPSC) was held in April 1975. Gibby Hatton rode Jack Lambie's streamliner at 69,8 kilometres an hour, coming second to the fastest speed of the day, 71,9 kilometres an hour, set by Ron Skarin in Kyle's machine. Every year since, the IHPSC has provided excitement and spectacular progress has been made as can be seen from the list of IHPVA World Records given here.

There have also been spectacular achievements on water and in the air. Hydrofoils with one rider challenge racing eights and, from a gloomy period when experts predicted that human-powered flight was pure fantasy (no human-powered aircraft had managed to hold altitude in a slow turn, and pilots faded from exhaustion within minutes), Greek national bicycling champion Kanellos Kannellopoulos kept Daedelus aloft for almost 4 hours and flew almost 120 kilometres from Crete to Santorini in April 1988.

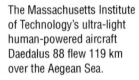

The Massachusetts Institute of Technology's ultra-light human-powered aircraft Daedalus 88 flew 119 km over the Aegean Sea.

The effect of the IHPVA on conventional cycling

As Kyle pointed out at the third IHPV Scientific Symposium, the bicycle industry did nothing for 30 years after the end of World War II, and the UCI unceremoniously banished a Swiss rider in 1976 for using a slick suit, smooth helmet and 'aero' tubing. But then the UCI began easing up until, by 1984, just prior to the Olympics, they sanctioned slick suits, airfoil tubing and helmets and the ancient disc wheel! As a direct result, world records have shown marked improvements and the industry has been irreversibly influenced. Greg Lemond's win over

Laurent Fignon on the final day of the 1989 Tour de France is directly attributable to his better use of areodynamics. Kyle, of course, says that these improvements are child's play by comparison with what is possible. Most of the information in this chapter is based on research by people associated with the IHPVA — notably Dr Kyle, who has made a plea to the bicycle industry to fund a chair of bicycle research at a large university.

The Argus Tour

I had taken to commuter and recreational cycling in 1976 when I read about the IHPVA, and wrote to Professor Kyle to subscribe as a member. At the time, Bill Mylrea and I were setting up the Western Province Pedal Power Association to lobby for bicycle facilities. The IHPVA philosophy so impressed me that I modelled the first Argus Tour on IHPVA rules, hoping to involve South Africans in this exciting era of discovery, the ultimate objective of which is not the testing of high-speed specials, but to make human-powered vehicles better: easier to propel, more practical and safer. The Argus Tour must be the finest testing ground in the world for a practical HPV: the winning machine has to be manageable in traffic, light enough to go up hills, stable in cross-winds, provide rider cooling, be unaffected by rain, and beat the country's best riders using the finest conventional equipment and working together in packs. The original rules had no restrictions on the vehicles (riders were divided into SACF members and non-members to enable both groups — for the first time — to compete in the

The Lightning F-40 with Tim Brummer (left), designer and builder of the machine, and Lloyd Wright (right), who rode it to set the course record for the Argus Tour in 1988.

same event) and there was only one overall winner. However, when it looked as if a streamliner might win, unconventional machines were put into a separate class. Later, there was an attempt to have them outlawed! Very few inventors have made use of the opportunity the Argus Tour gives them to design HPVs, and generally cyclists appear to be unmoved by Lloyd Wright's outright win in 1984, by Tom Thring's incredible performance in 1986, three weeks after major surgery, and, of course, by Lloyd's incredible wins in 1988 (by three minutes) and 1989 (by twelve minutes!). Any world history of human-powered land vehicle development must include these performances amongst the greatest.

What is aerodynamics?

Aerodynamics is the science which deals with air in motion and the reactions of a body moving in air. All sciences have to do with measurements. An understanding of aerodynamics is useful for a cyclist and those interested in human-powered land vehicles because it can enable them to measurably reduce the amount of power needed to move through air. Aerodynamics is also used to improve the stability of the moving vehicle. While the science of aerodynamics has become quite intricate, requiring years of study to master and access to expensive equipment, this chapter describes some simple concepts and inexpensive tests which cyclists and HPV builders should find useful.

A helium-filled blimp or hot-air balloon demonstrates *aerostatic* lift — floating in air — the Archimedes principle: *A body immersed in a fluid experiences an apparent loss of weight which is equal to the weight of the fluid displaced.* While it is easy to understand that a cork will float on water and a stone sink, it is not as easy to think of air, this harmless mixture of invisible gasses in which we live, as having sufficient mass to be of any consequence. Wet a finger and blow gently on it. OK, air exists.

What next? Before considering the weight of air we must clarify the difference between *weight* and *mass* by asking the question: *How much does one kilogram weigh?* The answer for us on Earth is that one kilogram mass weighs 9,81 newtons, due to the force of gravity. *Weight* refers to the *gravitational force* acting on that body. This force varies from place to place — one kilogram mass on the moon weighs less than one fifth of its weight on Earth. *Mass* refers to the property of *inertia* and is constant for a given body. However, because air is compressible, the mass of one cubic metre depends upon pressure and therefore varies with altitude, temperature and humidity. If you imagine, as most people do, that the mass of a cubic metre of air at sea level must be around 10 grams, you will be surprised to learn that the mass is more than a hundred times greater at 1 230 grams — almost one and a quarter kilograms.

The point about *mass* is that when making your way through air you have to work at overcoming the *inertia* of the air being pushed aside. The amount of work required increases as you move faster because the job has to be done faster. You are using force, as Sir Isaac Newton defined it at about the time Jan van Riebeeck was settling in at the Cape; Force is the acceleration of mass. $F = ma$.

The *weight* of air poses a different problem. One way to establish the weight of this cubic metre of air (1,23 kg x 9,8 = 12,05 newtons) might be to construct a box with inside dimensions of 1 metre x 1 metre x 1 metre, and then to weigh it

A flat plate moving through air creates high pressure ahead, an unstable low pressure area behind and considerable air movement. Chet Kyle: 'The key to high speed cycling is good streamlining and low frontal area.'

Standard bicycle/racing position with full fairing.

The tear drop shape is more apparent from the top.

when full of air and when empty. The problem is that the weight of the air above it can create an enormous force, making it difficult to construct a box strong enough. The weight of air can also be established by calculation: At sea level, a typical barometric pressure would be 1 017 millibars or 1,017 bars, which means 1,017 multiplied by the pressure exerted by a column of mercury 750 millimetres high. The weight of that column of mercury over an area 1 metre x 1 metre would be:

0,75 m x 13 536 kg/m³ x 9,81 = 10 152 kg x 9,81 = 99 591 newtons.

Frontal area greatly reduced by changing rider position.

You can sense this high pressure by trying to create a vacuum the size of a pea in your mouth. You can't!

The point about the *weight* of air is that it creates *pressure*, and when making your way through air you increase the pressure ahead and reduce the pressure behind. Because the air is fluid, you cannot move a block of air (like removing a brick from a wall) and leave an opening. Other air simply flows into the vacated area, and at sea level it is very difficult to prevent it from getting in! This pressure difference can become enormous. If it were not so, Boeing Jumbos and helicopters would not be able to fly.

Having shown that this invisible gas in which we are immersed has considerable substance in terms of *inertia and pressure*, we can show how a bicyclist has to work to push air aside. The bigger you are, the more air you need to disturb. The faster you go, the greater is the amount of air that has to be moved in a given time and the faster it has to be accelerated. And, if you shove the air vigorously aside so that it is set spinning long after you have gone, then that requires additional effort. As we know, the job of churning up air can be very tiring.

Prone rider position.

Working against air *inertia and pressure* would be less tiring if:

- There were not so much air — *air density* (ρ).
- You did not have to move so much air — *body size (A)*.
- You did not have to do it so fast — *air speed (v)*.
- The disturbed air calmly returned to its original position immediately after you had slipped through — *body shape* (C_d).

$$D = A \times C_d \times \frac{\rho}{2} \times v^2$$

These are the *four main components of air drag*, each of which can be measured separately to arrive at the total drag force. If you want to calculate the approximate drag force acting on a component, your whole bicycle, or your streamliner, methods to show you how are described in the Appendix, but you should first look at each of these four factors generally to get a background to the information you will need to gather. These explanations will also help you understand the suggestions for drag reduction given in this chapter.

Imagine you are on your bicycle, freewheeling down a long straight, smooth road of constant gradient on a calm day. Gravity provides the force which propels you faster and faster. As you go faster, the resistance caused by rolling friction and air friction increases until they together equal the gravitational force propelling you, and your speed stabilizes. This speed is called *terminal velocity*. How fast you go is clearly influenced by the steepness of the hill, the road surface (soft sand?), your wheels and tyres, additional luggage, and wind. Surprisingly, the combined rolling friction of bearings and modern tyres on a good road surface is very much smaller than the friction of the air.

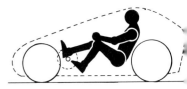

Supine rider position.

How do you increase your road/air speed without pedalling? The four main components of air drag will now be discussed in turn.

Air density in kg per m³	
Air temp. (°C)	*Multiply millibar reading by:*
5	0,001253
6	0,001248
7	0,001244
8	0,001239
9	0,001235
10	0,001230
11	0,001226
12	0,001222
13	0,001217
14	0,001213
15	0,001209
16	0,001205
16	0,001205
17	0,001201
18	0,001197
18	0,001197
19	0,001192
20	0,001188
21	0,001184
22	0,001180
23	0,001176
24	0,001172
24	0,001172
25	0,001168
26	0,001165
27	0,001161
28	0,001157
29	0,001153
30	0,001149

Air density

Measured in kg/m³, the symbol for air density is ρ. It is mostly affected by altitude, but also by temperature and humidity.

Most of the world speed records are set at high altitudes. Eddy Mercx went to Mexico City (over 1 800 metres), Gardner Martin went to San Louis Valley (2 300 metres), while others travelled to La Paz in Bolivia (over 3 600 metres!).

To some extent, the wake behind a cyclist can be regarded as a low-pressure zone, so, when someone comes pedalling past you, tuck in behind and try to ride in the low-density space. This effect is called *drafting* and is most noticeable when you're right up close (watch that wheel-to-wheel contact!) and have learned how to stay in the slipstream as it wanders from side to side. The effect is even greater behind a larger vehicle with a flat vertical back, such as a truck. However, the reduced air drag you experience is partly due to the forward momentum already picked up by the air around the cyclist or vehicle ahead of you, which reduces your relative air speed. The stoker on a tandem drafts the captain to mutual benefit. But, if you're doing a solo trip on the Garden Route, you can't exploit air density to go faster.

The formula requires the mass of one cubic metre of the air. Record the air temperature and ask the nearest meteorological office for their temperature and barometric readings for that time. Use the table given here to arrive at a suitable air density figure.

Body size

This is the size of the 'hole' being 'bored' through the air. It is called frontal area, symbol A, and is measured in square metres.

You can reduce your size. Put your nose on the handelbars, tuck in your elbows, put your knees together and wear tight-fitting clothes and you will pick up speed. Strictly speaking, you also simultaneously improve your shape so the effect of size is difficult to isolate. But it does work — air drag can be reduced in direct proportion to frontal area — halve your frontal area and you halve the drag force!

Measure the frontal area by projecting your shadow on a wall and get a helper to mark your outline. Shadow size can, of course, be distorted by your distance from the wall and/or the light, so use a large, stationery mirror to reflect sunlight (parallel beams) in the direction of travel.

Air speed

Here we consider the relative speed of you and the air. The scientific term for air speed is velocity, v, measured in metres per second.

Air speed is clearly a major component of air drag: no air speed, no air drag. However, the other important aspect of air speed, or velocity, is that drag does not increase in direct proportion to speed, but rather in relation to the *square* of the velocity. In other words, double your speed and air drag increases fourfold. Cyclists know that they can reduce air drag by reducing speed, but what we are looking for are ways of maintaining or increasing speed in relation to air without additional effort.

White Lightning, 1979. First human powered vehicle to exceed 55 m/h (80,45 km/h).

Velocity is quite easy to measure on a calm day when air speed is equal to road speed. Some electronic bicycle speedometers can be set accurately. Or use a stop-watch and measure the time between two known points.

Body shape

More importantly, how streamlined is the shape? The measurement is a number called a drag coefficient, symbol, C_d. Methods for measuring C_d are given in the Appendix.

The shape of the object has an enormous effect on the total drag. The object should have a shape which slips through the air causing the least amount of disturbance. Disturbed air may be air which has been needlessly set in motion. When a cyclist bucks down, he or she presents a more streamlined torso shape to the air and consequently disturbs less air. Loose clothing will flap, using the cyclist's effort to do so, and will leave disturbed air behind. Tight, smooth clothing disturbs less air, as do shaved legs and 'aero' components. To go faster, you want to disturb as little air as possible, and this can best be done by covering knobbly and fast-moving shapes with smooth fairings which part the air carefully and help it to return as nearly as possible to its original position. The effectiveness of streamlining is clearly shown by the performances of streamliners, some of which are discussed in this chapter. However, because streamlining is specifically forbidden by UCI (and SACF) racing rules, the full potential of streamlining cannot be used by cyclists who ride under these rules.

The variation in drag force between different shapes of equal frontal area is revealed in the coefficient of drag, or C_d value for each shape. The C_d can be determined for any shape for any given direction of travel and applies to the *shape*, irrespective of its size. C_d *is simply a ratio which shows how the drag of the particular shape compares to that of a flat plate of equal area, held at right angles to the airstream.* It is assumed that the flat plate has a C_d of 1. Therefore, given shapes X, Y and Z of equal frontal area, if shape X has a C_d of 0,9 and shape Y a C_d of 0,3, we can see that X has only 90 per cent of the drag of a flat plate, but three times as much drag force as Y in that airstream. (Note that the figures may vary at different air speeds). Similarly, if shape Z has a C_d of 0,1, it has one third of the drag of Y. Shape can refer to the cyclist only, the cyclist and bicycle, the bicycle alone, and so on. Because it is difficult for an amateur to predict how a new shape will behave in an airstream, the best approach is to test the actual object (or a scale model) and arrive at the C_d value after eliminating the other factors. Three methods of doing this are given in the Appendix.

Viscosity and laminar flow

There are two other characteristics of air flow which should be discussed: viscosity and laminar flow. The viscosity of air can be measured and variations related to temperature and humidity can be revealed. However, the variations are not great and, as is the case with altitude, it is impractical to move around to where the viscosity is lowest. Laminar flow is a concept which visualizes the surface of a streamlined body moving in still air; air molecules adjacent to the body will tend to be moved along with the body, and they in turn will try to drag with them the next layer of molecules. This procedure develops with a very small drag penalty until a stage is reached where the layers of air begin to shear and create turbulence — which results in a noticeable increase in drag. Successful laminar flow requires

Landshark, 1979. Gardner Martin's forerunner to Tour Easy, Easy Racer and Gold Rush — a du Pont prize winner and now in the Smithsonian Museum.

The Vector Single, designed by aeronautical engineers, raised the IHPVA 200 m speed record in 1980 from 82 km/h to almost 90 km/h at the IHPSC, and then went 94,77 km/h a few months later.

Steve Ball and Dragonfly II. Placed second at 9th IHPSC: 88,37 km/h.

131

1982 — the tenth IHPSC. Lightning X-2 (the winner) is in the foreground.

a properly streamlined body and relatively calm air. Many of the successful high-speed HPVs (Aeroshell, Dragonfly, Gold Rush, Lightning X-2, White Lightning, Vector, and others) used body shapes designed to take maximum advantage of laminar flow during record attempts where one of the pre-conditions for the recognition of a record is that there should be no wind. A cross-wind will disturb laminar flow, and because a machine for regular use will have to contend with cross-winds and otherwise turbulent air for most of the time, a body with good laminar flow for a commuting or touring HPV is very difficult to conceive. Important objectives for the design of such a body shape are small frontal area, minimum surface area, minimum turbulence when facing winds anywhere from 45 degrees left to 45 degrees right of direction of travel, and stability.

Stability

Stability relates to the position, direction and magnitude of the prevailing centre of pressure (air drag) in relation to the means of resistence. For example, when riding in still air, a disc front wheel has a relatively small air drag which is essentially in the direction of travel and is countered by the friction of both tyres on the road; if, however, the wheel turns too much to one side, there will be rapid changes in the magnitude and direction of the air drag force. A 27-inch disc front wheel on a standard bicycle with narrow handlebars is therefore both unstable and dangerous, but a 20-inch disc wheel on a recumbent with a long tiller and wide handlebars will be quite manageable.

Air drag and power formulae

We have seen that air drag acting on a bicycle or HPLV (human-powered land vehicle) is affected by four factors (air density, body size, air speed and body shape); and we have concluded that manipulating frontal area and shape are the best ways of reducing air drag, and thereby increasing air speed or reducing the power which the rider must provide. The mathematical relationship between these factors is given in this formula:

$$D = A \times C_d \times \frac{\rho}{2} \times v^2$$

D is the total drag force in newtons. (Divide by 9,8 to get kilograms.)
A is the frontal area in square metres.
C_d is the coefficient of drag for a vehicle — a number.
ρ is the density of air in kilograms per metre cubed.
v is the air speed in metres per second. (Divide km/h by 3 600 and multiply by 1 000.)

This formula shows that the total drag force, D, is directly proportional to the frontal area, A. Halve A and you halve the drag! Similarly, D is directly proportional to the drag coefficient. Halve C_d and D is halved. However, because velocity appears in the formula as velocity squared, it means that if v is doubled, D will rise four times! D values plotted against v are therefore parabolic.

This is only partly why there is such a marked difference in the power needed to go from 10 kilometres an hour to 20 kilometres an hour, and from 20 kilometres an hour to 40 kilometres an hour. There is another law of physics at work. In 1836, about the time Louis Trichardt's oxen were dragging his wagons around the Soutpansberg, the inventor James was born to Mrs Watt in Scotland. James was the fellow who found out how to measure the power output of steam engines in terms of force and velocity, which he called horse power. The SI unit of power used today is named after him.

Power (measured in watts) = Force (newtons) x Velocity (metres per second).

Suppose that a cyclist is able to produce a constant power output of, say, 500 watts, the power formula shows that the force with which he pushes forward will *decrease* as his speed increases! This has nothing to do with air drag, rolling friction or going up hills. It works for rockets in space where air drag and gravity might be regarded as zero. The disappointing truth is that as we gather speed and we need more force to overcome the rapidly increasing drag force, we find we have less and less force available! This can be shown mathematically like this:

From $P = F \times v$ we get $F = \dfrac{P}{v}$

Since D is a force in the same units as F we can say that when $D = F$

$$\frac{P}{v} = A \times C_d \times \frac{\rho}{2} \times v^2$$

and therefore $P = A \times C_d \times \dfrac{\rho}{2} \times v^3$

which means that power is proportional to velocity *cubed*, and that is why it gets so increasingly difficult to go faster. If you cannot reduce the drag component, then you have to produce more power — a lot more power! Imagine you are doing 40 kilometres an hour on the level and you want to increase your speed to 80 kilometres an hour. Doubling your power output will only get you to 50 kilometres an hour. Four times the power will get you to 64 kilometres an hour, and only *eight* times your power output will get you to double your speed to 80 kilometres an hour.

A composite graph showing six parabolic drag curves and three hyperbolic power curves excluding mechanical losses, usually about 5 per cent. It shows, for example, that the old roadster needs 100 watts to go 20 km/h, while the F-40 will go about 33 km/h on 100 watts.

Roadster **(M1):**	$A = 0{,}50$ m^2	$C_d = 1{,}10$	$C_r = 0{,}006$	Mass is 78 + 15 kg
10-speed tourer **(M2)**:	$A = 0{,}40$ m^2	$C_d = 1{,}00$	$C_r = 0{,}0045$	Mass is 78 + 12 kg
Aero Racer **(M3):**	$A = 0{,}39$ m^2	$C_d = 0{,}83$	$C_r = 0{,}003$	Mass is 78 + 11 kg
Aero Racer, drafting **(M4):**	$A = 0{,}39$ m^2	$C_d = 0{,}50$	$C_r = 0{,}003$	Mass is 78 + 11 kg
Lightning F-40 **(M5):**	$A = 0{,}44$ m^2	$C_d = 0{,}30$	$C_r = 0{,}004$	Mass is 78 + 15 kg
Vector single **(M6):**	$A = 0{,}42$ m^2	$C_d = 0{,}11$	$C_r = 0{,}0045$	Mass is 78 + 31 kg

C1 = 100**W**

C2 = 250**W**

C3 = 500**W**

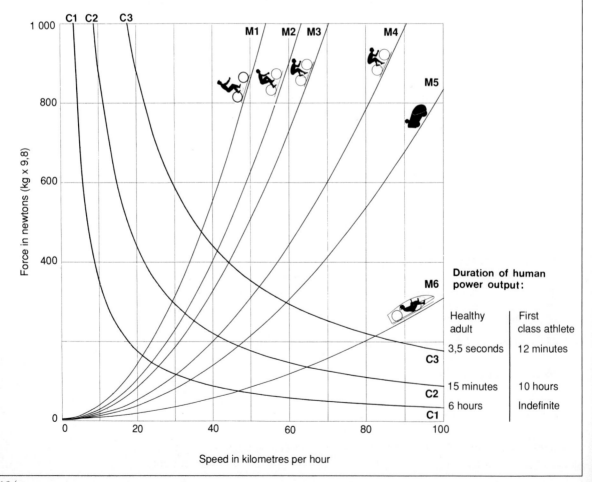

The ultimate UCI-sanctioned low-drag machine and cyclist, Steve Hegg of USA winning the 4 000 m pursuit in the 1984 Olympics in Los Angeles — a one million dollar venture!

Reducing aerodynamic drag: Practical guidelines for riders of ordinary bikes

Most of the effort of riding a bicycle, even at a speed as low as 15 kilometres an hour, goes into overcoming wind resistance. The higher the cyclist's speed, the greater the force of wind resistance. Drag forces acting on the bicyle and rider increase as the square of the cycling speed; ultimately, this means that doubling your speed requires an eightfold increase in power.

What practical ways are there of overcoming this? Wind tunnel and road tests have shown that the best way of improving aerodynamic efficiency is to use an enclosed, streamlined recumbent bicycle. But let's look at what a cyclist using a conventional bicycle can do to improve aerodynamic performance. There are four key methods:

1. Reduce the frontal area
Total air drag is directly proportional to frontal area, so it is important to try and reduce it. Tucking up into a hill-descent position with the hands on top of the bars, the chin resting on the hands, the cranks parallel to the ground and the knees together helps. The drag on a rider in this position riding at 56 kilometres an hour is about 3,3 kilograms (32 newtons); by contrast, the drag on a rider in an upright touring position is about 6 kilograms (59 newtons). Using aerobars helps you to keep in the hill descent position when cycling on the flat.

2. Streamline your body
Effective ways of streamlining yourself are to wear tight-fitting clothes, cover or tie up hair, shave the legs and wear an aerodynamic helmet. Mittens and shoe

covers designed to reduce drag will also help. Long hair may cost as much as 30 seconds in a 40-kilometre race. An aerodynamic helmet can reduce cycling time by about 15 seconds in a 40-kilometre time trial. By contrast, the racer's 'hairnet' helmet not only gives no protection, but also has greater drag.

Modifications and components that can reduce drag

Clipless pedals

Aerotubing (non-cylindrical, teardrop-shaped with thin leading edge)

Aero derailleurs

Aero rims (V-shaped; same width as the tyre)

Aero spokes (less spokes — 28 to 32; blade-shaped; radially laced; shorter length)

Disc wheel or 3-spoked wheel (A disc wheel should not be used on the front wheel in high winds.)

Narrower tyres (18 mm; glued firmly to rims with gap between tyre and rim filled with silicone.)

Narrower hubs

Streamlined waterbottles behind the seat

Quick-release wheel levers positioned parallel to the ground pointing to back of bike

Concealed brake cables

Pump positioned under the top tube

Shift levers repositioned on top of the down tube with cables routed inside the frame

---

Cherie Pridham on her time trial bike — bullhorn handlebars, aero helmet and a disc wheel all contribute to reducing drag.

Time savings in a 40 kilometre time trial resulting from aerodynamic modifications

Item	Time savings (seconds)
Aero bike frame	42
Spoked aero wheels	39
Aero handlebars	29
Front disk wheel	14
Rear disk wheel	14
Two disk wheels	67
Aero helmet	14
Aero clothing	14
Aero water bottles	14
Aero pedals	9
Aero cranks and sprockets	6

3. Streamline your bicycle

Use components with smooth surfaces and no protrusions or exposed angles. Relocate certain components; for example, cables can be routed inside the bicycle tubing or placed behind more aerodynamically-efficient shapes. Some time savings that can be made by using such equipment are listed here. (Many of these are expensive and only result in infinitisemal reductions in drag.)

4. Drafting

In most circumstances, the most effective way of reducing aerodynamic drag is to cycle behind other riders; this technique may reduce wind resistance by up to 40 per cent for the following rider if the gap between the cyclists is 0,3 metres and about 35 per cent if the gap is 0,5 metre — equivalent to a power saving of between 20 and 30 per cent for the following cyclist. (For more about the technique of drafting, see Chapter 7 — basic technique — and Chapter 14 — racing technique.)

There are a number of important things to note about drafting:

- Cyclists can travel considerably faster in a group than alone. By rotating the leading cyclist, who may cycle at 100 per cent or more of his VO_2 max for the short time that he is in the front and then recovers in the bunch when he cycles at only 80 to 90 per cent of his VO_2 max, the group as a whole travels faster. Thus a four-rider team can travel about 7 kilometres an hour faster over 4 000 metres than each rider can singly; twelve or more bicycle tourists of equal ability can probably travel between 2 and 6 kilometres an hour faster in a group than each can singly, provided that all are equally prepared to cycle in the lead.

- The drafting effect may last for up to five bike lengths. Thus the ruling in triathlons that cyclists may follow no closer than two bicycle lengths behind another cyclist does not prevent the following cyclist from enjoying some benefit.

- Following slightly behind and to one side of a leading rider, a manoeuvre which is legal in time trialling, can reduce the wind resistance of the following cyclist by about 25 per cent.

- A cycling break into a strong head wind seldom succeeds because following is so easy; a break downwind is more likely to be effective because drafting provides less benefit.

- The second rider on a tandem is, in effect, drafting very closely behind the leading rider. Tandem riders use on an average 20 per cent less power per rider at any speed than two separate cyclists do.

- Small wheels allow closer drafting, but as a wheel size decreases, rolling resistance increases, usually cancelling any potential advantage.

- Motor vehicles, depending on their size, increase cycling speed between 1 and 5 kilometres an hour when they pass within 2 metres of the cyclist; with 3 metres of side clearance the effect is much less (0 to 1 kilometre an hour). The effect is greatest with the largest passing vehicles like trucks.

    If a cyclist is next to a steady stream of traffic, his speed may increase by 5 to 8 kilometres an hour. Thus, in a time trial in traffic, the cyclist should cycle as close to the passing traffic as is safe.

Not quite right!
These riders have the advantage of aero helmets, a streamlined bike with disc wheel and the drafting effect of two riders on a tandem to help them reduce wind resistance. Tucking up into a hill descent position would greatly reduce frontal area and dramatically decrease wind resistance.

Tail or head winds

Winds speed up or slow the cyclist by approximately half the wind speed; thus a 2-kilometre-an-hour tail wind increases the cyclist's speed by about one kilometre an hour; a head wind of the same velocity will slow the cyclist by about one kilometre an hour. However, on an out-and-back course your best time will be on a calm day. A constant wind from any direction will result in a slower overall performance.

Only those winds within the trailing 160 degrees of an imaginary circle drawn around the cyclist will aid the cyclist's speed; winds from anywhere in the remaining 200 degrees (including head and side winds) will slow the cyclist.

CHAPTER TEN

CYCLING and your BODY

In this chapter you will see how your muscles work and how they get their energy from fuel stores. You will also learn how to increase the fuel stores before riding, and how to make them last longer. This will help you train intelligently and avoid some of the problems people encounter in riding.

The engine that makes your bike go is skeletal muscle. Like other engines, muscles burn fuel in the presence of oxygen for energy. They also produce waste products and heat which have to be disposed of. Unlike most other engines, the same delivery system that brings the fuel and oxygen **also** carries away the waste and the heat. This is your blood, pumped through the circulation by the heart. And the harder your muscles work, the more your blood is pumped to them, so that fuel supply and waste disposal keep up with the demand and match each other.

Muscle structure and function

A large proportion of our body-weight is made up of skeletal muscle. The skeletal muscles work in co-ordinated groups to move the bones at the joints. In any particular movement a group of muscles (the *agonists*) shorten (contract), while the opposing *antagonists* are reciprocally inhibited so that they relax and lengthen. For example, when you straighten your leg, the large group of muscles in the front of your thigh, the *quadriceps femoris*, or 'quads' are the agonists. As they contract, the hamstrings at the back of your thigh relax, and your leg straightens as the bones pivot around your knee. This pattern of contraction and reciprocal inhibition of opposing groups of muscles is co-ordinated by the nervous system.

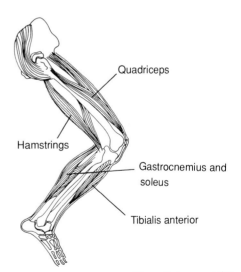

Quadriceps

Hamstrings

Gastrocnemius and soleus

Tibialis anterior

Figure 1: Leg muscles

Structure of muscles

The diagram shows how skeletal muscle is made up of long cylindrical cells, the *muscle fibres*. These are richly supplied by blood vessels and nerves. Muscle fibres are made of many tiny rods called *myofibrils*. These, in turn, are composed of millions of even smaller rods, the *myofilaments*. The myofilaments are arranged so that they overlap partially in such a way that they give the myofibrils

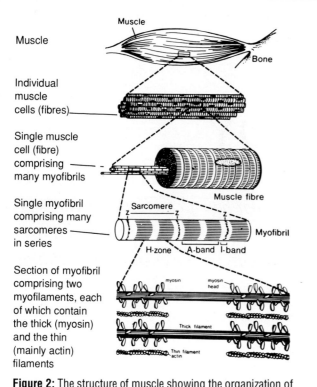

Muscle

Muscle

Bone

Individual
muscle
cells (fibres)

Single muscle
cell (fibre)
comprising
many myofibrils

Muscle fibre

Single myofibril
comprising many
sarcomeres
in series

Sarcomere

Myofibril

H-zone   A-band I-band

Section of myofibril
comprising two
myofilaments, each
of which contain
the thick (myosin)
and the thin
(mainly actin)
filaments

myosin

myosin
head

Thick filament

Thin filament
actin

Figure 2: The structure of muscle showing the organization of
the thick and thin filaments into sarcomeres, myofibrils and,
ultimately, muscle cells.

a striped, or *striated* appearance. The thin
filaments are made of a protein called
actin and two other proteins — troponin
and tropomyosin — while the thick filaments are made of *myosin*. When an im-
pulse reaches the muscle from the brain,
the actin and myosin react together so that
the filaments slide on one another to produce contraction. Muscles use *energy*
when they contract.

The combustion of the body's fuel with
oxygen takes place in the *mitochondria*.
These tiny structures within the muscle
fibres contain enzymes for converting the
energy in the food we eat into chemical
energy that the muscles can use. The mitochondria have been called *the power-
houses of the cell*.

The absorption and storage of fuel

The major energy-containing components
of our food are carbohydrates, fats and
protein. (Other essential dietary components are vitamins and minerals.) After a
meal, these are digested and then absorbed into your body and stored until
they're needed.

Digestion starts when food mixes with the juices in the stomach. From there
it's passed slowly to the intestines where the components are broken down into
small molecules which are readily absorbed into the bloodstream and carried to
their storage sites.

Dietary carbohydrates, such as starch, are broken down into the simple sugars
glucose, maltose, galactose and fructose. These sugars are all converted to
glucose in the liver. Some of the glucose can be used immediately for energy by
the cells (including the brain, which needs an uninterrupted supply); the rest goes
to the skeletal and heart muscles and the liver for storage as *glycogen.*

Fats are transported as bound fatty acids to the adipose (fat) tissues and
muscles for storage as fat. People have widely differing amounts of fat tissue. An
average healthy male has about 15 per cent of his body-weight as fat; highly
trained athletes have between 2 and 7 per cent. An important point is that fat is
an extremely efficient energy store: even if you are lean, the fat you do have can
provide more energy than your carbohydrate stores.

Dietary protein is digested to amino acids, which are used by tissues as
building blocks for growth and to replace protein lost by wear and tear. Amino
acids can also be converted to glucose by the liver when carbohydrate supplies
are inadequate.

To summarize: Some carbohydrate is used as glucose by the cells, the rest is
stored as glycogen in the muscles and liver. Fats are stored in the adipose tissue
and muscle. Dietary protein is usually used only to build tissue, but, when
necessary, it can be converted to carbohydrate for energy.

Energy for muscle contraction

Three metabolic systems inside the muscles are involved in the conversion of food energy to energy for muscle contraction: the phosphagen system, the glycogen-lactate system, and the aerobic system.

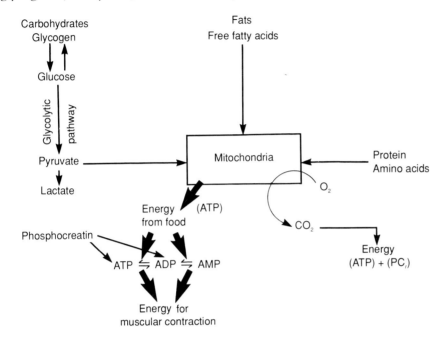

Figure 3: How fuel is converted to energy for muscle contraction.

The phosphagen system

The energy used by the muscles when they contract always comes directly from a chemical called *adenosine triphosphate (ATP)*. ATP stores energy in a readily accessible chemical form in what are called *high energy phosphate bonds*. In releasing this energy, ATP is broken down. The problem is that all the ATP in the muscles will last for only about two seconds of maximal effort. ATP is therefore continuously resynthesized from its breakdown products during exercise, and this needs more energy from another source.

Some energy is immediately available from another chemical with high energy phosphate bonds — *phosphocreatine (PC or creatine phosphate)* — which is in the muscle. Muscles contain more phosphocreatine than ATP. PC can release this energy very quickly to restore the ATP concentrations. The phosphagens (ATP plus phosphocreatine) provide enough energy for about six seconds of maximal exercise — a shortish sprint.

The glycogen-lactate system or glycolytic pathway

The glycolytic pathway does not need oxygen. It can generate ATP faster than the aerobic system, but not as fast as the phosphagen system. It's useful during exercise of high intensity when energy needs exceed the maximal rate at which oxygen can be delivered. It can supply enough energy for about thirty to forty seconds of maximal exercise. The problem is that it releases only about 3 per cent of the total energy contained in glucose and therefore wastes a lot of fuel.

In the early stage of the breakdown of glycogen, glucose is split into *pyruvate*, releasing enough energy for a little ATP production. This step requires no oxygen. The second step, which occurs inside the mitochondria and generates large amounts of ATP as the pyruvate is further metabolized in the presence of oxygen, belongs to the aerobic system (which is discussed in the next section). Some pyruvate does not enter the mitochondria but is converted into lactate. We used to believe that lactate was only produced by muscles when they did not have enough oxygen and that the lactate produced under these conditions was an important cause of fatigue. Many scientists now think that lactate is always being produced **and used** by the muscles as an energy source, and only accumulates in the bloodstream when it is produced faster than it can be consumed. From the blood it enters the liver, where it is converted back to glucose.

The aerobic system

In the aerobic system, glucose (via pyruvate — see the preceding section) and fatty acids derived from food or energy stores are burnt with oxygen in the mitochondria to provide energy for ATP production. Though it generates energy for ATP at only a quarter the rate of the phosphagen system, the aerobic system can go on for a virtually unlimited time — as long as the fuel and oxygen supplies last. It's a very efficient system: virtually all the energy contained in the fuels is released. It is the major energy system used in prolonged exercise.

How the energy systems relate to one another

Figure 3 on page 141 shows how the energy systems relate to one another. They are not mutually independent; all are used during exercise, but the emphasis on each varies depending on the circumstances. Exercise of high intensity needs large amounts of energy rapidly: the phosphagen system can fuel short bursts of maximum power for a few seconds; the glycolytic pathway comes in handy when you need power for longer surges and jumps, but wastes fuel; and prolonged exercise relies mainly on the efficient and economical aerobic system.

Fast twitch and slow twitch muscle fibres

The muscle fibres can be divided into two types, which are randomly spread throughout the muscles; these are called *fast twitch* and *slow twitch* fibres. Fast twitch fibres are larger and paler than slow twitch fibres. They contain more enzymes for the phosphagen and the glycogen-lactate energy systems and are therefore well equipped to deliver bursts of power. Slow twitch fibres are redder because they contain more mitochondria and more *myoglobin*, a protein that speeds up the rate at which oxygen moves through the fibre. They also have more of the enzymes involved in the aerobic energy system, and a richer blood and nerve supply. Slow twitch fibres are therefore ideally suited for endurance.

Some people are born with more fast twitch than slow twitch fibres, and vice versa. There's nothing much that can be done about this: training may alter the proportions by 10 to 15 per cent at the most. This is why some people are born sprinters, others long distance runners.

Three important properties of muscles

The *strength* of the muscle determines *how much force it can generate when it contracts*. It's measured simply in terms of how much weight the muscle can lift, and this depends mainly on the muscle's size and its contractile quality. The contractile quality of muscles from different people differ widely; thus some people with small muscles can be very strong.

Power and strength are different in that strength reflects how much a muscle can lift and power is the *amount of work the muscle can do in a given time* (that is, it is the rate of doing work.) It is measured in kilogram metres per minute (kg.m/min). One kg.m/min is the equivalent of lifting one kilogram to the height of one metre in one minute. The power of a muscle therefore depends not only on how strong it is, but on how fast and how frequently it can contract in a minute. The muscles can sustain their maximal power for only about ten to fifteen seconds.

Finally, we come to *endurance*. Endurance refers to the *length of time a muscle can sustain a given amount of work.* It depends a lot on how much energy is stored in the muscle in the form of glycogen.

Figure 4: Fast and slow twitch fibres, magnified 400 times. The dark-stained fibres are fast twitch and the lighter ones are slow twitch.

The lungs and circulation

We have seen that our muscles cannot exercise for more than a few minutes unless they use the aerobic energy system. For this they need a constant supply of oxygen (O_2) and fuel — the harder they work the more they need (and the more carbon dioxide (CO_2) and heat they produce).

The O_2 comes from the air we breathe. In the lungs the air enters tiny round airsacks called *alveoli*. These have very thin walls which allow the air to come into close contact with the blood over a large surface area. The red blood corpuscles (RBCs) contain a special protein, *haemoglobin*, which is specially shaped to take up O_2 from the lungs and release it to the tissues. The RBCs which

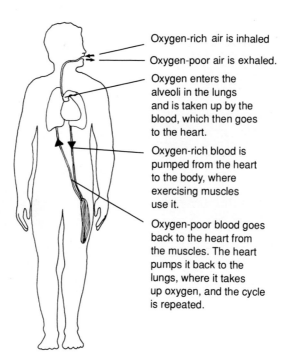

Oxygen-rich air is inhaled

Oxygen-poor air is exhaled.

Oxygen enters the alveoli in the lungs and is taken up by the blood, which then goes to the heart.

Oxygen-rich blood is pumped from the heart to the body, where exercising muscles use it.

Oxygen-poor blood goes back to the heart from the muscles. The heart pumps it back to the lungs, where it takes up oxygen, and the cycle is repeated.

Figure 5: The pathways by which air is transported from the air to the active muscles.

enter the lungs have released their O_2 and picked up CO_2 in the muscles. As they pass through the lungs, they release the CO_2 and fill up with O_2. The CO_2 is breathed out, the O_2 is taken to the muscles by the RBCs. The heart pumps the blood to the lungs, the muscles and all the tissues of the body.

How the body adapts to exercise

To meet the demand for more fuel and oxygen during exercise you breathe harder and your heart pumps more blood to the muscles that are doing the work. The following sections explain how these and other functions of the body adapt to exercise of increasing intensity.

Oxygen consumption (VO₂)

Oxygen consumption increases linearly as workload increases. As muscles work harder, more fibres are recruited, increasing the energy requirements. This, in turn, increases the rate of oxygen consumption progressively up to a point just before the maximum workload, beyond which there is no further increase in VO_2, even though exercise intensity may increase a little further. At this point the body has reached its maximal O_2 consumption — the VO_2 max. This is shown at point A in Figure 6. VO_2 max is usually expressed relative to body mass as millilitres of O_2 per kilogram body-weight per minute (ml O_2/kg/min).

In healthy, non-athletic males VO_2 max values of between 45 and 55 ml O_2/kg/min have been found. In top marathon runners the VO_2 max is usually around 70 to 85 ml O_2/kg/min. Similar values have been found in the few top cyclists that have been tested.

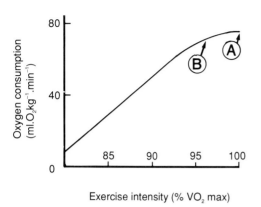

Figure 6

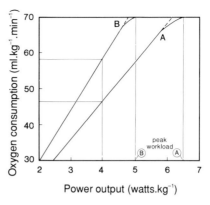

After Nadel (1988)

Figure 7

VO₂ max is a useful indicator of fitness, but it's not the only factor that determines cycling performance: some people reach their maximal exercise level before a virtual plateau in VO₂ is reached (point B in the diagram). Other important factors are efficiency, motivation, technique and tactics. For example, some riders can ride faster than others at a given VO₂. Such riders are said to be more 'efficient' — they burn less energy than others do at the same speed. In other words, they are more economical in their energy expenditure.

Efficiency relates partly to aerodynamics. At speeds of 32 kilometres an hour or more, at least 90 per cent of your effort goes into overcoming wind resistance. You can reduce wind resistance by paying attention to aerodynamics (see the section 'Reducing the oxygen cost of cycling' later in this chapter). Another factor that affects efficiency is wasting energy on activities that don't propel you forward: fighting with your bike, holding the handlebars too tightly or doing 'pushups' on them as you ride, jerky pedalling, and so on. Practise riding smoothly and develop your cadence to spin rather than push high gears. Learn not to waste energy.

Figure 7 shows the VO₂ at different cycling workloads in two cyclists who have similar values for VO₂ max. Rider A is more efficient: at any workload he consumes less O₂ than rider B. At the indicated workload (4 W/kg), rider B uses 60 ml O₂/kg while A uses 20 per cent less. Equally important, A achieves a higher maximum workload at his VO₂ max. A high maximum workload has been found to be an excellent predictor of athletic performance.

Factors limiting VO₂ max

Much scientific research has been done to discover why there is a limit to the rate at which we can consume O₂. Scientists have studied every step along the path of O₂ from the air to the mitochondria. They have studied breathing, the transfer of O₂ from the alveoli to the blood, its transport by the blood to the muscles, and the uptake by mitochondrial enzymes from haemoglobin. The evidence indicates that the limiting step is the rate at which the blood can carry the O₂ from the lungs to the muscles. This depends on two factors: the concentration of haemoglobin in the blood, and how fast your heart can pump blood (the *cardiac output* — see the section on heart rate and stroke volume during exercise). Others argue that it is muscle contractility rather than the ability to use oxygen that limits an athlete's performance potential.

Other factors that influence VO₂ max

Age: VO_2 max falls by about 9 per cent per decade after the age of twenty-five years in healthy, inactive people. People who keep up vigorous exercise throughout their lives may reduce this age-related decline to about 5 per cent per decade.

Gender: Females have lower values for VO_2 max than males. This is due partly to their relatively higher content of body fat (which increases mass without increasing VO_2), their smaller muscle mass, and their less 'powerful' muscles.

Training: A moderate training programme may result in an increase in VO_2 max of about 5 to 15 per cent. This range is very wide and largely genetically determined.

Altitude: With increasing altitude, the barometric pressure and the O_2 pressure in the air decreases. This causes a fall in VO_2 max of about 10 per cent for every 1 000 metres above 1 200 metres.

Heart rate and stroke volume during exercise

During exercise the amount of O_2 needed by the active muscles may increase almost instantaneously by as much as twenty times, while the requirements of the inactive muscles remain the same. Figure 10 shows how the heart increases the amount of blood it pumps and how this blood is distributed more to the muscles that are most active.

The heart rate (number of beats per minute) increases (Figure 8), and so does the volume of blood the heart pumps out with each beat (the stroke volume) (Figure 9). These two changes cause an increase in the volume of blood that the heart pumps each minute, the *cardiac output*. As described, this increase in blood flow is distributed towards those muscles that have increased O_2 requirements and the heart (Figure 10), and away from the more inactive tissues, including the kidneys, the liver and the intestines (Figure 11). The flow of blood to these organs is still enough to maintain their normal function. The signal for this redistribution of blood flow is provided by metabolic breakdown products released during muscle contraction. As a result, more O_2 and fuel are delivered to those muscles that are working the hardest, and more breakdown products and heat are carried away.

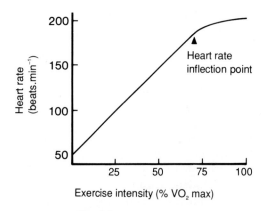

Figure 8

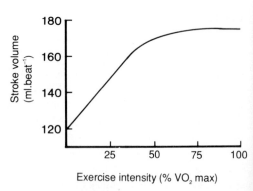

Figure 9

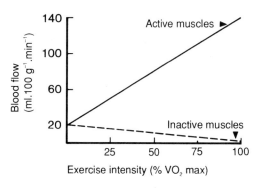

Figure 10

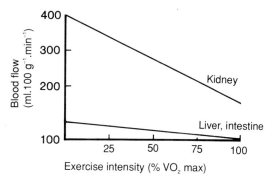

Figure 11

Notice that VO$_2$ and heart rate increase similarly as exercise gets harder. We can measure VO$_2$ in an exercise laboratory or simply count the heart rate and use either to express how hard any given level of exercise is (as a percentage of VO$_2$ max or of maximal heart rate).

Fuel consumption during exercise

During exercise the muscles burn fuel derived from all the storage sites described: glycogen is stored in the muscles themselves or in the liver, and provides carbohydrate (as glucose), and fat within the muscles or from adipose tissue provides free fatty acids. These are burnt in various proportions, depending on the circumstances. Let's take a closer look at the factors that influence the type of fuel we burn.

Of course, the *size of the carbohydrate stores* influences the type of fuel you burn: the larger the stores at the start of exercise, the longer they will last and you will have more carbohydrate relative to fat to burn for longer (see the section on filling glycogen stores in this chapter).

The *intensity and duration of exercise* are important factors. The *harder* you ride, and especially at over 75 per cent of VO$_2$ max, the more carbohydrate your muscles burn from their own glycogen stores. At lower intensity, relatively more carbohydrate comes from glycogen stores in the liver. The *longer* you ride, the more energy comes from fat as liver glycogen becomes depleted. Glycogen is broken down fastest at the beginning of exercise.

An important effect of *training* is that more energy comes from fat instead of carbohydrate early on in exercise. Carbohydrate stores therefore last longer in fit people, allowing them to carry on for longer.

The timing and composition of the *last meal before you exercise* also influences fuel utilization. A fatty meal is followed by a rise in the concentration of free fatty acids in the blood and these are available as fuel. A high carbohydrate meal (especially if it contains a lot of simple sugar like glucose, or even cane sugar, rather than complex carbohydrates like starch) results in high levels of insulin, an important hormone, in the blood. The insulin level may be elevated for up to ninety minutes after the meal. Insulin lowers the blood glucose level. It also inhibits the release of glucose from glycogen and of free fatty acids from fat stores. It is the 'anti-exercise hormone'. If you exercise when the insulin level is high, your muscles use their own glycogen and what glucose there is in the blood, and, since the mechanisms to replace blood glucose are inhibited, there's a serious

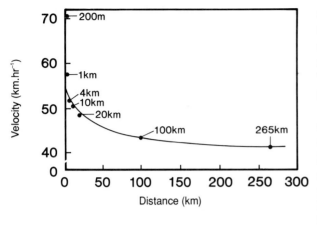

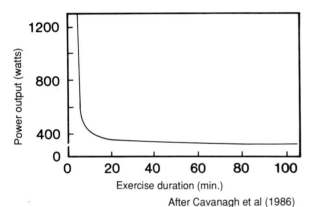

After Cavanagh et al (1986)

Figure 12: Top: The decline in the maximum speed that top cyclists can sustain as distances increase.

Figure 13: Bottom: The fall in the power output of top cyclists, depending on the duration of the exercise.

risk that the blood sugar will fall too low (hypoglycaemia). This will make you weak and light-headed, and it could make you pass out (see the section on making glycogen stores last longer in this chapter). You should, therefore, have your last meal at least ninety minutes before a major ride.

Caffeine causes an increase in the free fatty acid concentrations in the blood. This potentially beneficial effect lasts for three or four hours. It's inhibited by the presence of glucose (for instance, if you put sugar in your coffee). So coffee doesn't help much if you have followed an effective programme of carboloading before you ride. (Rather go in for the carboloading — it works, and the value of caffeine has never been proved.)

Glucose or other carbohydrates taken in during the ride do not reduce the rate at which you burn *muscle* glycogen, but slow the rate at which you use up *liver* glycogen. Eating or drinking carbohydrates on a long ride therefore makes your liver glycogen stores last longer and improves performance. But don't leave it too late: once you are exhausted, swallowing carbohydrate will certainly help; however, the intestines don't seem capable of absorbing carbohydrate as fast as the depleted muscles need it.

Carbohydrate stores and endurance

There is a close link between the amount of glycogen you have stored in your muscles and how long you can keep up exercise. For example, in one study runners who loaded up with carbohydrate for three days could run for 12 per cent longer at 70 per cent VO_2 max than runners who ate only their normal diets.

Filling glycogen stores: training and carbo-loading

We can use our knowledge to increase our glycogen stores before we ride and reduce their consumption during the ride. Let's look at the factors that influence stores: fitness and diet.

Training increases the amount of glycogen your muscles can store — think of it as increasing the size of your glycogen fuel tank. A high carbohydrate diet fills the tank. Most cyclists automatically tend to eat diets richer in carbohydrate when they train. All sorts of tricky dietary manoeuvres have been tried to get extra stores crammed in: periods of starvation, high protein food followed by high carbohydrate food, and so on. None of them work any better than simply eating high carbohydrate foods for three days before the big event, such as doughnuts, bread, sweets, and cakes. Potatoes and pasta which contain complex carbohydrates in the form of starch are particularly good.

On long hard stage-races, like the Tour de France, the riders' muscles become totally carbohydrate-depleted during each day's stage and fuel stores must be completely replaced by the next day if the cyclists are to perform well. Studies suggest that the best way of doing this is to ingest high carbohydrate drinks and snacks on the ride as well as during the remainder of the day.

Making glycogen stores last longer

We can also try to save glycogen during the ride. We have seen that muscle glycogen falls fastest early in the ride, and that it falls faster if you ride hard. Starting gently is, at least theoretically, a good way to protect glycogen stores. You can do this by having an easy warm-up ride before the race. Another possibility is to have a fatty meal three or more hours before the event to provide your muscles with free fatty acids, but this theory hasn't been scientifically proved.

You also need to protect your liver glycogen stores during a long ride. They are essential for maintaining adequate blood glucose levels. The brain, in particular, needs an uninterrupted supply of glucose from the blood to work properly; if blood glucose falls, you become shaky, weak, and light-headed. You may even collapse. Cyclists call this the 'bonk', and it happens most frequently on long rides of three hours or more. Untrained cyclists, especially those who do not eat high carbohydrate diets, and children may get it on shorter rides. To prevent it, carbo-load before the ride and ingest carbohydrate drinks or snacks during the ride.

Glycogen is not the complete answer!

All this may make one think that hypoglycaemia or muscle glycogen depletion are the only causes of fatigue during prolonged exercise. Unfortunately, this is not so, for while these factors may cause premature fatigue, riders will eventually become fatigued even if they don't become hypoglycaemic or glycogen-depleted. It appears that the contractile ability of the muscle falls progressively during prolonged exercise, possibly because of thermal damage to heat sensitive processes in the muscle. Fatigue of the nervous system may also play a part.

Replacing lost fluid

The best drinks contain about 6 to 10 per cent of a glucose polymer (a starch-like substance; examples are Caloreen, FRN and corn syrup), but you can use glucose or ordinary table sugar. There should also be a little salt in the solution (half a teaspoon of salt per litre) to replace what you lose in sweat. You should drink about 400 to 700 millilitres per hour, depending on the weather, your size and how hard you are riding. Don't wait until you are thirsty before you drink. If you do, you will never catch up with your fluid requirements.

Recently it has been found that adding sodium chloride (salt) to the solution that you drink is beneficial because it prevents the development of dehydration more effectively than does drinking water alone. But do not add more than half a teaspoon of salt to a litre of water.

It seems that during prolonged exercise, when the body loses both water and sodium chloride in sweat, it is forced to deplete its fluid stores in proportion to the developing sodium chloride deficit. If this did not occur and if the body fluid stores were allowed to remain normal in the face of this sodium chloride deficit, then dilution would cause the blood sodium chloride levels to fall with potentially catastrophic effects in runners and cyclists competing in races lasting more than four hours.

It follows that the only way in which dehydration can be prevented during exercise is to replace both the water **and** sodium chloride losses in sweat, *as they develop*. By contrast, there is no risk of developing a deficiency of either magnesium or potassium during exercise; thus neither need to be replaced during exercise.

The effects of endurance training on the heart, skeletal muscle and metabolism

How does exercise make us fit? What happens to our hearts and muscles when we train? We shall look at these two questions in turn.

The main effect of training on the heart is to increase the size of the chambers and the thickness of the heart muscle. The heart muscle is thicker in cyclists than in runners, though the chambers are the same size in both. This may be due to the work done by the arms, especially when cycling up hills when the arm muscles contract isometrically (i.e. without shortening) which increases the pressure against which the heart has to pump.

When the heart's chambers are larger it pumps more blood with each stroke (the stroke volume increases), and the heart rate becomes slower and the blood pressure lower at all levels of exercise, including resting. Interestingly, these effects are seen only when the trained muscles are used and not during experiments that stress untrained muscles, indicating that they are due more to the effects of training on the skeletal muscles than on the heart.

In fact, science tells us that what happens in the skeletal muscles during training is more important than the changes that occur in the heart. In previous sections some physiological and biochemical indicators of what happens in the muscles during training were mentioned. They are:

- An increase in VO_2 max indicating either that the heart has increased its ability to deliver blood to the muscles, or that the muscles have increased their ability to extract O_2 from the blood, or both.
    - An increased capacity to store glycogen in both muscle and liver.
    - A shift towards burning fat rather than glycogen as fuel at all workloads.
    - Lactate starts to accumulate in the blood at a higher percentage of VO_2 max.

Three adaptations in the skeletal muscles underlie these changes.

More blood capillaries

The number of blood capillaries that surround muscle fibres increases with training. This helps the delivery of fuel and oxygen to the mitochondria; it's particularly important for the uptake of free fatty acids since this seems to be the rate-limiting step in fat oxidation at exercise intensities greater than 50 per cent of VO_2 max.

Figure 14: The overall effect of training is to increase the ability to sustain a higher exercise intensity for a longer duration.

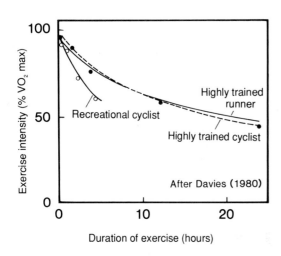

After Davies (1980)

Changes in metabolic pathways

With sprint training, the major adaptations are in the glycolytic pathway: there's an increase in the activity of the glycolytic enzymes and in the ability of the muscles to exercise in the face of acid accumulation.

With endurance training, the main change is an increase in the capacity of the aerobic pathways in the mitochondria. Structurally, there's an increase in the number and size of the mitochondria; the larger mass of mitochondria is able to produce more energy from fat, thereby sparing carbohydrate. They are also able to oxidize more lactate; therefore the accumulation of lactate in the blood occurs at a higher percentage of VO_2 max.

Adaptations in muscle contractility

Muscle power and contractility increase with all types of training. As you would expect, these changes have important implications for exercise performance.

The time course of adaptations to training and detraining

VO_2 max adapts very rapidly to training: most of the increase occurs within the first three weeks and then there is a further gradual increase which may continue for up to twenty-four weeks. The same thing happens if you stop training, with a rapid 7 per cent fall in the first two to three weeks followed by a more gradual fall of about 16 per cent over the next eight weeks. Actual performance can be maintained during de-training even if the exercise duration is reduced by up to two-thirds, provided the intensity stays the same.

Practical implications

We have seen that the effects of training occur only in those muscle fibres that are active during the training programme. It follows that when you train for a particular event you should concentrate on the correct muscle groups, and more specifically on the appropriate metabolic pathways in those fibres.

In this way you can tailor your training to match your goals. Sprint cyclists should aim to increase muscle contractility and sharpen the phosphagen system and the glycolytic pathway. Distance riders should aim to increase muscle mitochondrial mass so that the capacity of the aerobic system increases.

It is not necessary to maintain a high intensity of training all the year round; a reduction in mileage of up to two-thirds may maintain a reasonable level of fitness during the off season, provided the intensity remains high.

Lastly, the ability to adapt to training is genetically determined: some people respond very well, others don't, no matter how hard they try. Different people respond better to the various types of training. For this reason training programmes should be individualized, and some unfortunate people have to accept that they will never win the yellow jersey or beat their friends in a cycle race.

The regulation of body temperature during exercise

One of the main problems runners face in warm countries like South Africa is to be able to exercise safely in the heat. For cyclists hot weather is less of a problem because of the cooling effect of the higher wind speed, but in cold weather they have difficulties in keeping warm.

Human beings are *homeotherms*, which means that to survive we have to keep our body temperature constant within a narrow range (35 to 42 degrees Celsius) despite wide variations in environmental temperature and physical activity. During exercise as much as 70 per cent of the total chemical energy used by muscle contraction is converted to heat rather than movement. If your body temperature is to stay the same, it must lose as much heat as it produces.

Mechanisms of heat loss during exercise

During exercise the blood flow to the muscles increases, as I've described. The blood absorbs the heat generated by the exercise and distributes it throughout the body, but especially to the skin. In this way (and to a lesser extent by direct transfer from muscles near the skin) heat is conducted to the surface of the body. From the surface the heat is lost in three ways: by convection to circulating air currents; by radiation to any nearby objects that have a lower temperature than the skin; and by the evaporation of sweat. To produce cooling, sweat has to evaporate; sweat that doesn't evaporate results in no heat loss.

The efficiency of these factors depends on a variety of factors.

Intensity of exercise

The harder you exercise, the more heat you produce. The greatest risk of overheating occurs in events of high intensity and relatively short duration.

Environmental factors

Air temperature and wind speed influence the amount of heat lost from the skin. At high wind speeds large volumes of unwarmed air blow over the skin; this results in very efficient cooling by both convection and evaporation. Heat lost by convection and evaporation increases exponentially with wind speed. Consequently, the faster you ride relative to the wind, the easier it is to lose heat, even though you may be generating more by riding harder. This contrasts with running where effective wind speeds are much lower and the faster the athlete runs, the more difficulty there is in maintaining heat balance. The high wind speeds in cycling are so effective at cooling one that in cold weather there's a serious risk of overcooling. Of course, it's possible for cyclists to overheat when they are riding with the wind from behind, especially uphill.

At rest the skin temperature is about 33 degrees Celsius. If the air temperature is higher than this, heat cannot be lost by convection — in fact, heat is then transferred from the air to the skin. The only avenue for heat loss under such circumstances is the evaporation of sweat. But, under conditions of high humidity your ability to lose heat by evaporation decreases. And if you allow yourself to become dehydrated, you can't sweat as much and are in danger of overheating.

Finally, your body can actually gain heat by radiation from any objects in the environment that are warmer than you are. The obvious and most important example is the sun, but on hot sunny days a lot of heat also reaches you from the road and surrounding rocks.

Clothing and the wind-chill factor

Because of the risk of losing too much heat in cold weather, we need to understand how wind affects the 'coldness' of the air (the effective air temperature), and how to dress.

Clothing traps a thin layer of air next to the skin. Since air is a poor conductor of heat, this adds to the insulating properties of the clothing itself. The insulating qualities of different clothing can be measured and expressed in CLO units. One CLO unit is equivalent to the amount of insulation that provides comfort at a temperature of 21 degrees Celsius when wind speed and humidity are low. To survive in Arctic conditions Eskimos wear clothes that provide 10 to 12 CLO units.

The effective air temperature to which the body is exposed doesn't depend simply on how cold the weather is. Another important factor is the wind-chill factor. As we have seen, wind greatly increases the amount of cooling one gets at any given ambient air temperature. Figures 15 and 16 show how wind speed affects effective air temperature and how much insulation (expressed in CLO units) we need at different effective air temperatures. Say, for example, you go for a ride when the ambient air temperature is 5 degrees Celsius. You ride at 32 kilometres an hour (more or less equivalent to running at between 10 and 16 kilometres an hour). If you look at Figure 15, you will see that under these circumstances the effective air temperature would be –5 degrees Celsius. From Figure 16 you will see that, at this temperature, you would need about 2 to 3 CLO units of insulation to keep warm *while pedalling this hard*. But then you come to a downhill and you freewheel at 56 kilometres an hour. At this speed the effective air temperature drops to about –10 degrees Celsius, and because you are now resting and producing less heat, you will need 6 to 7 CLO units to avoid overcooling. At lower ambient air temperatures the effect is greater.

You may, therefore, encounter widely differing effective air temperatures on the same ride, and it can be very difficult to decide just how warmly to dress in cold weather. To provide 2 to 3 CLO units you would need to wear two cotton T-shirts, a long-sleeved cycling top, cycling shorts and longjohns or legwarmers, a hood, mittens, a ski mask, shoes and socks. You would still get cold on downhills. Experienced riders take with them a sheet of newspaper or plastic, which they put inside the front of their jersey to reduce wind cooling on downhills. This is also an excellent idea on cold mornings when you set out early and expect the day to warm up later — you then simply remove the paper or plastic and return it to your pocket for later use. A lightweight rainjacket that can be worn zipped or unzipped is also useful.

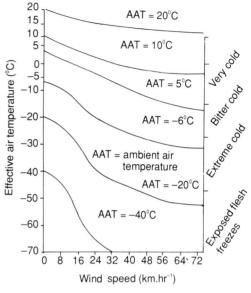

Figure 15: The effects of different wind speeds on the effective air temperatures at different ambient air temperatures.

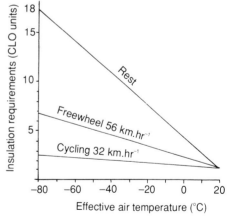

Figure 16: Insulation requirements during exercise at different effective air temperatures.

153

Heat acclimatization

When athletes who have trained exclusively in cool weather are suddenly confronted with hot, humid conditions, they suffer an immediate and dramatic impairment in performance. After training in the heat for seven to ten days, performance improves and returns to normal. This is known as heat acclimatization. Heat acclimatization is important; not only does it protect you from heat injury, it also gives you the edge over equally fit, but unacclimatized, rivals.

The important changes that occur with heat acclimatization are that heart rate, sweat salt concentration and body temperature during exercise decrease, while the volume of sweat increases. In addition, the rate at which lactate accumulates in the muscles and blood decreases.

The best way to acclimatize to heat is to do two to four hours of training in the heat daily for ten days. Heat acclimatization is retained for about two weeks and then lost slowly, unless you stay fit and train in the heat at least fortnightly.

Reducing the oxygen cost of cycling

The importance of aerodynamics, mass, friction and cadence

The main forces that retard a cyclist's progress include wind resistance, the combined mass of the rider and bicycle, rolling resistance and friction in the moving parts of the bicycle. Overcoming these forces requires effort. But there is a lot more to overcoming them than simply being fit, strong and well-fuelled; when you can, it is equally important to use techniques, tactics and equipment that *save you from having to expend effort.*

The effect that retarding forces have on a cyclist are described here; other sections of this book that deal with riding technique and choice of equipment give practical guidelines to overcoming them.

Aerodynamics and oxygen consumption

An important difference between running and cycling lies in the speeds at which the sports are practised. The highest speeds that runners achieve are around 45 kilometres per hour during 100-metre and 200-metre sprints. In contrast, competitive cyclists seldom travel at less than 40 kilometres per hour for any length of time, and they often reach speeds of 80 kilometres per hour and more. At these very high speeds, more than 90 per cent of the energy expended is used to overcome the resistance of the air through which the cyclist moves. This resistance is often referred to as aerodynamic drag.

Probably the most remarkable advances that have been made in the scientific studies of cycling techniques and bicycle design in the past decade have been to do with the effects of wind resistance on performance, and the ways in which it can be reduced. Chapter 9 describes many of these advances in more detail; it covers the history of the study into bicycles and aerodynamics, from the early perceptions of nineteenth-century cyclists to recent International Human Powered Speed Championships which have been held for experimental machines. These have resulted in a progressive increase in the maximum speeds

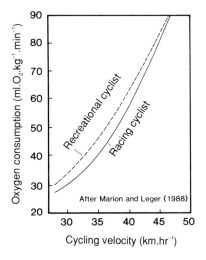

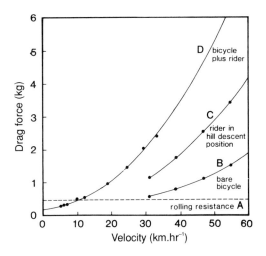

Figure 17: As this graph shows, oxygen consumption increases exponentially with increasing cycling velocity, and is marginally lower in highly trained cyclists than in casual riders. The drag forces determining the oxygen cost at different speeds are shown in the figure on the right.

Figure 18: At high speeds, 90 per cent of oxygen consumed goes into overcoming drag forces. This figure shows that the most important factor determining the drag forces (and therefore the oxygen cost) during cycling is the cyclist; it also shows how the drag forces (and therefore the oxygen cost) increase exponentially with increasing speed.

that modified bicycles can achieve, and have refined our understanding of how the ordinary bicycle and its rider can reach higher speeds without requiring an increase in oxygen consumption.

How wind resistance affects us

The faster you move, the greater the air resistance. This has a critical bearing on the increase in energy that is needed to overcome air resistance. The energy output required to overcome drag (air resistance) is equal to the product of the drag force and velocity; it increases as the cube of the cycling velocity. This means that in order to double your speed on a bike, you have to increase your power output eightfold.

In practice, cyclists partly counter this by using techniques such as drafting to reduce the enormous demands on their effort.

How much energy can you save?

A recent study by James Hagberg and his colleagues in Florida has quantified the savings in energy consumption that cyclists can make by using techniques or equipment that reduce the effects of aerodynamic drag. Their results are set out in the table on the following page.

They measured the rates of oxygen consumption of individual cyclists riding at speeds of 32, 37 and 40 kilometres per hour when the cyclists were either riding alone, drafting one or more cyclists in a straight line, drafting an eight-man pack, and riding a 'funny' bike with a 24-inch front wheel, a down-sloping top tube, cowbell handlebars and a rear disc wheel. The results speak for themselves. They also made the following observations:

- The oxygen cost of cycling increased by about 2,4 millilitres per kilogram per minute for each one-kilometre-per-hour speed increase, between speeds of 32 and 40 kilometres per hour.

Energy savings from drafting			
	Velocity (km/h)	Mean oxygen cost (ml O₂/kg/min)	Per cent saving
When riding alone	32	37,4	
	37	51,2	
	40	61,9	
When drafting 1 rider	32	30,3	19%
	37	36,5	29%
	40	46,1	26%
When drafting 2 or more riders in a line	40	41,8	32%
When drafting an 8-man pack	40	31,2	50%
When riding a 'funny' bike	40	48,7	21%
When drafting a truck	40	19,7	68%
Data from Hagberg et al. (1989)			

- The oxygen cost increased by 0,6 millilitres O_2/kg/min for each kilometre-per-hour increase in head wind speed, and decreased by the same amount for following winds.
- When cycling on the flat, the oxygen cost expressed relative to the cyclist's mass decreases by about 0,3 millilitres per kilogram per minute for each kilogram of increase in the cyclist's mass. The reasons for this are explained later in this chapter.

The influence of altitude

Altitude affects human performance in two contrasting ways. First, air resistance falls with increasing altitude. So performance in activities in which overcoming air resistance is important may improve when you are high above sea level. This is certainly true in sprint cycling.

Secondly, your VO_2 max falls when you are at high altitudes, so performance in activities in which oxidative energy production is important may be impaired.

On balance, then, what effect does altitude have? In runners, performance in events lasting up to about 100 seconds is improved by being at a higher altitude; after that, it falls. By contrast, a one-hour cycling record was set in high-up Mexico City (altitude 2 260 metres).

Chester Kyle has calculated that if one were considering only the benefits of reduced air resistance at that altitude, you could expect the cyclist to ride about 8 per cent faster than he would at sea level. In practice however, the increase in speed is about 3 to 5 per cent. This is because the benefits of reduced air resistance are partly countered by the body's reduced ability to utilize oxygen at high altitudes.

The influence of mass

Mass affects cycling performance in some unexpected ways. It will surprise many cyclists — especially those who pay dearly to hone milligrams off the weight of their equipment — to know that increased mass slows you down far less than aerodynamic drag does. Nevertheless, mass is significant; it is worth knowing just how much it does affect performance, and what you can and can't do about it.

Increased mass has four important effects:

- It increases rolling resistance.

- It slows hill-climbing speed.

- It retards acceleration.

- It increases downhill speeds.

Rolling resistance and mass

Objects have an inherent resistance to rolling. The degree of resistance depends largely on the area of contact between the tyre and the road. A wide, low-pressure tyre carrying a heavy load will deform where it makes contact with the road and will therefore have high rolling resistance. A narrow, high-pressure tyre carrying a lighter load will have far less resistance.

Rolling resistance increases in direct proportion to the weight that a wheel supports, and is is equal to about 0,3 to 0,5 per cent of the load on the wheel. It can be reduced by the following: smoother, harder road surfaces; larger diameter wheels; smoother and thinner tyre treads; specialized materials for the tyre wall and tread; and cycling in the straightest possible line.

Unlike wind resistance, rolling resistance is not influenced by cycling speed. On a road racing bike, the drag caused by wind resistance exceeds that of rolling resistance once you reach speeds of over about 13 kilometres per hour.

How much does mass slow cyclists down?

As mentioned earlier, increased mass retards cycling performance far less than aerodynamic drag does. Thus, for example, using aerobars (which increase mass but reduce drag) may do more for a cyclist's performance than using an ultra-light bike will. At the time of writing, the record time for the Argus Cycle Tour is held by Lloyd Wright, who rode a streamlined recumbent which weighed a lot more than the conventional lightweight racing bikes that he was competing with.

Chester Kyle has calculated that adding 3 kilograms (4 per cent) to an 80-kilogram bike/rider combination will have no effect on cycling performance in a race over a flattish road, over a distance of between about 3 and 40 kilometres. However, the situation changes when you have hills to contend with: if you rode up a 1,6-kilometre 10-degree slope at a typical racer's pace, and then rode down it again, that extra 3 kilograms could slow you down by about 22 seconds (nearly 3 per cent).

Big riders and small riders: which are faster?

Before going into the question of whether big cyclists perform better than small cyclists or vice versa, one fairly obvious point must be made clear: when heavy cyclists are compared with light cyclists, it's assumed that each has equal proportions of muscle and fat. If the heavy cyclist's extra weight is made up of fat, it will, of course, simply increase rolling resistance and not be a sound basis for any meaningful comparison.

Assessing the effect that increases in the weight of the *bicycle* has on perform-ance is a comparatively simple matter. But when you start looking at the differences in mass between different *riders*, things become more complex. There is a lot more to the issue than mass alone; you can't predict the effects of large differences in body mass between two cyclists without considering other factors that are inevitably linked to it.

A heavy cyclist will almost certainly have a correspondingly large body surface area. And this, of course, will determine his or her frontal area. Frontal area determines wind resistance, and is the single most important factor deter-mining the retarding forces that a cyclist has to overcome.

Studies into this have produced some unexpected findings:

- Although heavier people have more mass and volume than lighter people do, their body surface area doesn't increase linearly as a function of either mass or volume. Body area increases as a function of body-weight to the power of 0,85. Therefore, the surface-area-to-volume ratio of heavier people is less than that of lighter people.

There are two other points to consider here:

- Firstly, smaller people have a disproportionately higher ability to produce energy aerobically than larger people do. This is because they have a disproportionately larger surface area of lungs and blood vessels. So they have potentially greater cardio-respiratory reserves with which to service their smaller muscles. It has been found that in animals and in humans, VO_2 max scales as body mass to the power of 0,75 to 0,81. (This means that as body mass decreases there is a disproportionate increase in VO_2 max.)

- Secondly, when heavy cyclists get into a tucked racing position, they are better able to reduce their frontal areas than light cyclists are; so despite having a larger *surface* area, the *effective frontal* area may be no greater than that of the smaller cyclist. In fact, frontal area is scaled as body-weight to the power of only 0,55. Relative to frontal area, the oxygen cost of cycling at any speed is often the same for large and small cyclists.

Assuming that all other variables are equal, it follows that when they are cycling on a flat road, heavier cyclists clearly have an advantage. This is because they have greater muscle mass with which to overcome the same aerodynamic drag that smaller cyclists are faced with.

In one study, it was shown that relative to their body-weights, large (weighing over 80 kilograms) cyclists used about 22 per cent less oxygen when cycling at speeds of between 16 and 32 kilometres per hour than did light cyclists (whose average weight was under 60 kilograms). In absolute terms, the heavier cyclists did use about 10 per cent more energy when cycling at those speeds than the lighter cyclists did, but the difference was far less than the 25 per cent difference in mass. This theory is borne out by the fact that most top sprint cyclists are big.

To summarize these two points, the smaller cyclist has the advantage of a VO_2 max that, relative to the size of his muscles, is greater. The larger cyclist has roughly the same effective frontal area and the same aerodynamic drag as the smaller cyclist, but he has bigger muscles with which to overcome it.

On the road, what effect does this have? It depends much on the gradient.

The effects of mass on hill-climbing

It has already been shown that large cyclists have an advantage on the flat. But the tables are turned when it comes to climbing. As speed falls, the aerodynamic advantage enjoyed by heavy cyclists lessens. The energy needed to move a mass up a gradient increases in proportion only to the mass being moved — in other words, the mass of the bike and its rider. So the oxygen cost of cycling up a hill is, relative to body-weight, the same for heavy and light cyclists.

For reasons already gone into, the VO_2 max of the smaller cyclist is likely to be greater than that of the large cyclist. And that is what gives him the edge in the mountains.

Descents

Once cyclists reach the summit of a hill, their fortunes are reversed again. On downward gradients, the heavier riders have even more of an edge over their light rivals than they did on the flat; the high speeds reached on descents make their aerodynamic advantage all the greater.

Mass and bicycle size

A heavy cyclist has yet another advantage. The increased weight of the bicycle he or she needs is proportionally small; even if he is 40 per cent heavier than another rider, the larger bike he rides will only be about 10 per cent heavier.

The total picture

How does all this balance out? Overall, is it better to be big or small? Much depends, of course, on the route (not to mention a host of other variables, such as determination and skill, which have had to be left out of this argument). When the climbs and descents on a ride are equal, the smaller cyclist has an overall advantage; though the ascending and descending *distances* may be equal, the *times* involved in going uphill and downhill will be quite different, with the ascents taking far longer.

When two cyclists weigh the same as each other, but one is taller, who has the advantage? Theoretically, the shorter one does because his surface area — and therefore his frontal area — is less.

Friction and oxygen consumption

A roughly-moving chain uses up more energy than a smoothly-moving chain does. When you realise that it is you, the rider, who is generating that energy, it becomes clear how important it is to have components working smoothly. Friction in the contact surfaces of a bike's components account for a loss of about 5 to 15 per cent of the power you produce. Choosing high quality components, ensuring that they are properly adjusted, and that they are lubricated with light oil rather than heavy grease all helps to reduce energy-waste.

Cadence and oxygen consumption

Laboratory tests have shown that the most efficient cycling cadence for most riders lies somewhere between 70 and 100 revolutions per minute (rpm). Above about 100 rpm, there is a measurable loss of efficiency.

Researchers think that trained cyclists naturally opt for the cadence at which they are most efficient, in the same way that runners and swimmers do. It is also thought that the cadence they choose is determined partly by the composition of their muscle fibres. At higher cadences, it is the fast twitch muscle fibres which are most active; it follows that cyclists who are endowed with a high proportion of fast twitch fibres will most likely choose higher cadences.

Optimum cadence (the cadence at which you are most efficient) depends partly on muscle fibre composition, but also on the speed a cyclist is trained to ride at. The most efficient cadence for someone who generally rides at touring speeds — say 20 kilometres per hour — is usually about 60 to 80 rpm; for a racer whose average speeds are high, the most efficient cadence will be correspondingly high.

Reducing oxygen consumption: A summing up

The main forces that retard cyclists — namely air resistance, rolling resistance, mass, and friction have been dealt with. But it is important to realise that there are other things that may be minor in themselves but that all add up and make the cyclist expend effort unnecessarily: just two examples are incorrect saddle height and crank length. Efficient riding demands not only techniques that conserve energy, but good fit on a fine-tuned bicycle.

The medical benefits of cycling

There is good scientific evidence that exercise maintained for life reduces the risk of coronary heart disease and, possibly, also of cancer. After walking, cycling is probably the activity that has been used most widely for the rehabilitation of people suffering from various medical conditions. It can be done under supervision on a stationary cycle in controlled conditions, such as an exercise laboratory in a hospital. As the activity doesn't involve carrying the body's weight, the risk of injury, even for frail people, is low; in contrast there's a significant risk of injury in running. This gentleness of cycling — the low level of stress it puts on the bones and muscles and joints — makes it an ideal form of exercise for older people.

The major benefits of exercise in rehabilitation are improved fitness and self-esteem. For people with limited exercise tolerance due to heart or lung disease the changes that improved fitness induce in their muscles means that they can exercise harder and for longer before they reach their disease-imposed limits.

CHAPTER ELEVEN

CYCLING INJURIES

Cyclists' injuries fall into two main groups: traumatic injuries (in other words, the grazes, bruises or fractures that result from accidents) and non-traumatic injuries (usually the result of long hours in the saddle, faulty riding technique, riding an unsuitable bicycle or inadequate personal hygiene and care of cycling clothes; typical examples are numb hands or feet, or a painful rear). Traumatic injuries give the greatest cause for concern. Compared with most other sportspeople, cyclists are remarkably free of non-traumatic injuries.

Traumatic injuries

There are no accurate or comprehensive figures for the incidence of traumatic injuries in cyclists. Most studies of the subject are concerned with major injuries that require hospitalization or that result in death, although it is known that the majority of cycling accidents are too minor to be recorded on any police or hospital records.

However, bicycles have been ranked at the top of the United States Consumer Product-Safety Commission's Hazard Index of products associated with injuries.

Figures on accidents are, of course, a useful indicator of what the most effective measures for preventing accidents are; these measures are covered in detail in Chapter 8, which deals with safe riding techniques.

The dangers of the bicycle

In the first bike boom, cycling was credited with being a cure for constipation, gout, paleness and headaches. Sir Arthur Conan Doyle (not only the creator of Sherlock Holmes, but also a doctor and a keen cyclist) advised his female patients who were suffering from *ennui* to ride bicycles. An American temperance reformer even advocated cycling as a cure for drunkeness.

But there were also warnings of its dangers. Letters to medical journals of the time — some serious, some tongue-in-cheek — spelt out the risks:

There is no safety in a bicycle. At all ages and to both sexes it offers under the guise of a pastime an insidious allurement to deformity and disease ... surely the bicycle is to be looked upon as a menace which threatens us almost from the cradle to the grave, and a machine more to be avoided than a roulette wheel.

Editorial: *Boston Medical and Surgical Journal*, October 4, 1894.

Site and nature of injuries

Of the injuries that are treated in hospitals, about 20 per cent are fractures, about 30 per cent are bruises or contusions, and the remainder are lacerations and abrasions. More than half of all injuries are to the head and face, and the likelihood of injury to these parts is highest in accidents which involve a collision with a motor vehicle.

Head injuries

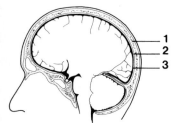

The importance of head injuries is that they are present in about 80 per cent of cyclists who die in cycling accidents. In addition to being by far the most common cause of death in cyclists, head trauma also accounts for about 70 per cent of hospital admissions that result from bicycling accidents. In American and Canadian studies, bicycle-related injuries have been cited as the single most common cause of traumatic brain injury in children.

1. skull
2. dura mater, a tough membrane
3. cerebrospinal fluid

Most cyclists who have suffered head injuries were not wearing helmets at the time of their accidents, yet studies suggest convincingly that as many as 90 per cent of head injuries could be prevented by the widespread use of good head protection. It is significant that so few children wear helmets, yet it is they who, statistically, are at greatest risk of injury.

The brain is one of the most delicate structures in the body, and has the consistency of a firm jelly. Under normal conditions it is protected from injury, firstly by the skull, secondly by a shock-absorbing fluid within the skull, and thirdly by a tough membrane which holds it together. These protective structures fail, however, when the skull is subjected to violent rotational forces — as, for example, when the head is struck by a side blow in a boxing fight, or when it is suddenly decelerated, as occurs when a cyclist's head makes contact with a road or a motor vehicle. Under these circumstances, the brain may rotate, tearing delicate structures, and it will ultimately strike the inside of the skull. The extent of the damage caused is directly determined by the rate at which the brain decelerates to a stop. Accordingly, the main purpose of a helmet is to reduce those deceleration forces.

There is a very wide variation in the effectiveness of helmets on the market, and it is critically important to choose one that meets with recognized safety standards. Guidelines to choosing helmets are given in Chapter 16.

Using a good helmet makes you eight or nine times less likely to suffer from a head injury should you be involved in an accident.

First aid treatment of common injuries

Abrasions or *grazes* are a fairly common result of falling and sliding over tarred road surfaces. Most are minor, but these injuries have the potential to be nasty; it's therefore wise to protect vulnerable areas such as the palms of the hands by wearing gloves. Likewise, it's sensible to wear a T-shirt under your cycling top for the extra layer of protection it affords. One of the reasons racers shave their legs is because it is so much easier to clean smooth grazed legs than it is to deal with hairy skin.

A minority of abrasions are fairly deep, with gravel, dirt and oil embedded in them. The most important aspect of treating them is to remove all the dirt from the wound. If it is very painful, a local anaesthetic should be used. After cleaning, the wound should be covered by an antibiotic spray or ointment until the skin layers have recovered enough to be watertight and resistant to infection.

About 10 per cent of racer's injuries are *lacerations* or injuries to the skin surface and underlying tissues, especially muscle. As foreign substances are often driven deep into the muscles, there is a high risk of infection, and it is essential to have appropriate medical care to ensure that dirt and dead tissue are removed, the wound is drained and, if necessary, stitched.

An interesting observation by a colleague is that many of these lacerations occur in tissues overlying the bony prominence on the outside of the hip — a point which frequently strikes the ground hardest in an accident. He suggests that extra chamois material in the cycling shorts overlying that area could reduce the severity of these injuries.

Contusions are bruises of deep tissues, particularly muscle, that often occur with other injuries. They result from damage to small arteries which bleed into the bruised tissues. Bleeding can be reduced by applying ice to the area for about twenty minutes, up to six times a day. Afterwards the area should be bandaged firmly.

Most cyclists' cuts and bruises are not serious and have no lasting effect. Sometimes, however, an area of firm scarring, a muscle *knot*, remains, particularly when a large area of muscle that is actively involved in cycling, such as the quadriceps or gluteal muscles, is damaged. This hard, knotty area that remains after the acute injury has healed may cause persistent discomfort that responds only to one form of treatment — a physio-therapeutic manoeuvre known as cross frictions. In this procedure the injured area of muscle is massaged firmly in a side-to-side direction across the underlying bone. The pressure applied to the muscle is increased progressively during the course of treatment. The treatment is exquisitely painful, but absolutely effective.

Fractures

The most common *fractures* of racing cyclists are of the ribs and clavicle (collarbone). Among commuting cyclists arm and leg fractures occur more often. The fractured limb should be splinted to avoid movement at the site of the injury, and it should have medical attention straight away.

There are two important points to be aware of regarding fractures. Firstly, fractures of the ribs or clavicle can puncture the lining of the lungs, which results in the sudden onset of breathing difficulties; this requires urgent medical attention. Secondly, head injuries frequently occur in association with neck injuries, particularly fractures of the cervical vertebrae. The danger here is that while the head injury is usually obvious, with the patient either being aware of it or being confused or unconscious, the neck injury may not be apparent. Yet simply moving the patient may cause the fracture to move and sever the spinal cord, leading to irreversible paralysis. The golden rule must be that every cyclist with

---

The bicycle face

... habitual violation of the law of the Sabbath may result in the worn, weary, and exhausted face called the bicycle face. ... due to the severe strain of violent exercise on seven days of the week ...

Editorial: *Medical Record*, August 12, 1895.

---

a head injury should be assumed to have a neck injury and must be treated appropriately. That is, they should be moved onto a stretcher only by trained people who know how to control the neck during the transfer to the stretcher and who will continue to control the neck until the patient is under medical care. They should then be taken straight to hospital. A cyclist who is unconscious should be assumed to have a neck injury and must be moved in the same way.

Children and injuries

A few types of injury are fairly specific to children:

- There have been several cases of children being struck in the abdomen by the handlebars as they fall forward in an accident. In most cases the injury has initially appeared minor, and the child has been sent home even after being carefully examined by a doctor. However, the subsequent develop-ment of more serious symptoms, such as vomiting, collapse or severe abdominal pain, may be signs of serious internal injury and they indicate the need for admission to hospital immediately.
- Rupture of the urethra (the tube through which urine passes) has been reported in a few children who have been struck in the crotch by the top tube. For young children it may be advisable to ride a bike with no top tube, or one that has a bent tube.
- Feet may easily be caught and ankles twisted in turning spokes when children are carried on the top tube or on a rear carrier that is not designed for this purpose.
- There have been claims that the gimmicky design of some children's bicycles has been to blame for accidents. The 'high rise' bike, (popularly known as the Chopper) was a case in point in the 1970s. The lesson to be learned is to base the choice of children's bicycles on stability and reliability and not on fashion.

Non-traumatic or over-use injuries

Over-use injuries are due to the wear and tear your body undergoes, or to pressure on your tissues during prolonged exercise. Such injuries are rare among cyclists, but they occur in about 70 per cent of runners. For this reason most of the scientific knowledge about them is based on what happens in runners rather than cyclists, and we still have much to learn.

Bicycle heart

There must be few of us who have not seen the ill effects of over-exertion on a bicycle. ... The heart produced is of large dimensions and of thick walls — a condition which may, perhaps, give little uneasiness to its owner, but which a medical man will view with considerable distrust and apprehension.

Editorial: *The British Medical Journal*, April 2, 1898.

Cyclist's knee

Cyclist's knee is a painful condition thought to be similar to runner's knee. It results in discomfort and pain at and below the kneecap (patella) when you ride. The most likely cause is inflammation at the spot where the infra-patellar ligament is attached to the lower edge of the patella, but other structures in the knee may be involved. The inflammation may be due to two causes: incorrect alignment of the leg and particularly the feet, and overloading of the ligament.

Incorrect alignment: If your feet point outward or inward too much and are rigidly held in this position by cleats, it may result in abnormal stresses in the ligaments of the knee. Similarly, if your foot is pronated (in other words, if you are flat-footed), the arch will flatten during the downstroke and cause the kneecap to point inwards excessively. This movement, repeated thousands of times, is believed to be one of the causes of cyclist's knee.

Overloading: Pushing high gears for prolonged periods puts an excessive load on the ligaments attached to the patella. Another cause of increased load is riding with the saddle too low — the knee is too flexed during the entire pedal cycle, which puts extra stress on the patella and ligaments.

Prevention and treatment: Cyclist's knee can usually be prevented by paying careful attention to the correct sizing and setting up of your bike: make sure your saddle is at the correct height and that your cleats are fitted so that your feet are in a comfortable, neutral position when you ride. Ride sensibly, develop a fast cadence, and avoid high gears, especially if you're unfit. Rarely, it may be necessary to fit in-shoe supports to correct foot pronation, and some riders have found it necessary to fit pedals that allow the feet more freedom to move.

If you are afflicted with cyclist's knee, you should reduce the amount of riding you do until the problem is cured, and pay special attention to the preventative measures that have been described. Some cyclists have had the cartilage at the back of the knee-cap surgically scraped in an attempt to cure cyclist's knee. In almost all cases this has been the wrong treatment; it is seldom that the pain caused by cyclist's knee arises in this area.

Injuries due to pressure

Your body makes contact with the bike in three areas: the handlebars, the pedals and the saddle. In all three places prolonged or excessive pressure on nerves and other tissues can give rise to troublesome injuries. Some of these, if not treated early, may cause serious harm.

Excessive pressure on a nerve cuts off its blood supply, depriving it of oxygen and nutrition and interfering with its function. This condition is called *ischaemic neuropathy*. It causes feelings of numbness or pins and needles in the affected area at first, followed by weakness and paralysis of the muscles. If the blood supply is allowed to return reasonably quickly, the nerve recovers rapidly, but serious, sometimes permanent, damage can occur if the pressure is prolonged or repeated.

Pressure between hands and handlebars: Two important nerves, the ulnar and the median nerves, may be compressed between the bones of your hands and the handlebars. *Ulnar neuropathy* is the more common of the two. It causes numbness and pins and needles in the ring and little fingers. *Median neuropathy* affects the thumb, index and middle fingers. With prolonged pressure, weakness of hand grip and loss of co-ordination may occur, especially if it is repeated over a few days of continuous riding.

These injuries tend to occur if the bike is the wrong size or incorrectly set up so that too much weight is carried on the hands. They are more likely if the handlebars are not well taped or if you don't wear padded gloves.

Prevention: Choose a bike that is the correct size, and set it up carefully. Pay particular attention to saddle position and handlebar stem length. Keep your handlebar tape in good condition, and use padded cycling gloves. If you still have problems, you can fit padded handlebar covers or use gloves with extra padding. On long rides change your position on the handlebars frequently: use the brake hoods, the bends, the tops and the drops. Using aerobars may help because you can rest on your arms, relieving the pressure on your hands. *Don't ride long distances on successive days if your hands keep going numb — sort out the problem first.*

Feet, shoes and pedals: The stiff soles of cycling shoes are designed to distribute the pressure from the pedals over the entire surface of the bottom of your foot, thus reducing the incidence of foot problems. Even so, pressure from the hard moulded synthetic soles of some modern cycling shoes on the small *digital nerves* in the feet may result in numbness of the toes and pain in the feet. This tends to happen on long rides over flat terrain, and especially if your shoes are too tight. Your feet may swell on long rides and aggravate the problem.

To prevent the injury, make sure your shoes are comfortable and fit properly. Don't pull laces or velcro too tight. It may be necessary to use an insole to spread the pressure over a wider area.

Perineum and saddle: The weight of your upper body on the saddle is carried on two bones called the *ischial tuberosities*. They make contact with the saddle through the *perineum*. The perineum consists of skin and the tissues underneath (subcutaneous tissues), with the *pudendal nerve* and the tube through which you pass urine (the *urethra*).

Among new cyclists it is common to have a sore perineum after riding the first few times. This quickly wears off if your bike is correctly sized and set up. But prolonged exposure to heat, sweat, friction and pressure may cause the skin of the perineum and the genitalia to become raw and prone to bacterial infection. Infection may start in hair follicles and spread, causing boils and other horrible sores. To prevent these you must keep your shorts clean and the chamois in good condition. Personal hygiene is also important. Sores in this area that don't settle down quickly need medical attention.

Pressure from the saddle can become a major problem when nerves, subcutaneous tissues or the urethra are affected. It is worth spending money on a good quality saddle. 'Anatomic' saddles for men and women are shaped to minimize pressure on the midline perineal structures. Women have a wider pelvis than men and special women's anatomic saddles are available that are wider than those made for men.

Care of cycling shorts

There are many ways of cleaning your shorts and keeping the chamois soft. One excellent method is as follows: Wash the shorts regularly with mild soap; while the leather is still wet, rub in a liberal quantity of lanolin cream, and then hang them up inside-out in the sun. The sunlight kills bacteria and the lanolin will be absorbed, making the chamois as good as new.

Since the earliest days of the bicycle, designers have worked at producing a comfortable saddle. This is one of the ideas that didn't work:

Bicycle Saddle for the Use of Either Sex

UNITED STATES PATENT OFFICE
BICYCLE AND MOTOR-CYCLE SEAT

Patented May 19, 1925   1,538,542

Application filed February 16, 1924. Serial No. 693,327

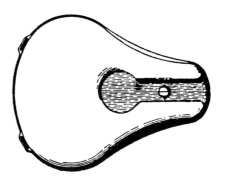

...It is a primary object of my invention to provide a bicycle or motorcycle saddle having a suitable cavity properly located to allow comfortable clearance for the private organs of the male rider, said saddle having also a channel adapted to allow clearance for the female rider's private organs, to prevent pressure at the opening of said organs due to the weight of the rider, and tending also to keep said organs in a naturally closed state, the sides of said channel being substantially parallel and bell-mouthed ...

Referring to Fig. 1, a somewhat circular cavity is formed on a medial line of the apparatus as a whole, at the junctions of said extension with said larger seating portion. Said cavity is of suitable size, shape and location to comfortably receive the private organs of a male rider and more particularly the testicle region of such rider. Said opening is of bell-mouthed formation, the bell-mouth character thereof being formed on the upper portion of said opening. Such bell-mouthed formation is particularly useful to the comfort of the male rider both during the riding act and also during the mounting or dismounting acts, said organs being slidably lodgeable or dislodgeable in relation to said opening when same is thus covered or uncovered by angular movement as compared to what may be called a vertical straight-away movement ...

Perineal nodules (saddle sores) are painful lumps that tend to occur in riders in heavy training who do long rides regularly. Prolonged and repeated pressure causes chronic changes in the subcutaneous tissues of the perineum, resulting in hard, tender nodules. These grow and become extremely tender if neglected. Microscopically they are seen to consist of areas of dead tissue surrounded by inflammation. They may also become infected. The chances of getting them are less if you keep your shorts in good condition and take particular care to keep the chamois clean and soft.

At the first sign of a nodule, stick a corn plaster over it so that the nodule lies in the hole in the plaster. These usually stay put for a few days and take the weight off the nodule while you ride. If you have acted in time, this is usually all that is necessary, and the nodule will disappear, but if it gets worse, stop riding for a while.

Rarely, an operation may be necessary to remove nodules, but if you get to this stage, it is a disaster. You will end up with scar tissue in the weight-bearing area, and this is bound to cause new problems: scar tissue isn't very strong and doesn't do well under pressure.

Always take painful nodules on your backside seriously and do something about them the moment they start. Once they become established they can be a major nuisance.

The *pudendal nerve* may be caught between your pelvic bones and the saddle. This causes local numbness and loss of sensation in the genitalia. Check saddle position and tilt, and if this doesn't help, try an anatomic saddle. Some people believe that cycling may damage the nerves (or some blood vessels) involved in sexual function, but the issue of whether cycling causes impotence has not been resolved.

The *urethra* is the tube that runs between the bladder and the outside of the body: you pass urine through it. Abnormal pressure on the urethra results in inflammation (*non-specific urethritis*). The symptoms are the urge to pass urine frequently and urgently. The stream may be poor and it may burn. These symptoms may be due to an unrelated urinary tract infection and you should see your doctor and have your urine checked. Stop cycling until it resolves.

In general: If you have a bike that is the right size and it is correctly set up, you are unlikely to develop non-traumatic injuries. Ride sensibly and pay attention to basic riding technique. Develop a pedalling cadence of at least 60 revolutions per minute and avoid high gears. If you still develop signs of an injury, act early to prevent it getting worse. Some very promising cycling careers have been destroyed by letting them ride!

Muscle cramp

Some people are prone to crippling muscle cramps which consistently occur after they've ridden a certain distance; you find some riders who can ride for, say, 90 kilometres and who, almost without fail, are then attacked by cramps which are severe enough to force them off the bike. It's probable that these unfortunates have a minor muscle abnormality.

There is no certainty about what causes muscle cramp. Theories that it is caused by a lack of salt have never been substantiated, and are very likely wrong. It is possible that depletion of glycogen from the muscles combined with severe muscle fatigue causes cramp during exercise. And untrained riders are a lot more prone to cramp than fit riders are.

Although we have to accept that some riders are simply born more susceptible than others, you can do much to prevent cramp by training, especially over long distances, and by getting enough carbohydrates before and during your rides, and by seeing that you drink enough to replace lost fluid.

If cramp does attack you on a ride, you may be able to keep going by slowing down and easing up on your use of the cramping limb. But it's more likely that you'll be forced off your bike. Rubbing the muscle may help, though rest is a more certain remedy. When the cramp has passed and you are back on your bike, avoid taxing the muscle.

Doing stretching exercises (which are described in Chapter 13) seems to cure people of nocturnal cramps; it's quite possible that this will also help prevent exercise-induced cramp.

CHAPTER TWELVE

THE RACING scene

This chapter gives an overview of racing in this country — how it began, how it is organized now, what types of races are ridden, and how to join a racing club yourself.

No matter how fit, unfit, fat, lean, strong or weak we are, there lurks within all of us a competitive streak, a will to win. That compulsion to test one's abilities against those of others is inherent in human nature, and drives us to performances that, when considered objectively, seem almost unnatural. Think, for example, of what goes into riding the Tour de France's 4 000 kilometres over the twenty-five or so days that the race takes. Something of that spirit is at the heart of all racing, and it compels many of us to back our dreams of victory with tens of thousands of kilometres of hard slog in training.

A short history

When bicycles were invented, one of the first things people did on them was to try and go faster than anyone else. This obsession with speed and competition has been with cyclists ever since.

The world's first bike race was ridden in 1868 on the St Cloud track in Paris on wood-and-iron front-wheel driven bicycles which were popularly known as boneshakers. Thirteen years later South Africa's first organized cycle race took place in Port Elizabeth. By the time this historic Eastern Cape race took place, the bicycle had evolved into a relatively sophisticated piece of engineering — the high-wheeler or penny farthing — and our pioneer racers are almost certain to

169

have ridden machines that sported the technical innovations of hollow tubing, solid rubber tyres and ball-bearings.

Local interest in bicycle racing spread like wildfire, especially among the British troops stationed here, and the arrival of the safety bicycle in the second half of the 1880s gave racing further impetus. Soon there was regular organized racing in most major centres, and a rougher version of it existed in numerous outposts. In 1892 a controlling body called the South African Cyclists' Union was formed; a year later local cycling was linked to the world racing scene when South Africa became affiliated to the International Cycling Association. Later it was affiliated to the Union Cycliste Internationale (UCI) — otherwise known as the International Cycling Union.

By 1896 the Wanderers Amateur Cycling Club in Johannesburg was considered the strongest in the country with over 250 members; Johannesburg was even described in a British cyclists' magazine as the centre of world cycling, though this was almost certainly an exaggeration.

A pacer, *circa* 1895.

The Wanderers, Johannesburg, 1891: the line-up for the 25-Mile Championship of South Africa.

South Africa's first world champion sportsperson was a cyclist: Laurens Meintjies was a Wanderers rider who broke 16 records in America and is reputed to have initiated the technique of riding behind a pacer to get the benefit of reduced aerodynamic drag. The pacers used then were cycles rather like extra-long tandems built to take several riders; they reached high speeds, and were used in much the same way that modern motor pacers are.

Since the first boom in the popularity of cycle racing here (1890 to 1910) the sport has had several ups and downs. It has never captured the public imagination in the way that rugby or cricket have, but as the list of South African triumphs shows, South African cyclists have had some remarkable achievements.

Photo J. E. Bruton.   Cape Town.

MR. JACK ROSE,

OUR WORLD'S CHAMPION, AND HIS SPRINGBUCK RACER.

PAST AND PRESENT.

Some South African cycling triumphs

1893	Laurens Meintjies	World Road Race Champion
1897	Jack Rose	World 25-Mile Record
		World Hour Champion
1912	Rudolph Lewis	Gold Medal, Olympic Games
1934	Ted Clayton	Berlin Olympics
		— Silver Medal for 10 Miles
		— Bronze Medal for 1 000-Metre Time Trial
		— Bronze Medal for 1 000-Metre Sprint
1938	Hennie Binneman	Gold Medal, British Empire Games,
		100-Mile Road Race
1938	Sid Rose	Bronze Medal for 10 Miles
1952	The Springbok team, which included Ray Robinson, Bobby Fowler, R. Estman, Jimmy Swift and Tom Shardelow won a Silver Medal for the Team Pursuit at the Olympic Games in Helsinki. Robinson and Shardelow won the Silver Medal for a tandem event.	

The South African Cycling Federation

The South African Cycling Federation (SACF) was formed in 1957; it is the officially recognized national body representing racing cyclists in the Republic. The SACF Executive holds congresses in winter and summer when representatives from provincial member organizations meet to discuss such matters as a national racing calendar, sponsorship, racing rules and the selection of national teams. The Federation is directly connected to the Department of Sport and Recreation, the RSA Sports Trust, the SA Olympic Council and the Springbok Colours Council. Cycle racing in South Africa is based on the rules of the International Cycling Union, but due partly to our international isolation, the SACF has adapted these to suit local conditions. The addresses of the SACF and of some of its affiliated clubs are given in the Appendix.

International isolation

The quiet but steady growth in the popularity of cycle racing locally has been despite the severe blow that the sport was dealt in 1963 when the International Olympic Council barred us from the Games because of our government's racist policies. In 1970 the UCI barred South African cyclists from any officially recognized international competition for the same reason. (It is ironic that cycling is perhaps the one sport which in many areas and for a long time was genuinely free of racist controls.)

Though the annual Rapport Tour and other races attract some foreign riders, and local riders have more than held their own in racing seasons in Europe recently, the bans on us are very inhibiting; it is tricky and often impossible to race openly overseas if you have a South African passport. Overall, the lack of international competition has set local racing back seriously. To give an example: because there is so little opportunity or motivation to specialize in particular types of racing, local riders don't reach their full potential. Take kermesses: overseas, so many of these races are ridden that anyone with a talent for them has numerous opportunities to perfect his technique. Here there are few such opportunities.

As a measure of how much international exposure and success popularizes cycling, consider what happened in the USA. Until recently, the American public, like the average rugby-watching South African, barely knew that cycle racing existed. Then the Americans unexpectedly produced a crop of world class cyclists; when they rode off with coveted

Ted Clayton

cycling medals at the 1984 Olympics and Greg Lemond won the Tour de France for the first time in 1986, the media started giving exciting and well-informed coverage to the sport, and the popularity of racing in America skyrocketed.

Racing and the recreational boom

Apart from international isolation, there are other reasons why cycle racing hasn't really fired public enthusiasm. I feel our lack of a large public following is partly because cycling isn't a recognized sport in schools — though there has been progress recently in this area, especially in the Eastern Cape. Another reason is that the media doesn't do it justice; the subtle, and sometimes spectacular excitement of the sport can only be communicated by a commentator who understands the rules and the strategies, and knows something about the riders — their personalities and their racing histories. If you have ever watched good overseas coverage of say, the Tour de France, you will know what I mean. And, of course, people are put off getting started because of the sheer expense of equipment.

But I am hopeful that competitive cycling will get a greater and greater spin-off from the recreational cycling boom; fun rides organized with the help of Pedal Power Associations attract literally thousands of novice riders — many of them potential racers: a recent Argus Tour, for example, drew over 12 000 riders — more than ten times the number of members the SACF has in the entire country. I feel sure that there is much common ground between racers and fun riders, and that if there was closer co-ordination between Pedal Power and the racing organizations, there would be benefits for all.

Each race is a fiesta ...

This description of racing in Europe comes from *A Natal boy in Italy* by Barry Clegg:

And always there are the fans, thousands of them packing the villages en route, screaming their support and abuse. Debating and arguing the merits of various riders and reliving their own and the exploits of the greats of the past. It is impossible not to be infected by the excitement and enthusiasm, the preceding phalanx of support-vehicles and motorbikes, police and commissars, then the breakaway, the stragglers and the frenetic caravan of team vehicles pounding the horns and klaxons and taking crazy risks to get to the riders, but accidents are rare. The policing of the race and the crowds is fantastic, the roads are free for the racers, and any vehicle trespassing is sharply and often forcibly ejected into a convenient space.

Each race is a fiesta, the wine flows and the meat cooks, everybody who is anybody is there, whole towns turn out for the occasion, and long after the race is finished, the prizes presented, the riders tucked into bed, the revelry continues. Post-mortems on each race and different riders are kept alive by media coverage: television, radio and whole pages in national and local newspapers say something about most races that took place in the country.

How to join organized racing

If you want to get into organized, regular racing, I recommend that the first thing you do is join the South African Cycling Federation. An SACF licence will entitle you to ride in the many races sanctioned by the Federation. Usually there is an event every week in all the major centres; these are listed in a national racing calendar which the SACF makes available at the beginning of each year.

To join the SACF, you simply approach a local cycling club which is affiliated to it (there's a list of clubs in the Appendix at the back of this book); ask for an SACF licence form, fill it in and send it off. The SACF or the secretary of your club will let you know in due course if you have been accepted as a licensed rider.

Categories of riders

There are several categories of riders under SACF rules. Most race meetings cater for all of them.

Scholars (or, if you go by the word in the SACF rule book, **schoolboys**, though girls can and do ride successfully in events in this category)**:** This group is split into under-11s, under-13s and under-15s. The maximum race distances for the respective categories are 20 kilometres, 30 kilometres and 40 kilometres, and gear ratios are restricted to a maximum of 78. (See the gear ratio chart in the Appendix for an explanation of that.) One reason for the gear restrictions of younger riders is that they help to iron out the great variations in strength and physical development that you often find among adolescents of the same age; being limited to high gears means that a spiderweight twelve-year-old has a chance of holding his own in a race against a powerful hunk of the same age. Because low gearing forces riders to spin their pedals at a rapid cadence, this rule also ensures that youngsters have a sound grounding in good pedalling technique, and it helps to prevent the injuries to muscles, joints and tendons that high gearing can cause. Racing on a bike fitted with gears that allow you to exceed the maximum ratio is cause for disqualification in a race.

Under-17: This category used to be called 'Juvenile'. Gears are restricted to a maximum ratio of 83, and race distances are not more than 60 kilometres.

Juniors: These are riders aged under 19. Gear ratios are only restricted for track racing, the maximum ratio being 91.

Seniors: These are riders over the age of 19; there are no gear restrictions.

Veterans: Riders over the age of 35 who are licensed as amateurs are in this category. Cyclists mature slowly and there is a surprisingly slow fall-off in performance related to age. The veteran category is a popular and lively one, and racing is usually handicapped in A, B and C groups, determined by age and ability. Competition is tough, riders are determined.

Ladies: Licensed women riders compete in so-called Ladies' events or, on invitation, in Juveniles' and Veterans' events. The rules at present seem fairly flexible, but with the growth of exclusively women's racing associations (such as the Western Province Ladies' Cycling Association, which is affiliated to the SACF) better provision is being made for women and the rules will probably tighten up. Women's cycling is growing rapidly, especially in the Cape, and this is a category with much potential.

Professional: Riders over the age of 21 with valid professional licences are in this category. The South African Pro category was founded in the early 1980s in an attempt to raise standards. It was also done in the hope of enabling riders to compete internationally. To no avail. Both professionals and amateurs with South African passports have been barred from international competition. Like riders in the amateur categories, professionals are governed by the SACF.

Unlike professionals in countries where there is big money in cycle racing, our twenty or so pro riders don't earn enough from their riding to live on, and most have other jobs — which makes it difficult to put in the training that top international riders, whose only work is riding bicycles, do. In contrast with the situation here, the Professional Cycling Union in Europe is well established and highly organized; members enjoy direct payments in the form of salaries and appearance money as well as fringe benefits like pensions.

The rules that legitimize income from racing are relatively flexible here and the distinction between amateur and professional categories is fairly narrow; of course it is easier for professionals to earn money directly from racing, but amateur cyclists can also be sponsored.

Amateurs and professionals are generally allowed to ride in the same races.

The road and the track

There are two main categories of cycle racing: road and track. Road racing is the more popular sport among participants and spectators alike, and organizers have placed more emphasis on it.

Until recently, road and track seasons were kept quite separate: track events were ridden from October to April and road events from April to October. Many found this an illogical division as road cyclists were having to fit their long training rides into the short days of winter. Moreover, until recently the racing calendar had no off-season; as many cyclists here don't specialize but race through both seasons, this meant that for them, there was no quiet time of year in which to unwind, rest or even prepare for the next season.

But as from 1990, track and road seasons overlap. Most road races and tours are scheduled for mid-August through to the end of November. Minor track events are also scheduled for this time. From December to the end of April the emphasis is on track racing, but there are also short, fast road races such as kermesses and criteriums. There is an off-season in June and July.

Road racing

Road racing takes several forms and demands a variety of skills.

Tour or stage racing: Stage races are the most demanding of all cycling events. They are held over a prescribed route which is divided into component stages; these are usually ridden over at least two days though they may, like the Rapport Tour, take as long as ten days. The world's greatest stage race, the Tour de France, takes three weeks and is ridden over about 4 000 kilometres.

The overall winner is the rider who has the least accumulated time over the full race. After each stage this leader wears the coveted *yellow jersey*. Within a stage race there are often secondary competitions and awards. Examples are:

- The title of *King of the Mountains*: This goes to the rider who has accumulated the most points for mountain primes. (A prime — pronounced preem — is a 'hot spot' somewhere along a stage, and there is competition to reach it first.)
- Prizes for winning *individual stages*.
- A prize for the rider who has accumulated the most *points*; points are allocated to those who have been placed in *stage finishes* or in 'hot spots' during stages.
- Last, and definitely least, is the *lanterne rouge* (red jersey) which is awarded to the rider who comes last overall.

Riding day after day at peak performance makes immense physical demands on riders and requires intense psychological motivation. The longer and more demanding a tour, the more important the role of team work becomes; the yellow jersey needs all the support he can get from team mates to ward off the opposition. Team tactics are numerous: team members may shelter their chosen leader from wind so that he conserves the energy he will need for the final winning effort;

riders may on occasion deliberately slow down the pace by riding in the front and blocking riders who may try to speed it up.

Some team members are also required to carry extra food and water for their leader, lend wheels or bikes if necessary, and should the leader have a puncture, their job is to shepherd him back into the pack.

Important stage races in South Africa are the Rapport Tour, the mountainous Eastern Transvaal Tour, the Garden Route, the Southern Transvaal and the Western Transvaal Tours.

Single-stage races: Most road races are single-stage events; distances vary in the senior section from 60 to 180 kilometres. Usually there are no hot spots or primes. The overriding aim is to win — which is not necessarily the same thing as riding fast: depending on the road and weather conditions and the overall style of the field of riders, dominant teams may deliberately restrain the pace of parts of the race if it ultimately helps them to win. (If this statement sounds somewhat contradictory to you, the section on team tactics in Chapter 14 should clarify it.)

In most provinces there are weekly road races during the season. In addition, the SACF calendar includes single-stage races that have the status of National Classics like the Ladismith to Bergville Classic and the Star 100 Classic.

In Europe famous one-day events are The Milan–San Remo, the Milan–Torino and Paris–Roubaix, which is notorious for its long sections of bone-shaking cobbled roads.

Criterium racing: Criteriums take place around short circuits of between about 600 metres and 2 kilometres, which are repeated; total distances are usually between 20 and 80 kilometres. City blocks, parks and even supermarket parking areas often make good courses. Criteriums usually involve negotiating one corner after another at high speed, and they demand total concentration. Prime or prize laps are usually indicated by a whistle which is blown during the race on a

Kermesse racing

surprise basis — you never really know when to expect it, and this gives the race a constant edge of competitive tension.

These races have excellent spectator appeal: the riders reappear often on the circuit, and because the distances are short, the riding is usually fast and exciting. They are easy to arrange since all equipment and publicity material can be assembled on site. Well-known South African criteriums include the Zoo Lake Classic, the Il Campione and the Chris Willemse series in Cape Town.

Kermesse racing: 'Kermesse' is popularly used in South Africa as a synonym for criterium, but strictly speaking, it is a circuit race on a larger circuit of between 2 and 15 kilometres long.

Time-trial events: The time trial is often called the race of truth. Riders set off individually and ride against the clock. No slipstreaming or drafting is allowed from any source. So, unlike the rider in a bunch who can be sheltered by other riders during much of a race, the time trialler has only his own skill and fitness to depend on. Time triallists make the best use that they can of aerodynamic equipment: pointed helmets, smooth, tight-fitting clothing and aerodynamically designed bicycles — smaller front wheels and/or disc wheels are common on time-trial courses. Francesco Moser, who in 1989 broke the world hour record (he covered 51,151 kilometres in that time) did so with the aid of specially-designed equipment and clothing. For several reasons time-trial bikes are not used in standard bicycle racing: the shortened upturned handlebars are considered dangerous and the disc wheels cause handling problems.

Time trial distances vary, but provincial championships are usually ridden over 40 kilometres for seniors.

Time triallists need specialized skills such as being able to hold a crouched, aerodynamically efficient position throughout, a fluid pedalling action and the judgement to pace efforts so that speed is steady over the entire distance. As time trials often feature as stages in tours, and can have a critical impact on the final race result, it is important for racers to have the versatility to ride them well.

Time trialling is less popular than most other forms of racing here, but in Europe and the UK it attracts a lot of interest.

Team time trials: Skilled slipstreaming and team work in sharing the lead are all-important in these events, in which average speeds of up to 50 kilometres an hour are reached. The 100-kilometre team time trial is an important Olympic event.

In team time trials within stage races, each member of a team is considered to have finished in the time that the team winner does; in other words, you are given maximum credit for your role in helping the team winner.

Hill climbing: The rules are much the same as for time trialling, but it's up, up, up all the way, favouring the lean, light, strong and dogged.

Competitive fun rides: Where there are active Pedal Power Associations (PPAs), there are fun rides organized for almost every weekend, barring the depths of winter. Though they attract many riders who simply amble along enjoying the view and the conversation, they also have a hot competitive side to them. There are no restrictions on gearing and participants are welcome, irrespective of age and equipment. Some fun rides have a special category for registered riders.

Falls and accidents are far more common in these events than in registered races. Predictably, there are far more falls in the section for unregistered racers — a group which is generally less disciplined but often just as fast as the registered riders.

A time trial stage of the 1988 Rapport Tour — the Southern Sun/M-Net team in action: (from left to right) Mark Beneke, Alan van Heerden, Tony Impy, Gary Beneke, Willie Engelbrecht.

However, safety standards have improved a lot in recent years, thanks largely to the tireless efforts by the PPAs under whose auspices most of these rides are organized. As a service to fun rider sponsors/organizers, PPAs offer practical help and safety guidelines based on the experience that they have gained while helping to run hundreds of such events. It is sensible to check before entering a fun ride whether or not it is PPA-sanctioned. Registered cyclists often enjoy fun rides, as they provide a refreshing change from the demands of serious racing. Recently some fun ride organizers have enticed professionals to ride among the amateur enthusiasts. The pros add lustre to events and are able to give informal advice to less experienced cyclists.

Track racing

Track racing is a very different game from road racing. It is done on a bike with a single fixed gear and no brakes; you slow down by back-pedalling. As speed is paramount, the bikes are stripped down to the lightest and barest essentials.

Track events take place on an enclosed wooden or concrete oval track with banked sides. Circumferences range from 166 to 550 metres. The shorter the track, the steeper the banking should be.

The only cycling track of Olympic standard in this country is the Cyril Geoghegan Stadium in Durban — but unfortunately Durban's debilitating humidity isn't conducive to record-breaking. It is a pity that there are no indoor tracks in this country as many events are washed out by rain. Indoor track racing (usually on smaller wooden tracks) is an exciting spectacle, and in Europe six-day events attract crowds of up to 70 000.

Track races are shorter and tactics are arguably even more important than in road racing. Here is a list of most of the popular track events ridden in this country:

Devil-take-the-hindmost: The last rider crossing the line on each lap is eliminated until only three or four remain. These then sprint for the line. This race is a test of tactical judgement and speed.

Points race: There are various versions of this test of consistency, stamina and sprinting power. Points are usually allocated to the first three riders across the line at specified lap intervals. The rider with the most points at the end of the race wins.

Distance races: These are fairly straightforward events over specified distances; they may be as short as 500 metres or as long as 40 kilometres, with different distances demanding different tactics.

Time trials: *Individual time trial:* Cyclists ride alone against the clock, and the rider who clocks the fastest time wins. The usual distances are 500 metres, 1 000 metres, and 3, 4 and 5 kilometres. The best time triallers tend to be riders who specialize in training for these events.

Team time trial: There are usually four riders per team, and the lead is shared on a rotational basis. The third rider across the line determines the team's time. The standard track distance is 4 000 metres. At the time of going to press, the world record for the team time trial on the track is 4 minutes 12 seconds, with an average speed of about 60 kilometres an hour — which is pretty close to flying.

Madison: This is the most exciting, sometimes the most confusing, and probably the most dangerous of all track events. Riders enter as teams of two and the race is a constant relay with one rider racing while the other sits out or cruises slowly around the top of the banking. Riders change over either by touching or by hand-slinging each other into the mainstream of the race. The length of each relay distance is entirely at the discretion of the riders. Madisons demand the full spectrum of track-racing qualities — speed, stamina, experience, courage and caution.

Match sprint: This event usually confounds the uninitiated spectator. The winner is the first person to cross the line, but how long it takes to do this is almost irrelevant: as a result, there are often deliberate slowing tactics as each rider saves energy and tries to get into a good position to make a break for the finish line towards the end of the race. The official distance of 1 000 metres is contested by two (usually) to four riders. Riders draw lots and the loser leads for the first lap, unless an opponent chooses to take over. At the end of the first lap there is usually a sudden slow-down, where the leader does his best to con the opposition into taking the lead. Being behind in the early stages of a 500-metre sprint has the advantages of being in the slipstream of the rider in front and of having a full view of the impending strategies of others. It is extremely difficult, but not impossible, for the front rider in an equal match to lead out and win the race. These races are extremely tactical and are usually intensely fast over the last 200 metres. Power, cunning, quick reflexes and a strong nerve are prerequisites for a racer who competes in these events.

Coaching in South Africa

The SA Cycling Federation has appointed a committee to set up a national coaching scheme, but so far not enough money has been available to really get this going. The SACF sets exams for coaches at A, B and C grades, and most provincial teams have managers and/or coaches assigned to them.

My feeling is that priority should be given to coaching at grassroots level; if the sport is to develop, more good, trained coaches should be available to young riders — ideally through schools as well as through clubs. There are, fortunately, many veteran or ex-cyclists involved at club and provincial level who do, on a mainly informal basis, train others and give them the benefit of their experience.

CHAPTER THIRTEEN

TRAINING
for racing

This chapter discusses why you need to follow a training programme if you want to race and it gives guidelines for setting one up. There are probably as many training programmes as there are riders; no single programme works for everyone. But if you apply the principles outlined here and in Chapter 10, you should be able to devise a programme that fits in with your ambitions and your other commitments.

Read Chapter 10 before you read this chapter. It discusses the physiological changes which take place when the body is stimulated by physical activity. If you know what is happening to your body when you are out on your bike, you'll be able to apply the principles of training more intelligently and you'll be in a better position to judge how to adapt a programme to suit yourself.

Your performance in racing depends on:

- Your physical and athletic ability.
- How well you have conditioned yourself physically.
- Your knowledge of technique, tactics and strategies.
- Your mental attitude and psychological state.

The relationship between these four aspects varies from individual to individual and also depends on the level of competition. Being in good physical condition is obviously a basic requirement; if you have done your training and are well rested and strong, you will be able to control and predict your body's performance during an event. Techniques and tactics are also very important; many races are won not by the strongest or fittest riders, but by those who match physical ability with clever strategy.

Some basic principles

Before you start a training programme your general health should be good. If you are over thirty or have any doubts about your health (especially if you have ever had a heart murmur or high blood pressure or kidney problems) you should consult your doctor.

Your fitness and strength will only improve when you exercise at intensities that stress your body. But start out sensibly: progress gradually, climbing the training ladder step by step. Give yourself a chance to rest and recover properly. And remember that cycling is a specific sport; cross-training in other sports will help to make you fit but will not necessarily improve your cycling ability.

A sound programme which spells out how and when to train is a good idea. A novice cyclist may not know enough about his or her body to be able to 'listen to it' with any real confidence. With experience, athletes get to understand the whims, needs and reactions of their bodies and learn to adapt prescribed training programmes to achieve the results they want.

Monitor progress by keeping a daily record of what training you do and how your body reacts. This is best done by checking your pulse rate and weight. If anything out of the ordinary is noted, you can take the appropriate steps.

Pulse

Count your pulse for one minute immediately after you wake up every day. You will find minor variations from day to day, but as you get fitter, it should gradually become slower. Greater variations may be a sign that something is wrong. If it varies from, say, 50 beats per minute one day to 60 the next, it could be attributed to disturbed sleep, the onset of illness or because the body has not recovered from the previous day's exercise and needs rest.

Weight

The percentage body fat of a top male racing cyclist should ideally range between 4 and 8 per cent. For women it's higher — about 8 to 12 per cent. Body fat percentage can be tested at any good gymnasium.

Weigh yourself at the same time every day, preferably immediately after getting up in the morning. In the early stages of training, you should notice a gradual decline in your weight, which will stabilize once you adapt to the programme. But you should still aim to bring the percentage down to under 8 per cent (or under 12 per cent if you are female) as excess fat is unproductive and only hinders your efforts.

Example of a training and racing diary

MONDAY _6 August_

Pulse/a.m. _50_   p.m. _70_   Weight _70 kg_

Distance ridden today _125 km_   Hours slept _7½_

Course _Rolling hills for ½ the distance; 1 steep hill._

Weather _Warm but windy_

Workout type _LSD_

Nutrition _B: muesli, milk, fruit; L: egg salad/bread; Snack: banana; D: pasta, salad, bread, a beer._

Remarks _Put in effort on hills; struggled a bit on steep hill. Headwind on way back. A little tired afterwards but recovered quickly._

Sleep

Although individual requirements vary, an athlete in training should get at least eight hours of sleep nightly.

Tips for young and adolescent cyclists

Young children and adolescents should only ride competitively if they enjoy it. The motivation should come from their own free will and natural enthusiasm, and never from parental or other outside pressure. It is far more important for them to concentrate on the basic techniques of cycling (which will stay with them forever) than to win races at this stage of their lives.

During adolescence both body and mind undergo tremendous changes, and it is vital for people who coach young riders to understand these changes and the problems that go with adapting to them. A rigidly enforced, strenuous physical programme can make young riders burn out or crack.

At this age physical capabilities appear to be determined more by size and relative maturity than by the level of training; a large, well-developed rider with no previous training may beat smaller youngsters of the same age who have trained rigorously. As puberty advances, the effect of training increases. I have often seen a weak schoolboy rider suddenly transformed into a powerhouse junior, and conversely, seen excellent youngsters fade in the senior ranks.

When I was twelve and started cycling, I was often lapped in five-lap track events. Discouraged, I gave up cycling after a year or so, and played other sports. My interest in cycling revived fairly spontaneously when I was sixteen. This time round I competed with seniors and, to my surprise and pleasure, did well. In retrospect, it's clear that as a twelve-year-old, I wasn't ready in mind or body for racing.

How to assess the intensity of your training

The intensity of exercise can be scientifically measured and expressed as a percentage of your maximal heart rate (MHR). This is described in more detail in Chapter 10 ('Heart rate and stroke volume during exercise'). Essentially, the harder you exercise, the higher your MHR and the faster your heart beats. Your muscles only become stressed or overloaded when you exercise at an intensity that produces a heart rate of over 60 per cent of your maximal heart rate (MHR), and at 70 to 75 per cent you achieve optimum aerobic training. This is the level at which most of your training should be done.

You can have your maximal heart rate measured accurately in an exercise laboratory, but this isn't really necessary because for most people it is equal to 220 minus their age. So if you're thirty years old, your maximal heart rate is about 190 beats per minute, and you should aim for a heart rate of between 133 and 143 beats per minute when you are doing long, steady distance riding.

A variety of electronic devices are available that monitor your heart rate when you ride. Though it is not always easy, you can measure it yourself with sufficient accuracy by counting your pulse (use the pulse in your wrist or the one in your neck) for six seconds and multiplying the result by ten. Personally, I prefer using a monitor, and I find it adds interest to training sessions.

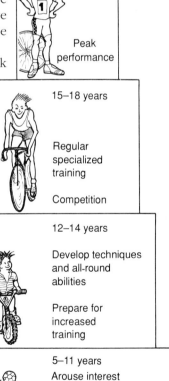

Adult

Peak performance

15–18 years

Regular specialized training

Competition

12–14 years

Develop techniques and all-round abilities

Prepare for increased training

5–11 years
Arouse interest
Develop co-ordination
Develop basic skills
Emphasis on enjoyment

Coaching young cyclists.

Exercise intensity can be classified according to heart rate as follows:

- low intensity training — 60–70% MHR
- medium intensity training — 70–75% MHR
- high intensity training — 75–80% MHR
- maximum intensity training — 80–100% MHR

VO$_2$ max — defined as the number of litres of oxygen that an individual can consume in one minute per kilogram of body-weight — is measured in millilitres per kilogram per minute.

Your VO$_2$ max is largely genetically determined but can be improved by increasing your cardiac output through training. See Chapter 10 to find out more about VO$_2$ max and cardiac function during training.

Illness and accidents

If you are ill or recovering from an illness, even a cold or flu, your body will need all its resources to help it recover. Don't train when you're sick. If you are on medication, consult your doctor about whether you can continue training, and at what intensity.

After an accident or a hard fall, the body needs rest to recover from the shock. Avoid high intensity work-outs for a few weeks afterwards. If you feel that you're in a fit state to race, go ahead, but don't expect top performance while you are recovering.

HINAULT'S NOT WHAT HE'S MISSING

For Lee Fox

I love to ride my bicycle,
I love to keep in shape,
I skim along the country roads
On all fours like an ape.

Though clouds above are scudding and
The roadside hums with life,
To me it's just a canvas that
I cut through like a knife.

My posture's parabolic as
My feet pump up and down
And all I see while training is
A tyre tread turning round.

An optional moral
I am, you'll note, in every way
A man like all the rest:
Oblivious of life itself —
Preparing for a test.

by Gus Ferguson

Fuel for racing

This is dealt with in far more detail in Chapter 10, but it is worth recapping basic rules here. Fuelling yourself properly is largely a matter of common sense; make sure you understand the basic principles of it, and avoid gimmicky fad diets.

- Never race or train hard on a full stomach. Try to have your last meal at least three hours before the start.
- Pre-race meals should consist mainly of complex carbohydrates and little or no fat.
- During tours, protein intake must be restricted to meals at the end of each stage.
- In races or training rides that are longer than 80 kilometres or that take longer than two hours, you should re-stock your fuel supplies by eating carbohydrate-rich snacks at regular intervals and in small quantities. I recommend corn syrup. Regular feeding tends to keep your blood sugar level constant.
- Be very careful not to get dehydrated. It can happen unexpectedly and suddenly, especially in the heat, and it can easily put you out of a race. Getting enough water is even more important than getting enough to eat.

- If you eat a normal, healthy diet you are probably getting all the vitamins and minerals you need. But I prefer to make doubly sure by supplementing my diet with a multivitamin tablet, a B-complex tablet and slow magnesium every day. In long races and in hot weather I find that it is helpful to add some vitamin C to my water-bottle. Some athletes — particularly women — need extra iron, but it is advisable to have your blood checked rather than take minerals unnecessarily.

  I also find amino acid supplements help in the recovery process after intense training; I recommend taking them after training sessions. If you are in any doubt about your vitamin and vitamin intake, consult a doctor or nutritionist.*

Stimulants and medicines

Many tonics contain stimulants that are not allowed in cycle racing, and commonly-used medicines can contain drugs that may impair alertness or be illegal in terms of racing rules. Cough mixtures, for example, contain forbidden drugs such as codeine and ephedrine.

Caffeine is a legal stimulant: a cup of coffee half an hour before the start of the event can make you more alert. But taking caffeine is controversial as it's thought to have side effects such as cardiac arrhythmia, insomnia and headaches.

Illegal drugs

Reliable witnesses have claimed that the most notorious dopers in cycle racing have also been known for the number of crashes they have; the short-term boost that drugs may give you can be wiped out by reduced alertness, an altered sense of judgement and long-term health risks. Doping makes fair competition impossible; there can be little satisfaction in winning a race in this way. Moreover, it has killed cyclists and it is illegal. Defaulters risk having their licences suspended.

Doping tests are conducted in many major cycling races, and a number of racers here have been exposed by them. Perhaps it is because of this that cycle racing has had something of a tarnished reputation where drugs are concerned. But I feel that in the past, administrators of other sports have closed their eyes to illegal drug use in order to keep a clean image — and that cycle racing has become something of a scapegoat.

Clothes

If you have any uncertainty about the weather when you set off for a ride or a race, it's safer to dress warmly: modern fabrics make it easy to stuff surplus clothes into your back pocket if you start feeling hot. A light rainjacket, for example, will keep out wind but be no trouble to you if you don't need it. When the weather is not quite cool enough for tights or long sleeves, rubbing on a layer of liniment

* CO-AUTHOR Tim Noakes argues that pill-taking among healthy people who have access to good diets is unnecessary, and that it encourages a potentially risky dependence on 'medical props'. He adds that there is no evidence that amino acid supplements are necessary or that they aid performance. The cheapest and most effective way of taking amino acids is in the form of quality protein foods such as fish, eggs, meat and dairy produce.

will help to protect you. One of the best ways of insulating your front from cold air at the start of a ride is to stuff some layers of newspaper inside your jersey; this method is not only free, but disposable.

Always wear a vest or T-shirt under your cycling jersey. This will absorb sweat and regulate temperature, and give you an extra skin if you should fall.

For the cooler seasons of the year, I recommend getting an all-over thermal suit. This will keep you warm without making you overheat, and it isn't bulky. For time trials, kermesses, track races and short road races, a one-piece skinsuit is comfortable and aerodynamic. Unfortunately these lack pockets.

Make sure your cycling pants fit snugly, and wear braces if necessary to keep the chamois against the crotch to minimize any chance of being chafed. Bib suits are an alternative to braces.

Methods of training

All good training programmes include a variety of training activities which you should be familiar with in order to devise a good training schedule.

General formula for a training programme.

Long, steady distances (LSD)

Training over long distances at an easy sub-race pace is an excellent foundation for the racing season because it improves aerobic performance and 'puts miles in your legs'. Distances covered should be longer than the event you are training for. A typical LSD distance for a road cyclist would be 125 kilometres in a training session. The heart pumps at around 70 to 75 per cent of the maximal, and time is unimportant.

Continuous fast training

The pace is faster than in LSD training. Distances are not as long, but should be longer than typical race distances. This form of work-out increases endurance and gradually conditions the body to withstand race pace. Doing 'Sunday rides' in a big group of racers is a good way of getting in this type of training; the pace is continuously fast with riders sharing the work by riding in one anothers' slipstreams. This type of training also instils race rhythm and improves bunch riding.

Intervals

Interval training involves a series of hard efforts over a given distance with a controlled number of rest periods which allow for partial recovery. An example of an interval work-out is twenty-five 750-metre intervals broken up by 30-second rests; the intervals would be at a pace that would bring the heart rate up to about 85 to 90 per cent of maximum.

Fast interval training involves a harder pace with longer recovery intervals. An example is twenty 750- to 1 000-metre intervals with two-minute rest intervals. The heart rate should be about 90 to 95 per cent of maximum. Fast interval training helps to prevent fatigue when you are short of oxygen.

Slow interval training increases endurance, but doesn't contribute much to speed. Set distances are ridden slower than race pace with short recovery periods.

To avoid overtraining, young and unfit riders should make sure that the heart rate returns to below 60 per cent of MHR before starting the next interval. Don't overdo it, and never do more than two hard interval work-outs a week.

Both forms of interval training, especially the slow variety, also develop the aerobic capacities needed for longer time trial events.

Repetition riding

Set distances of 2 to 4 kilometres are ridden at fast speed, close to race pace, with rest periods long enough to allow almost complete recovery. The longer the distance, the slower the cyclist rides.

Sprint training

In sprint training you repeat short sprints. This means riding at maximum speed, an all-out effort for 75 to 100 metres, then having a relatively long rest period to ensure full recovery.

Acceleration sprints

Acceleration sprinting involves a gradual increase from a slow, steady pace to an all-out effort. The distance of the sprint should be 200 to 250 metres, split in roughly equal parts between easy effort, medium to hard effort and all-out effort. Enough of this training will increase both your speed and endurance.

Acceleration sprints are a useful exercise in cold weather, because the gradual increase in speed diminishes the risk of muscle injury. Again, rest periods must allow complete recovery.

Set sprints

A set of sprints, followed by a decent rest period, will develop speed and endurance. A typical example is:

- sprint for 75 metres
- ride at medium pace for 75 metres
- sprint for 75 metres
- cycle very slowly for 75 metres
- sprint for 100 metres
- medium pace for 100 metres
- sprint for 100 metres
- cycle very slowly for 100 metres
- sprint for 150 metres
- medium pace for 150 metres
- sprint for 150 metres
- rest and recover

Repeat the programme when you are fully recovered. This training develops the capacity to withstand acid build-ups in the muscles and is a good foundation for demanding events like the Madison, the Devil and points racing.

Speed play or fartlek

Fartlek is a Swedish term meaning 'speed play'. This form of training is often used in running. In cycling it means riding longish distances — on track or on road — at a variety of speeds. When done correctly, it develops all-round ability.

The essence of fartlek is play. A typical fartlek programme involves all the previously mentioned kinds of training, in an informal but competitive atmosphere. If it is done properly, this training is psychologically stimulating and fun, so that the work done is almost unnoticed. It is particularly useful for older riders, especially when there is the problem of apathy towards training. Many professionals favour fartlek over the more rigid and dedicated regimens. The fast/slow pace is well suited to training for middle to long distance riding (60 to 100 kilometres).

Strength training

I must issue a warning before describing this training: unless you are well conditioned to cycling, strength training in high gears can be dangerous to the joints, especially the knees; it would be foolish for novices, young riders or anyone who knows he or she is prone to knee injury to do it.

Cycling is essentially an aerobic sport, but sometimes during races you need to call upon strength reserves, for instance, when sprinting up a steep hill or when riding a one-kilometre prologue time trial. The method of developing strength is simple. Go out and find a long, gradual hill of about 5 kilometres and use a big gear of, say, 53 x 14 where the maximum cadence possible is about 35 rpm. The total time of each effort should be about 15 minutes, with a rest period of the same length. Three to four such sessions at a time are enough, and don't do this training more than once a week.

You should warm up thoroughly first, and remember that strength training needs longish recovery periods of up to two days. If you have any doubt about whether to do strength training or not — don't; if things go wrong, the consequences may be serious enough to keep you off your bike for a very long time.

Motor pacing

This is a form of speed training when the cyclist rides behind a sheltering vehicle such as a motor cycle, scooter or car. The reduced air drag enables you to ride much faster than racing pace, and sharpens speed skills. Many professionals train behind a motor bike when they are aiming to reach peak fitness.

There is no point in pacing behind a vehicle larger than a car because the effect created tends to be artificial in racing terms and training effects are reduced. And it is not advisable to motor pace more than twice a week as this is a high intensity work-out.

Be warned: motor pacing is dangerous. Both the cyclist and driver have to be pretty experienced. Another cyclist is usually the best person to drive the motor vehicle.

Indoor training

Training on rollers, wind-trainers or stationary cycles is an option when the weather is lousy. Rollers develop the ability to spin (pedal at high cadence) as the friction on them is less than on the road. They can be used as a warm-up device, especially for track events, and can also be used to loosen up or warm down after a hard race or training.

On wind-trainers the load can be altered to simulate road conditions and wind resistance. They also provide some cooling.

The main disadvantage of using these devices is that the scenery will probably numb you with boredom. They are usually used indoors and cause rivers of sweat. Stationary bikes offer a limited range of positions and can cause aches and pains.

Supplementary training routines

You can improve cycling performance through such activities as circuit training, stretching exercises, weight training, mountain biking and swimming. An all-round, well-conditioned cyclist will usually outperform the 'pure' cyclist, provided that mileage on the road is not sacrificed for supplementary routines. In supplementary training, concentrate on strengthening the muscle groups used in cycling: the triceps, deltoids, back muscles, abdominals, gluteus maximus and all leg muscles.

The activities described here can be done all the year round to supplement riding on the road, and during the off-season they will help maintain strength, suppleness and a degree of fitness.

Stretching exercises

Stretching exercises increase suppleness all over the body, preventing specific cycling problems that arise from the cycling position, such as stiff and round shoulders. Suppleness allows more freedom of movement, which is useful in all types of riding, especially in high intensity efforts. It also helps to prevent injuries from falls or sudden movements. And stretching stimulates the circulation, which helps the recovery process. Try to include stretching exercises in a daily routine.

Stretching exercises

These exercises are excellent for maintaining the supple body you need for cycle racing. Try to do four or five of the exercises shown here a day, and aim to work through all of them twice in a week. The exercises are meant to be done slowly and gently — don't push your body to the point of pain. Hold each stretch for about 30 seconds and do each exercise about five times.

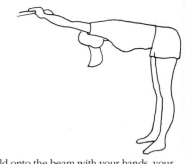

Hold onto the beam with your hands, your feet slightly apart. Keeping your legs and arms straight, bend forward as far as you are able. This will stretch your calf muscles.

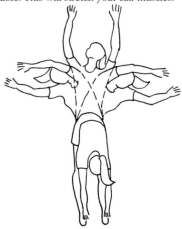

Lift your right leg (not too high) up in front of you onto a beam. Keep your left leg straight and your left foot at right angles to the beam. Slowly bend toward your raised leg, getting your body as close to the leg as you can. Feel the muscles stretching at the back of your raised leg. Repeat with your other leg.

Lift your right leg onto a beam, at a right angle to your body. Your left foot should be parallel to the beam. Slowly bend sideways towards your raised leg. Repeat with your other leg. This will stretch the muscles in the inner side of your raised leg.

Stand with your arms stretched above your head and your feet slightly apart. Bend to the left (as far as you can go); bend to the front and touch your toes; bend to the right (as far as you can go); straighten.

Sit on the floor. Put the soles of your feet together. Hold your feet together with your hands and pull yourself forward, stretching your back and groin muscles.

Rest your forearms against a wall, with your left leg stretched out behind you and your right leg slightly bent in front of you. Push your hips towards the wall. You should feel the calf muscles in your straight leg stretching. Repeat with your other leg.

Sit on the floor with your legs spread wide apart. Bend forward slowly from the hips as far as you can, until you can feel the muscles in your thighs stretching.

Squat with your right leg bent (foot flat on the floor, directly below your knee) and your left leg stretched behind you, with left knee resting on the floor. Lean forward as far as you are able. Feel your hamstrings and groin muscles stretching. Repeat with other leg.

Sit with your legs outstretched in front of you. Bending your knee, bring your left leg over your right leg (with your left foot on the floor on the right side of your right knee). With your left hand on the floor behind you, twist your upper body towards your left arm. This will stretch the muscles of your back and buttocks. Repeat on the other side.

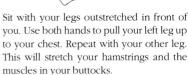

Lie with your shoulders flat on the floor, arms outstretched. Bend your left knee and bring it across your body. Put your right hand above your bent knee and pull your thigh down to the floor. Your face should be turned towards your outstretched left arm throughout. Feel the muscles stretching in your back and thigh.

Lie face down on the floor, arms stretched out above your head. Lift your left leg up behind you as high as you can, and hold it there with your left hand. Repeat on the other side.

Sit with your legs outstretched in front of you. Use both hands to pull your left leg up to your chest. Repeat with your other leg. This will stretch your hamstrings and the muscles in your buttocks.

Sit on the floor with your legs spread wide apart. Keeping your back straight, turn your upper body to face your left leg and bend forward from the hips to clasp your left foot with your hands. This will stretch your hamstrings and the muscles in the sides of your back. Repeat on the other side.

Sit with your left leg stretched out in front of you and your right leg bent (knee pointing outward and sole of foot against left thigh). Bend forward from the hips and clasp your left foot in your hands. Feel your hamstrings stretching. Repeat on the other side.

Sit with your right leg stretched out in front of you and your left leg pulled up behind you. Lean back slowly, keeping the back straight. This will stretch your quadriceps. Repeat on the other side.

Stretching hints:
- Warm up with callisthenic exercises or a quick activity such as skipping.
- Hold each stretch for thirty seconds: stretching should be a controlled, sustained exercise with no jerky bouncing.
- Stretching exercises must be progressive, but never stretch to the point of pain, only to a feeling of tightness.

Circuit training

Circuit training includes a variety of exercises — some using gym equipment — designed to improve muscle strength and tone. These exercises help to improve your power-to-weight ratio, and they help you to climb and sprint better as your upper body muscles become stronger. They also help to improve neuromuscular co-ordination.

Ideally, circuit training should be done in a well-equipped gym under the guidance of a trained instructor. If you can't get to a gym, free-standing exercises can be done at home.

Circuit training tips:
- Always warm up and warm down; this can be done on a bicycle or stationary bike.
- Try to do an hour of circuit training three or four times a week; the hour includes time taken to warm up and warm down.
- Expect some pain and stiffness after your first few work-outs.
- Go for high repetition and light weights.

Swimming

Swimming is one of the most holistic athletic activities known. It conditions all muscle groups. Try to incorporate two swimming sessions in your weekly programme — possibly after your circuit training. Five hundred metres per session is ample.

Mountain biking

Mountain biking — especially when it is off-road — is an ideal supplementary activity. It improves handling abilities as well as overall fitness, and gives you a refreshing break from the drudgery that can creep into ordinary training. Try mountain biking on your rest day.

Weight training

This should only be done with the guidance of a qualified instructor. Weights are used to strengthen specific muscle groups; the ones to concentrate on in cycling are shown in the diagram.

Progress should be gradual — your first few sessions should use lighter weights to allow muscles to adapt and to develop the correct lifting techniques. Don't do weight training during the racing season as it takes a long time to recover from it.

Circuit training — free-standing exercises

Stand with your hands on your hips and your feet slightly apart. Bend knees until you are squatting. Leap into the air, throwing your arms and legs out. Resume a squatting position.

From a press-up position (arms straight), jump forward so that your knees are between your outstretched arms. Jump back to your original position.

With hands on hips, step up onto a 40 centimetre step, right leg first; stand still for a moment, and then step down, right leg first. Repeat, with your left leg first. Your pace should be rhythmic.

Lie face down with your arms at your side. While stretching your arms straight behind you, lift your chest and legs off the ground.

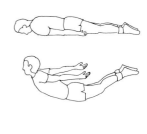

Circuit training in a gym

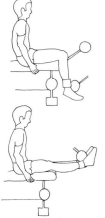

Leg extension: with one or both legs

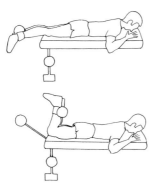

Back extension: with one or both legs

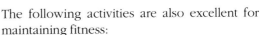
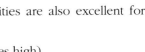

Back hyperextension

Bent-arm pull-over

Chin-ups: with front or reverse grip

The following activities are also excellent for maintaining fitness:

- Skipping (lift knees high).
- Sit-ups (put your hands behind your head and get someone to hold your feet down).
- Running (do stretching exercises beforehand, start gently and wear the correct shoes).
- Rowing.
- Swimming (good all round exercise).
- Ball games (develop strength and co-ordination, but avoid contact games).

Weight training

Power clean
Strengthens back, shoulders and legs.
1. From a squat position lift the bar to thigh height and then to a high chest position, flipping it back into your hands.
2. Flip the bar forward again and, keeping it close to the chest, lower it to the ground (squat position).
3. The whole movement should be fast, smooth and continuous.

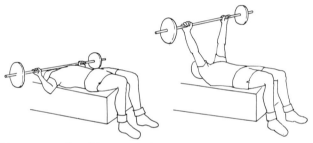

Bench press
Strengthens upper arms, shoulders and chest
1. Lie on a bench with your feet flat on the floor.
2. Get a helper to hand you the bar. Clasp it with arms straight and knuckles facing you.
3. Lower the bar until it almost touches your chest. Breathe in. For safety's sake, don't hold it above your throat.
4. Breathe out as you push the bar upward again.

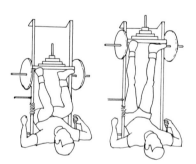

Leg press
Strengthens thighs and hips
1. Lie on a mat under the leg press and hold onto the uprights.
2. Bend your knees until your feet are flat on the underside of the press.
3. Breathe in as you straighten your legs.
4. Breathe out as you lower the weight. Repeat.

Press behind neck
Strengthens shoulders, upper back and arms, and sides
1. With your hands wide apart, palms facing forward, lift the bar from thigh height to chest height.
2. Push the bar upwards, extending your arms, and lower it carefully to behind your head until it rests on your shoulders.
3. Press the bar up to extend arms fully once again and then lower the bar to the starting position.

Half squats
Strengthens thighs, calves and buttocks
1. With your arms and feet wide apart, lift the bar onto your shoulders (as you did in the 'press behind the neck' exercise).
2. Keeping your back straight and your heels on the ground, bend your knees until you are halfway between standing and sitting.
3. Straighten up again.

Safety rules

Weight training can be dangerous so keep the following rules in mind:

- Ask a qualified person to supervise your first few sessions.
- Be sensible: don't compete with someone else, but progress at your own pace.
- Always spend at least 10 minutes warming up (for example, stretching exercises or skipping).
- Make sure that the collars that hold the weights in place are secure.
- A weight that cannot be lifted fairly easily is too heavy for you and could cause injury.
- Co-opt a helper or use squat stands when lifting heavy weights.
- Wear firm shoes rather than 'takkies', and make sure that the floor surface is non-slip and free of any hazard.
- Wear sensible clothing (tracksuit or T-shirt); loose flapping clothing can be dangerous.
- If you have excessive pain or any swelling of the joints, cut down on weight training and work up again more gradually.

Typical weight training programme:

- Start by warming up to the point of sweating with skipping, stretching, cycling and free-standing exercises.
- Do three sets of twelve repetitions per exercise. (I do 3 x 12 each of leg presses, leg extensions, leg curls, seated calf raises and half squats with straight back, with two-minute rests between sets.) The weight used should allow the last repetition to be just manageable. This will usually mean that you are using 65 per cent of your maximum lift.
- This should be followed by 3 x 15 squat jumps from a three-quarter squat position. Jump as high as you can; this develops explosive power.
- Warm down by stretching.
- Try to do two or three work-outs per week, each lasting an hour, including warm-up time.

Massage

This is not exactly a form of supplementary training — but it can be a valuable adjunct to training. A thorough massage — ideally, two or three times a week when you are racing — will help to relax you, get the circulation going and rid the muscles of toxins.

A good time for a massage is about two or three hours after a race or high intensity training session.

A pre-event massage should take the form of a light rub to relax the nervous athlete. Rubbing on a warming ointment such as one containing wintergreen oil, and giving a vigorous slapping will help to get the blood in the legs to circulate and give a passive warm-up. If the weather is cold, rub on a thick liniment which will help to keep the legs warm and act as a water repellent. (Note that you shouldn't apply any oil-based embrocation in hot weather as it will stop sweat from evaporating.)

Off-season training

In the June/July off-season you should incorporate other types of training into your yearly programme, but don't neglect your cycling. Try to cycle at least five times a week to keep fit. As you won't be racing, concentrate on supplementary programmes and try, if possible, not to put on too much weight. Keep below 12 per cent body fat.

Principles of setting up a programme

Do what is good for you as an *individual*. Don't be influenced by the comments and training routines of others. Treat the training programmes in this chapter merely as guidelines. They are designed for the ambitious racing cyclist, and can be scaled down to suit your needs and the time you have available. Set realistic goals for yourself. Begin by asking yourself a few basic questions:

1. *How much time can I devote to cycling?*
Can you spend six hours a day on your bike, or six hours a week? The answer has important implications for your goals. If you have a busy job or family commitments you will probably not make it to the Tour de France and will have to scale down your dreams, perhaps to a three-hour Argus Tour. Or a four-hour Argus Tour. It doesn't matter. The important thing is to get your priorities right and to feel great when you achieve your goal.

2. *What type of athlete am I?*
Are you physiologically more suited to long distance, aerobic-based events, or to the anaerobic demands of sprinting, or are you a middle of the road athlete? You can find out what type of muscle fibre you have — and therefore what type of athlete you are — by having a muscle biopsy done. In practice, most people find out through practical experience. (There is more about this in Chapter 10.) In competition you soon find out if your body favours stamina or speed. Once you know your relative strengths, you can specialize and concentrate on your strengths.

3. *What races should I go for?*
Do your short-term objectives lead to greater medium- and long-term goals? Are victories in minor events important or are they unnecessary for reaching your ultimate goal?

A young rider's short-term goal should be to learn basic technique in cycling, which is a vitally important foundation for adult racing, and not to win every race.

The importance of rest and recovery

In training, the body needs time to recover and repair muscle damage. Always follow a high-intensity training session with a rest day. Rest days need not be inactive: they can include light training or a diversion like mountain biking. Such 'active rest' is more beneficial than complete rest, because stimulating the circulation helps repair muscle damage more quickly.

Full recovery after hard training requires about forty-eight hours of rest. So for two days prior to an important race, you shouldn't train hard. You may find it beneficial to have a light ride on the day before a race. Experience will teach you what is best for you.

Since cycling is nothing like as traumatic to the tissues as long-distance running, recovery doesn't take as long as it does in runners. Also, in cyclists, muscle glycogen reserves are not depleted in the way that they are in runners; on the easier downhill sections, for example, cyclists have a chance to replenish their fuel stores as they go. Thanks to this, cyclists can compete in long stage races and cover distances of 200 kilometres a day for two or three weeks; by comparison, a runner in the Comrades marathon would need days to recover enough to do even a fairly minor run.

Developing spin or cadence

At the start of a training programme, use small gears and maintain a high cadence to develop good pedalling technique. Try to maintain about 100 revolutions per minute (rpm) in long, steady distance training sessions. As you get fitter, you can use bigger gears.

In preparing for a race you should always use cadences that are comfortable. An efficient road cadence is 85 to 95 rpm, and when climbing hills, this should drop to between 65 and 70 rpm.

In track sessions, concentrate on higher cadences. A cadence above 110 rpm develops the necessary leg speed needed for short, fast events.

(Cadence is covered more fully in the next chapter.)

Distance and intensity

The distances you ride in training should be proportional to the events you are training for. In pre-season LSD training you should ride distances that are longer than actual races, at 65 to 75 per cent of your maximal heart rate (MHR). As the racing season gets closer, cut the distances down and increase intensity. Road cyclists should cover an actual race distance at least once a week during mid-season training.

Six weeks of LSD is enough to provide a solid foundation, and mid-season training fine-tunes fitness with high intensity work-outs. During racing you will find out what your weaknesses are and will be able to judge whether you should concentrate on longer distances or higher intensities.

Training by racing

Preparation is important, but I believe that cyclists should also race as much as possible. Racing is in itself an excellent form of training and is the best way of finding out what weaknesses you may have. Racing also improves your tactics, which are vital for the big events. It also provides the essential race rhythm.

I regard myself as a lazy trainer and I use races and fun rides to get into condition.

Overtraining

You are overtrained when your body has been pushed beyond its limits in your efforts to raise its limits. When your body starts refusing to do what is asked of it, it is merely demanding time for recovery.

Overtraining is common but the symptoms are not always easy to recognize. Watch out for the following:

- Unusual increases in your pulse rate on waking or going to sleep.
- Sore legs and heavy breathing during cycling and other activities such as climbing stairs.
- Excessive thirst.
- Insomnia.
- Continual tiredness, listlessness and apathy, and poor appetite.

The treatment of overtraining is simple: rest until the symptoms disappear. But if the symptoms persist, see a doctor. You could be suffering from an infection or a lack of minerals, or there could be any of several other causes.

Often enthusiastic athletes are terrified to stop training and turn a blind eye to the symptoms of overtraining. But prevention is better than cure. Never embark on a training programme expecting immediate results — progress is usually slow.

Training for specific categories

Whatever category you are in, remember that your training programme should be based on this foundation: first you need to get basically fit with low intensity training to maximize aerobic output; then you can concentrate on anaerobics, speed and achieving your competitive peak.

Women: The only factor that stops women from performing as well as men athletically is biological: women have proportionally less muscle and more fat — between 12 and 16 per cent — and there are other differences, such as the number of red blood cells and the size of the lungs. But training principles are the same, though training distances may be scaled because race distances for women are shorter than they are for men.

Juniors: Young riders should train less intensely than older riders. I would recommend that adolescents scale down to about 75 per cent of the programmes outlined and that they leave out on-bike weight training. Younger riders seem to get into condition far more quickly than older riders do.

Veterans: Generally race distances are shorter, although veterans are a tough bunch. If there are to be any adaptations to the programme, training should be more speed orientated.

A racer's programme for the year

Start by looking at the calendar and deciding what events you want to win or do well in. With good planning you can reach peak performance twice a year. Peaking is an art itself: you need to rid yourself of as many distractions and hassles as possible so that top physical condition coincides with peace of mind and mental determination.

If you are planning your programme around the SACF racing calendar, it would be sensible to plan your year like this:

- First preparation period: December, January and February.
- First peak: March, April and May.
- Second preparation period: partly off-season — June, July and August.
- Second peak: September, October and November.

First preparation period

December and the first half of January should be a recovery period after the previous peak. Train and race casually, cycling about four times a week. Do circuit training.

From mid-January you should concentrate on losing unwanted weight, developing speed on the track and experimenting with new techniques.

A programme for February is suggested here:

- Monday: An active rest day.
- Tuesday: 25-kilometre warm up followed by a high intensity work-out such as Fartlek — two hours in total.
- Wednesday: 100 kilometres of long, steady distance (LSD).
- Thursday: A 30-kilometre warm-up followed by acceleration sprints — total time two hours.
- Friday: 60 kilometres of LSD at a high cadence.
- Saturday: 80 kilometres of LSD at a high cadence.
- Sunday: A 30-kilometre warm-up and then a race.

First peak

The main races in this half of the year are in this 12-week period. In March follow the same routine as in February, but consider including motor pacing during the last two weeks of the month to sharpen your speed. The fine-tuning begins now, so race more seriously and as often as you can to sharpen your competitive instincts.

An ideal training programme for April and May is given here:

- Monday: Active rest.
- Tuesday: Motor pacing and set sprints — total two hours; massage.
- Wednesday: 120 kilometres of LSD at a high cadence.
- Thursday: Motor pacing and sprint training — total two hours; massage.
- Friday: 40 kilometres of LSD and rest.
- Saturday: Race.
- Sunday: Race; massage.

A typical annual training programme

	JAN	FEB	MAR	APR	MAY	JUNE	JULY	AUG	SEPT	OCT	NOV	DEC	FREQUENCY
Stretching exercises													Daily
Circuit training													3 × per week
Swimming													2 × per week
Weight training													3 × per week June/July
Cycle training													Daily except June/July
Racing			IMPORTANT EVENTS					IMPORTANT EVENTS					As often as possible

Second preparation period

In June and July concentrate on LSD work-outs totalling about 400 kilometres a week and do weight training. In August, step the LSD up to 700 kilometres per week, shed unwanted weight and sharpen pedalling technique that may have become dull during weight training sessions.

Second peak

All the major tours are in the period September to November. Most top racers ride a tour almost every week at this time, so there is a danger of overtraining. Midweek training should be a maintenance programme without over-exertion as you will need time to recover, especially if you are travelling in addition to racing.

The first two weeks of September should include a sharpening of training methods. If you have access to a pacer, try long intervals behind a motor bike. In the last two weeks, do some strength training on your bike and a series of short uphill sprints. Race as often as possible.

In October and November race, rest, do maintenance training, race, rest and win, win, win.

Preparing for a tour

The physical demands on a tour cyclist are great. Because of this, the preparation period must be tailored accordingly. My suggestions are:

- Analyse the route of the tour at least three weeks before the start and focus your training on the specific demands of the event. If it's hilly, do climbing training and shed any grams of surplus weight you may be carrying.
- Have an intensive training week, starting two weeks before the tour.
- The week preceding the tour should consist mainly of LSD rest rides, giving the body time to recover to its full strength.

A three to three-and-a-half hour Star 100 or Argus Tour for working people

This training programme is for people who would like to do well in a ride such as the Star 100 or the Argus Cycle Tour, but whose jobs or other commitments make it impossible for them to follow the ideal training schedule set out in this chapter.

Almost any male with a modicum of natural ability, a reasonably good bike and some training should be able to do a 100-kilometre tour in three to three-and-a-half hours; females are blessed with less muscle, and for them, three-and-a-half to four hours is a more realistic time to go for. If you're over about fifty, it might be wise to allow yourself a bit more time. And whatever age you are, check that you are medically fit before you embark on a training programme.

Step 1: Let's assume you are new to cycling and unfit. Start out gently, with short rides. Avoid hills if you can; if you can't, make sure your bike is fitted with a low gear — for example, 42 teeth on your small front chainwheel, and 28 on your largest rear sprocket; ride up hills just fast enough to avoid getting off and walking. Do 1 000 kilometres like this, and use the time to make sure your bike is correctly adjusted for you. Get the feel of pedalling smoothly, and get your behind used to the saddle. Then, and only then, increase your efforts. Expect this stage to take three to five months.

Step 2: Build up to doing 300 kilometres a week by two months before the event. This should include one long ride — about 100 kilometres on Saturday or Sunday; if you ride 40 kilometres a day before or after work, or on the way to work during the week, you will be clocking up the required distance. Allow at least two, but preferably more, months for Step 2.

Step 3: Keep up your 300 kilometres a week, increasing the distance if you wish. Include about an hour of interval training each week; this should be preceded by a good warm-up. Add regular stretching exercises to your programme. Try to race in a fun ride every weekend, using these to practise the slipstreaming techniques described in Chapter 7 and the bunch riding techniques described in Chapter 14.

It'll help to be familiar with the training principles described in this chapter, even if you have to accept that they must be drastically modified to fit in with your lifestyle.

CHAPTER FOURTEEN

RACING TECHNIQUE
and
STRATEGY

*This chapter is about racing and winning. It is also for those who are not
serious about winning but who enjoy learning and using winners'
techniques and tactics simply to improve whatever level of competitive
riding they are at. Indeed, many of us are not out on our bikes for any
prize, but for the exhilaration of speed, the camaraderie in rivalry, the joy
of being fit and the exquisite exhaustion at the end of a hard-ridden race.*

Cycle racing is a tactical sport, a complex mixture of strength, skill, strategy and opportunism. It is not always the strongest rider who wins. If you want to race well rather than merely ride fast, you have to be able to analyse a race as you are riding it and be able to react effectively. This chapter discusses basic techniques for competing in informal as well as in serious racing, and it goes on to cover more sophisticated strategies.

One of the first things to understand about racing is that it is unpredictable. The way a race goes depends not only on the form you are in, but on the wind, the weather, your team mates, and the ability and even the mood of your opponents. Success depends very much on the way you cope with these and a host of other variables. The more versatile you are and the better you can adapt your techniques to suit different situations, the better you will do.

It takes strength, speed, alertness and skilful bike handling to hold the pace and hang in through the constant changes in a race. You need to know what your own strengths and weaknesses are when climbing, sprinting, time trialling or whatever, and be able to make full use of this knowledge during competition.

The demands are not only physical. Even more important than strength is knowing how to conserve energy, even if it means keeping behind an opponent, and knowing when to attack. The ability to read a race — to predict the moves of others — is also important: if you can do this, you will be tactically ahead of the competition and will have an advantage over those who merely follow the strategies of the bunch. Quick, independent thinkers often win races even when they are less fit or less strong than their less experienced competition.

Cyclists also have to cope with psychological stress: almost all racers know the what-the-hell-am-I-doing-here syndrome, and we have to brace ourselves against the powerful temptation to give up when the going gets really gruelling.

You will probably never be master (or mistress) of all the skills that successful racing demands. I know no one who is. In my experience, all cyclists have a chink in their armour. But the more experienced racers are, the better they are at disguising their weaknesses by bluffing or using countering tactics. Remember that nobody is unbeatable; one of the strategies of skilful racing is to look out for your opponents' weaknesses and use them to your advantage. And you can be sure that if you let your pedalling falter or if your expression betrays the fact that you are suffering, **your** opponents will attack.

The rest of this chapter discusses basic racing techniques and strategies in competition. The information in it will, I hope, save the novice cyclist a lot of time and effort wasted through mistakes. But it can't take the place of a personal coach, nor can it take the place of first-hand experience. And nor can it cater for every individual's needs. The methods described in this chapter have worked well for me, and I believe they would work well for most riders. But if they don't suit your style or your ambitions, you should feel free to adapt them to suit your own requirements.

Technique

The art of pedalling

A smooth, fluid, efficient pedalling action is absolutely vital to success. If you think about the distances a racer covers in training and competition and the fact that most of his or her riding is done at a rapid cadence, you will realize that the pedals are turned millions of times in a year and billions of times in a career. A minute amount of energy saved per revolution adds up significantly, and in racing it can mean the difference between victory and defeat. If you take a close look at the pedalling techniques of top riders you will notice that despite differences in style, their pedalling action is always efficient and unruffled.

Good pedalling action only develops through practice. And it usually requires conscious effort — checking and correcting — before it comes naturally.

Before you can concentrate on improving your pedalling you should make sure that your position on the bike is correct. This is essential if your leg muscles are to transmit maximum power to the pedals. Guidelines to correct position are given in Chapter 5. Minute adjustments to your position may have to be made to compensate for your particular bone length and musculature. If you are in any doubt about your position, try to get an experienced racer, preferably a coach, to monitor your riding over several days. And remember that most racers need to continue making minor adjustments to their riding positions from time to time as muscle, ligament and tendon configurations change gradually over the years.

While I am on the subject of position, it is worth mentioning that current opinion among some experts is that the riding position of most European racers (which is one that has long been accepted as being right) is too low. American engineers claim to have proved in laboratory tests that many European cyclists would benefit in terms of power output if their saddles were raised by 3 to 4 millimetres.

There are two main schools of thought regarding pedalling. One school favours the 'ankling' technique while the other favours what is called the 'toes down' method. My feeling is that you should use both methods as each has advantages in different situations.

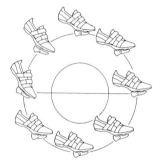

'Toes-down' method of pedalling.

Ankling: In theory, this method of pedalling entails dropping the heel below the level of the toes as it approaches the top of its revolution. The opposite foot is simultaneously pulling up with its toes pointed down. One foot is thus pointing down as the other is pointing up. The object is to get some 'push' into the upstroke, just before the 12 o'clock position, and to overcome the 'dead spot' when the cranks are in the vertical 6 o'clock position, when little or no power is transmitted to the pedals.

However, this theory has been challenged by researchers at Penn State University who claim (fairly convincingly) that this action is seldom perfected even by experienced cyclists. It **is** a difficult technique to perfect, as you have to co-ordinate the actions of the quadriceps muscles, which push the pedals down, with those of the hamstrings, which pull them up. However, these muscle groups are large and powerful, and through ankling they can be better used than in the 'toes down' method, which places more strain on the less powerful lower leg muscles, such as the soleus, tibialis anterior, and gastrocnemius.

Perhaps the best advice to give is that you should keep the objects of ankling (the push forwards at the top of the pedal stroke, and the push back at the bottom of the downstroke) in mind as you pedal.

Ankling is useful when the cadence is low, for example, during climbing.

'Ankling' method of pedalling.

The toes down method: The foot remains in an unchanged position relative to the pedal throughout each revolution — the toes always lower than the heel. This method is best used when your cadence is high and when you want speed.

When you start a training programme, favour low gears and concentrate on high cadence work. This applies especially to young riders, as they are particularly prone to injury if they pedal in low gears. Learning to spin the pedals is an essential part of developing speed, and the earlier you do it in your cycling career, the better. Some coaches even suggest that road cyclists train in a fixed gear in the early part of the season as this forces you to keep up a rapid pedalling action.

Though powerful riders have been known to get away with a rough style of pedalling, weaker riders can't: they, more than anyone, should remember that smooth pedalling is one of the skills that can help to make up for a lack of power.

Making the most of your gears

Intelligent gear selection is closely allied to efficient pedalling technique, and it is an equally important skill in racing. There is no hard and fast rule for choosing the right gear for the terrain. Your choice will depend partly on your pedalling style, the gradient, how tired you are, your strength, the wind and on whether you are riding alone or in a bunch. It is a subtle skill that comes mainly with experience, though the following guidelines should help you to master the technique fairly quickly:

- For most of your riding, choose comfortable gears which allow you a cadence of between 85 and 105 revolutions per minute (rpm) on flattish roads.
- Though some training at very high cadences is a valuable way of gaining suppleness and conditioning the muscles to speed, cadences of over 110 rpm are not efficient when you are actually trying to ride fast. So in races, keep below this.
- When approaching hills, drop to a smaller gear **before** you start climbing, and continue to change down as you climb higher. Try to keep your pedalling light at the beginning, and as you climb, shift into increasingly bigger gears. As you approach the summit, where the speed usually hots up, move into a larger gear for maximum power. On long hills, expect your cadence to drop to between between 60 and 75 rpm. Remember that higher cadences save your legs; the lower the gear you use, the less force you need and the less time your legs will need to recover.
- Keep your momentum up on a steep hill and resist the temptation to let up as you approach the summit.
- During long tours, using low gears will encourage fast recovery.
- When sprinting, ensure that your gear is properly engaged — a slip of a gear can lose a race.
- An indexed gear system (described in Chapter 3) is invaluable because it prevents unintended gear changes.
- Smaller gears and a high cadence are essential in races where the pace changes, such as in Madisons, kermesses and criteriums.

Braking

During racing, an experienced cyclist only uses brakes in emergencies as experience develops the ability to anticipate bunch movement. Remember that braking results in a loss of energy. If you **must** use your brakes, use both. Take stock of your speed before you get to corners so that you don't find yourself having to brake on them; the stresses of braking and cornering together can destabilize a bike and cause a crash.

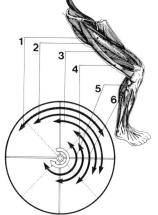

1 Rectus femoris

2 Gluteus maximus

3 Vastii

4 Hamstring

5 Gastrocnemius

6 Soleus

Sequence of leg muscles used in pedalling.

If you have to stop in a hurry, keep your weight well down over the back wheel to ensure that you are not pitched forward.

Descending hills

Downhill racing is an art in itself, requiring a combination of iron nerve and skilled technique. Here are guidelines for some basic downhill techniques:

- Try to keep your weight over the back wheel to prevent bouncing over rough patches in the road.
- Always approach corners from the outside to the inside and try to follow a good line. (See the next section, 'Cornering'.)
- Relax, but keep a good grip on the handlebars.
- Adopt a low, streamlined position.
- If you have to brake, use both brakes, though it is preferable to slow down by sitting up slightly and using your body as a windbreak.
- Take note of traffic signs which might indicate hairpin bends, sharp corners or potholes.

- Wet roads can make descents very tricky — be careful.
- Watch out for stones or glass as a downhill puncture is a frightening experience.

A final word of advice: don't risk too much on descents when there is nothing to gain by, for example, leading the pack downhill. Rather relax and merely try to stay with the group. But, if you have broken away on your own and the finish line is near the bottom of a mountain pass, go for it and descend at your maximum speed. Remember too that an individual cyclist will descend a mountain pass with tricky corners faster than a bunch of cyclists, who will be slowed down by caution.

Cornering

Fast cornering can give you a valuable edge over your rivals, especially in races such as kermesses. Try the following techniques:

- Follow the straightest line possible through the corner, using if you can, the full width of the road. Being able to follow your own line usually means having to be in the lead or second position (unless, of course, you have dropped right off at the back).
- Lean your body to steer the bike and don't turn the handlebars.
- Learn the limits to how far your bike can lean. Know when you can pedal through a corner without your pedal striking the road, and when you can't. If your pedal does knock the road, it is likely to destabilize you; this is one of the most common causes of crashes in races.
- Stay away from painted road lines, which are usually very slippery.

Technique of cornering. Notice how the riders lean into the corner.

- Place your weight in the centre of the bike for good balance.
- Always check that your tubulars are well glued on before a race. If you have a puncture during a race and have to replace your tubular, remember it may not be secure enough for you to risk fast cornering.

Hill climbing

Hill climbing techniques vary, depending on the style and abilities of the cyclist. You should develop your own strong points. There are two commonly used climbing styles: In the first, you hold a steady pace to the top — a style that I prefer as I am less strong on hills, and tend to suffer on them. This style suits the smooth pedaller. The second method is to attack in spurts. This method is used by specialist climbers. They dictate the pace and force the weaker climbers to react in the hope that they will crack.

Here are some tips for hill climbing:

- Try to ride a climb at the front of the bunch. This is especially important if you are unsure of your climbing strengths. Unlike the leader of the bunch on flat roads, you will not be bearing the brunt of any great wind resistance. Your position at the front will hopefully secure you against being dropped off the back later, should your pace slow down; at the worst, you may find yourself dropping to the back of the bunch — which is a lot better than being dropped off it entirely.
- Concentrate on smooth pedalling. Any roughness will result in loss of momentum, which is the last thing you can afford on a hill.
- Control your pace so that you don't burn yourself out or blow. Slowing your pace down ultimately loses you far less time than it takes to recover from blowing.
- As climbing is slow, wind resistance diminishes as a factor, so you are free to choose a comfortable riding position rather than an aerodynamic one. In other words, sit more upright on the bike and enjoy the chance it gives you to breathe easily.
- Good climbers have strong shoulders, arms and abdominal muscles, especially if they spend a lot of time riding out of the saddle and pulling on their handlebars. It helps to develop these muscles through exercises off the bike.
- Try climbing when you are seated and when you are out of the saddle. One of these styles may suit you better than the other, and if so, you should train for it. However, you are more likely to use both styles, partly because the changes in position give welcome breaks.
- Get into a good rhythm with smooth pedalling and deep, controlled breathing. This helps to keep you going longer.

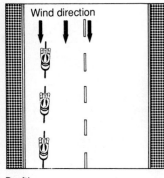

Drafting

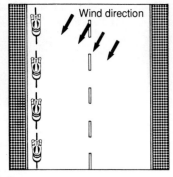

Gutter grovelling

■ Finally, try, if you can, to attack positively on hills. This often scares the opposition into passivity.

Riding in a bunch: techniques and tactics

Cycle racing is a strange balance of rivalry and mutual dependence. For the greater part of a race, riders keep in packs, co-operating with each other in temporary alliances. A loose (and often abused) code of etiquette demands that each rider takes his or her turn to ride in the front of the bunch to break the main force of wind resistance and to shelter those behind. Success in racing depends very much on how well you use bunch tactics to your advantage, to conserve energy until the critical moments of breakaway, attack or sprint.

As Chapter 9 (which covers aerodynamics) points out, when you ride in the slipstream of other cyclists you are often using about 25 per cent less energy than the riders in front, yet you are travelling at the same speed. This tactic enables bunches of riders to travel at far higher speeds than those attainable by a lone rider.

The following section gives guidelines to slipstreaming tactics and discusses typical situations that you are likely to come across when riding in a pack.

Positioning within a bunch

The direction of the prevailing wind determines where you will get the maximum benefit from riding in the slipstream of the riders ahead. The diagrams on this page show what the best positions are in relation to wind direction.

Drafting or pacing: In its simplest form, drafting (the system in which riders take turns to be in the front of a group, sheltering those behind) involves a line of cyclists riding into a head wind. This line is called a pace line. In an efficient pace line, each rider has a short spell at the front and then drifts back to the end of the line, gradually moving up it in a rotation system until it is his or her turn to take the lead again. A bunch of riders follows the same principles, but for obvious reasons the procedure is less simple.

Echelons: An echelon is a staggered pace line, angled into the wind. Its purpose is to protect riders against cross-winds, as opposed to head winds. Riders have to be spread across much of the road for it to work. If you are training on public roads, there is an obvious danger of being wiped out, and the technique has to be used with discretion. Riding in a tight echelon can be nerve-racking and dangerous; it demands concentration, alertness and skill.

The better your position in the bunch or the echelon, the more sheltered you will be and the more energy you will conserve. And the closer you keep to the rider in front — a tactic known as wheel-sitting — the greater the benefit of riding in your opponents' or team members' slipstreams will be.

However, there is more to positioning than simply taking shelter. If, for example, you want to break away from a wheel-sitter or a bunch, you have to find a position which hinders your opponents' attempts to cling to you. One way of preventing wheel-sitting is by riding close to the road edge; this is known as 'gutter-grovelling'. You should also try to get a feel for how well the bunch is co-operating: if apathy, team tactics or plain politicking is preventing the bunch from working well together, it will make it easier for an alert rider to break away.

Typical bunch formation

A bunch usually takes this shape: The workers are in front while the majority of the bunch, who have chosen not to work, ride behind; at the back of the bunch are the stragglers and the hangers-on.

The advantages to *being among the workers* are firstly, that you can join a breakaway group without being boxed in by slower or reluctant riders; and secondly, you are in a better position to anticipate attacks by opponents and you have a far better view of the terrain ahead. The disadvantage, of course, is that you are using up energy.

In the *middle of the bunch* you can cruise along easily. But in amongst the masses manoeuvrability is limited, you can become stuck in a position, and it is here that most falls occur.

The *rearguard* are in the worst position. These riders get caught in the concertina effect of acceleration and deceleration and have to constantly adjust to the pace dictated by others. Usually the riders at the back are the weakest and they have to use up most of their energy closing the gaps that open up when the pace hots up. When this happens they have no advantage of group protection.

It is obvious that the best place to be in a road race is within the working group. But, you have to make a contribution. Be careful not to overwork.

Typical bunch scenarios

- An echelon forms in front of a following bunch. The riders who are excluded from it receive no shelter and get blown off.

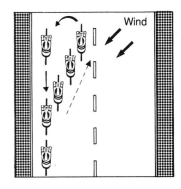

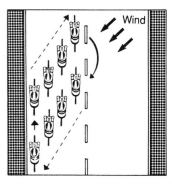

A single echelon (top) and a double echelon (bottom). The arrows show the rotation followed by the riders. Riders in an echelon are not only sheltering from a side wind, but also from the effect of a head wind that is created by their own speed.

Racing jargon

blowing: overdoing effort and then being forced to slow down by lactic acid build-up and by depletion of energy

breakaway: a break by one or more cyclists who leave the main bunch and get ahead

bunch: group of cyclists who bunch together to shelter from wind

dead-wheel: the rider in front slows down to slow the pace of a following rival

drifting: slow movement to the side

echelon: a line of cyclists, staggered diagonally to shelter from cross-wind

gate-closer: a rider who closes an echelon from behind

gutter-grovelling: riding on the side of the road to prevent wheel-sitting

jump: accelerate powerfully in short bursts

yellow jersey: the leader in a tour (after each stage)

lead-out: a team bunches around a sprinter to provide protection, and shepherds him to a good position for sprinting to the finish

presenting a tricky wheel: riding unpredictably to shake off a wheel-sitter

prime: (pronounced 'preem') a minor race within a bigger race; some races have what are called 'hot spots' along the route, and reaching them first carries a prize or helps you accumulate points

switching: leaving a gap alongside you that is just big enough to tempt a following rider to squeeze his wheel in, and then you close it to cut him off

wheel-sitting: riding very closely to the cyclist in front of you

It is difficult to force yourself into an established echelon, as the rotating riders will block you out. The only way to get in is by sprinting to the front and taking your place in the lead.

Often there is also a rider who closes the echelon from behind, preventing others from getting in. This 'gate-closer' does not have to pace, but allows the riders in the echelon who are drifting back to rejoin the forward-riding queue.

- In a cross-wind, one rider may attack and ride in a position that makes it impossible for those behind to find shelter in the slipstream. Those immediately behind will be strung out along the road edge, all taking the wind.

- A group of about six riders forms a tight echelon, splits the main bunch and breaks away. The right response from riders who are not in the front bunch is to form another one. But usually the initiative taken by the first group causes confusion and it is often difficult for the second group to get their act together quickly.

- Some riders in the group try to take advantage of the slipstream without doing their share of the work. This can result in an overall slowing down of the race if the working riders are unhappy about carrying shirkers to the line.

- A rider in the working line of an echelon can deliberately slow it down for tactical reasons by cutting back on his pace. It is usually considered unsporting to interfere with a working echelon, and this may make other riders frustrated and even aggressive. But on the other hand, racing is about winning, and spoiling tactics are part of the game.

Breakaways

Once a working group breaks away from the main bunch, it is very difficult for those behind to catch up, even though they may be equally strong and fit. Try to develop an instinct for predicting breakaways. Some tips are:

- Note where all the top riders are positioned. If you see them moving up to the front of the working group, follow them.
- If there is a hill ahead, try to move to the front. As I've already mentioned, there is far less wind resistance at slower, uphill speeds than there is on the flat; being in front will cost you little or no extra effort, and you will be in a good position once you are over the summit.
- It is often a good idea to move towards the front before a prime, even if you are more interested in winning the later part of the race than the prime itself. Commonly, breakaways follow immediately after a prime when riders who have not contested it, attack.
- When there are cross-winds, keep as near to the front as you can; the better riders are likely to form an echelon which will be difficult to get into unless you are in a good position when they break away. Riders in an ordinary bunch will not be as well sheltered as those in the echelon.

Going for victory: sprinting out of a bunch

It is in the last few kilometres that the real drama of the race, the sprint for the finish, starts.

Your ability to sprint depends on the proportion of fast-twitch fibres in your muscles, your training, your determination, your position in a race and your tactical know-how.

In planning a sprint in a road race, a good rule of thumb is to aim to be in the top ten about 5 kilometres from the finish. In the last kilometre, try to move to the top five. At the 400-metre mark, the third position is a good place to be in. When you do make your move for the line on the last stretch, give it 100 per cent of the power in your leg muscles and pull hard on the handlebars.

To make sure your speed doesn't tail off, sprint for a point beyond the real finish line. And remember that races can be won by 'throwing' the bike forward at the very last moment.

In order to get into a position that makes a good sprint possible, it is essential to avoid being boxed in by others. This is easier said than done because, to save the energy that a sprint demands, you should keep out of the wind until the critical moment when you put all you have got into a surge for the finish.

Dictating the sprint: a winner's tactic

The timing of a sprint is usually dictated by the best sprinters in the bunch. A sprinter who can get away and stay away from the following riders will benefit from a long sprint. A sprinter with a powerful jump — in other words, someone whose strength lies in brief bursts of acceleration — will usually try to keep the sprint as short as possible by blocking any breakaway by other riders.

The dreaded wheel-sitter

In sprinting you are often faced with something of a paradox. On the one hand you want maximum efficiency. So it makes sense to follow as direct a line as

Sprinting for the line.

possible to the finish, with no effort wasted by careening about the road. But on the other hand, you may have a wheel-sitter hanging in behind you, plotting to overtake you just before the finish line. Getting rid of the wheel-sitter may force you to take a very indirect line. Try surprising him or her with a tricky wheel; in other words, vary your pace unpredictably, or move sideways or into small gaps ahead to try and shake the parasite off.

Sometimes you can con your opposition into a move that forces them into a box. One way of doing this is by leaving a gap that is just big enough for a bike to fit into and then closing it when your opponent takes the bait. This is called 'closing the door'. Violent switching (swerving from side to side) is cause for disqualification but a gentle 'drifting' is legitimate.

A final word of advice on sprinting: anything can happen in the last metre. Never sit up or ease off until the line is crossed. And never give a victory salute until you actually cross the line. Too many big races have been lost by sprinters throwing up their hands in celebration, only to be passed in the last few centimetres.

A summary of tips for the individual cyclist

Much of what has been covered so far concerns the rider on his or her own in a race. The advice assumes that you have the strength and the fitness to make choices in the all-important matter of positioning yourself well. I'll briefly recap what I see as tactical priorities in individual racing:

- Riding in a bunch is what racing is all about. Positioning yourself intelligently in the group conserves vital energy and allows you to capitalize on the errors of others. A good idea for a novice is to tag onto an experienced rider to learn how to manoeuvre in the bunch and not be caught unawares by a breakaway.
- Try to cultivate an instinct for the way others are planning to ride the race. Observe what they are doing, and plan a strategy that fits in with that.
- Learn to work in an echelon and to force your way into working groups.

Team tactics

As slipstreaming, echelon riding and pacing play such crucial roles in cycling, it follows that riders can team up to help each other. A formal team organizes its tactics so that one of its members can win. But, of course, cycling is unpredictable: whatever tactics are used or strategies planned, spontaneous decisions often have to be made during the race. For instance, the team leader may be having a bad day or may be caught at the back of the bunch when a breakaway occurs; a decision may have to be taken for another member of the team to take the leading position and try to win.

Team members are expected to defend their leader to the utmost, sheltering him, particularly in cross-winds, and even carrying his food to save him effort. Leaders are under constant threat and have to be able to respond with all they've got when necessary.

Once a rider in a tour has established a lead, the team usually protects him almost all the way to victory. This may make it seem easy for the rider in the yellow jersey to win, but this is not so. The responsibility of maintaining the lead is onerous; in addition to the pressures of trying to win the race, the leader has to maintain the team's spirit by not taking all their graft for granted, yet also assert authority in tense or confused moments.

In short races and kermesses, team tactics are not always critically important. But in tours and stage races, they play an essential part in gaining advantage and ultimately victory, and they largely determine the outcome of important races.

There are many tactics that teams use. Here are some of the most frequently used ones:

- One or two team members may initiate a breakaway. This break will only be allowed to gain distance if the remaining team members agree that their co-riders in the break are doing well enough to win. If the riders who have broken away are joined by opponents who are known to be better sprinters than they are, then the break has to be slowed and prevented from gaining too much distance. The gap can be closed either by team members in the break slowing down the pace, or by those in the following bunch closing the gap. When the break is caught, a stronger group from within the team can take over and break away. This is a common pattern in a road race.

- If riders in a team make a break that looks successful, the remaining team members usually try to slow the chasing bunch down by grouping at the front and interfering with working echelons.
- Teams often set a fast pace up a hill to give their specialist climber an opportunity to break away. This is especially important when the climb involves a prime. The Portuguese teams were experts at this tactic during the Rapport Tour between the years 1983 to 1986. They would form a team echelon before the climb, and as soon as the hill was reached, the protected climber would make a move, and the opposition were not able to follow.
- In a sprint finish, a team member can give a 'dead-wheel' to a dangerous opponent, which allows the team's sprinter to grab the initiative before the opposition realizes what's happening. A dead-wheel is when the rider in front slows down or decreases effort instead of accelerating and protecting the rider behind.
- Towards the end of a race, a team may bunch around their chosen sprinter to provide protection. With one or two kilometres to go, the team moves forward and increases the pace with their sprinter sheltered. With team protection, there is no chance of the sprinter being boxed in as team mates will move out of the way when the sprinter's explosive effort is needed. This is called a 'lead-out' or a 'team-train'.

To recap a point made earlier, the success of a team depends on the willingness of its individual members to commit themselves fully to their roles. They not only have to be quick-minded in implementing winning strategies, but they also have to dedicate their Herculean efforts to a shared victory and not seek personal glory or be jealous of the actual winner. However, a fair team leader allows team mates to win sometimes as this is essential for morale.

How individual riders can counter team tactics

If you are racing as an individual, it can be very difficult to compete against well-organized teams. But in some ways, individuals with talent and tactical know-how have distinct advantages in riding alone. There are many tactics that can either neutralize your rivals' team work or capitalize on it:

- If you are in a break where all the teams in the race are represented, there is no strategic reason why you should contribute to the working. Just sit and save energy. (If your conscience tells you this is unsporting, remind yourself that the other riders have the advantage of team support.) Remember, too, that there will probably be no concerted chasing from a following bunch as all the teams will be blocking to let the break gain distance.
- If a team is leading out their sprinter, try to follow his wheel and then pass him on the finishing line. But don't expect him to submit to this easily.
- When a breakaway group doesn't include members of all the teams, you can expect members of the unrepresented teams to try to close the gap between the dropped bunch that they are in, and the group ahead. Don't use up your energy here by taking an initiative and closing the gap; leave the main work to them, and take shelter behind them.

One advantage of being an individual is that prize money does not have to be split.

Techniques and strategies for specific events

(The events themselves are described in Chapter 12.)

The individual time trial

The key to good time trialling is good judgement of what pace you will be able to hold; remember that you will be on your own, with no one to shelter behind. Don't start too fast or end too slow, and try to keep your speed uniform. And be prepared to drive yourself: time trialling can be lonely and dispiriting.

A good warm-up is essential, but don't use too much energy during this. Motor pacing is a good idea, as riding in the slipstream allows you to reach racing speed without using up the vital energy that you will need in the race. Sometimes I warm up on heavy wheels and then change to racing wheels just before the start; I find it gives me a useful boost by making me feel faster.

Here are further tips:

- Concentrate on smooth pedalling action. Begin with a low gear, which will help you to accelerate, and maintain a cadence of 95 to 100 rpm. Keep up your fast momentum on short hills, sprinting through them if necessary.
- Adopt a low-profile aerodynamic position and use aerodynamic equipment.

Individual time trial

- I prefer to do time trials on a fairly empty stomach and to depend on liquid nutrition.
- Ideally, your heart rate should be just below your anaerobic threshold level. I recommend using your heart monitor during your training sessions so that you get to know when your lactic acid turnpoint is likely to occur.
- Cycle along a straight line — it saves vital seconds.

Team time trials

Many of the principles that apply to individual time trialling apply to team trials. The obvious difference in team events lies in the fact that a smooth-working echelon or bunch is essential for success. Riders who are suffering should let the rest of the team know so that they can rest behind the front riders a bit rather than slow the pace down through exhaustion. Here are points that have not been covered in the previous section that should be noted for team events:

- The time or distance ridden by the lead rider in a time trial should be determined by the strength of the wind. For example, in windy conditions the rotated lead should be about 250 metres whereas in windless conditions, this could go up to 400 metres.
- The smaller the team, the longer the distance that each rider should pace. This allows for longer recovery periods when you are not pacing. The more

riders there are in the team, the shorter the pace distance of each can be, and the more efficient the working action of the echelon is.

- Team riders should try to use similar gear ratios for matched rhythm. It also helps if they are of similar physique and temperament.

Kermesse racing

Kermesses tax nerve, concentration and skill to the utmost. Novices always find them difficult. Some advice for kermesse racing is:

- Try to get to the front of the bunch and stay there. Kermesses are characterized by numerous tight corners, and to negotiate them safely and fast, you should be amongst the first three riders so that you can choose your own line through the bend. Riders stuck in the bunch travel far more slowly round the corners, as there is a bunching, concertina effect. By the time bunch riders get round the corner, the front group is usually far ahead.
- The corners provide opportunities to attack. Approach a corner in front of the bunch, accelerate 40 metres before the bend, corner fast and sprint out of it. Your opposition may not anticipate your sudden acceleration, and by the time you are round the corner, you could be well ahead. Races are won by employing this very simple tactic.
- Select a slightly smaller gear than you usually race in and stick to it throughout the race. Gear changing is time-consuming and diverts concentration.
- Breakaways succeed better in kermesses than in any other road events. This is because the corners allow the lone rider to ride faster than the group, in contrast to the usual situation when bunches can easily outride individuals.

Kermesse racing

The closer the circuit, the easier it is to break away. When training, practise your jump — in other words, accelerating in powerful bursts.

- Attack after primes, when the competition may be letting up slightly.
- Before the race, check that your tyres are glued on!

Tour racing

I have said it before, but it is worth repeating that team tactics play a critical part in tour racing, particularly in the later stages of a tour. Usually the first few stages are merely trial stages in which better riders begin to reach peak form, and the teams are concentrating on trying to predict the race and plan their strategies.

Preparation: It goes without saying that you should only enter a tour when you are fit, well prepared, well rested and, if possible, relaxed. Study the routes beforehand, make plans and ride accordingly.

The magic of the yellow jersey: If you are part of a strong team, a solid tactic is to try to gain race leadership as early as possible in the tour. The yellow jersey has a magic about it that brings its own strength and can make a rider far exceed his or her usual abilities. And the pressure of being the leader can make you more determined. If you are reasonably confident of your strength and that of your team, and the opportunity to take an early lead arises, go for it — even if it doesn't fit in with your original strategy. Many underestimated riders have only developed into formidable cyclists after acquiring the yellow jersey.

If, on the other hand, you are a member of a weaker team, it may be more sensible to aim to gain leadership later on in the tour so that the strain that protecting you places on your team members will be less onerous. And if you stand no chance of winning the tour overall, aim to win stages. There's far more glory in winning a stage than in finishing in a respectable but unremarkable position like eighth overall.

During the tour: Long tours are a process of steady elimination. Slowly but surely riders are forced to drop out by accidents or by poor strategies or tactics. It helps to ensure that you stay in the race if you always plan for the next stage. If you are tired and your muscles need a chance to recover, drop your gearing and take it easy for a while. Remember to do stretching exercises, and have a massage at night to help eliminate toxins from the muscles. Be careful of what you eat, and always drink from your own clean water bottle. Food poisoning or diarrhoea can be disastrous on a tour.

Remember that your priorities on a tour are riding, sleeping and eating, and try not to let anything interfere with those. Top-level racers couldn't perform the way they do if it were not for their backup crews and managers who deal with hassles like maintenance of equipment, luggage organization and accommodation arrangements.

Track racing

Track racing is a specialized sport, and detailed coverage of its techniques and strategies is beyond the scope of this book. It really requires some training by a coach; your local club may have a coaching scheme.

The aspects of track racing that take the most getting used to are that you are riding with fixed gears and without brakes — usually on a track peopled by other speeding, brakeless riders. Despite the great differences between track and road racing, some training on the track will be useful to you on the road: it's an excellent training ground for developing judgement and alertness, accurate handling and mercurial cadence.

Race psychology

The need to place mind over matter is clichéd but essential advice for the racing cyclist. No matter how fit, strong or skilled you are, it is one's psychological state, and particularly motivation and determination, that make the critical difference between winners and losers.

Libertrau listed the following psychological factors as determinants of optimum performance in sport generally, and I would agree that they apply to cycle racing: emotional arousal; motivation; stress tolerance; ability to relax; anxiety level; personality attributes; interpersonal relations (with coach and team); concentration; general adjustment; attitudes towards one's self, others, winning and losing.

You can see the workings of psychology in the difference between performance in training and performance in racing: like many others, I find it hard to drive myself in training, and I seem to suffer far more on these rides than in competition. But there is something about a race that brings out my best performance. Likewise, there are riders who always beat me in a prime sprint, but when it comes to the final finish line, I nearly always find that I get over it first, because that is where my goals are focused.

Coping with stress

Cyclists who compete without really being serious about winning usually find that the exercise is a great reliever of everyday tensions: it clears your mind, gives you a terrific sense of well-being, and has you sleeping like a baby. But if winning is important to you, competition can be stressful because it carries with it fear of failure. In sportspeople stress is also caused by the conflict between commitment to the sport and the demands of family, work and leisure. It's important to resolve conflict-related tensions: there's a clear connection between anxiety and poor performance.

Nervousness expends unproductive energy — a common problem with young sportspeople. Learn to relax before and during competitions. One pre-race relaxation technique is called 'calm image scenery'. You get into a comfortable position, close your eyes and imagine your favourite holiday spot or beautiful scenery; imagine that you are there and that the sun is shining and you are pleasantly warm. Another useful relaxation technique is to alternately contract and relax your muscles. There are many other methods of relaxation and meditation; find one that suits you and use it.

Driving yourself

When you're really suffering on a race, when the pain is excruciating and the distance seems endless, you have to find ways of forcing yourself not to give up. I am kept going by the thought that things are just as hellish for the other riders. (A lot more hellish, I hope.) Mental rehearsal of winning also sees me through moments of gasping desperation: in my mind's eye, I am roaring across the line, arms raised in victory, trailing glory. Apart from raising my faltering morale, it helps in the tactically important task of hiding any suffering from the opposition. Being confident and showing it (or faking it, if you have to) also helps to make your team members confident and supportive.

Race routine — being prepared

It's very frustrating to discover just before the race that you're missing something as vital as a pair of shoes or a front wheel. Develop a pre-race routine in which you:

- Check and clean equipment.
- Eat sensibly, depending on what sort of race you'll be riding.
- Pack race food — corn syrup, apples etc. — and full water bottles.
- Relax — no need to be aggressive **before** the event.
- Know where and when the start is and arrive early.
- Use the check-list given here to check the contents of your cycling kitbag. (Commonly forgotten items are shoes, helmets and licences.)

Check-list: Cycling kitbag

One-day competitions

Cycling clothes:
Racing shorts
Racing jersey
Two spare vests/T-shirts
Helmet or cap
Gloves
Socks (2 pairs)
Racing shoes (2 pairs)
Arm and leg warmers
Braces
Bib
Wet weather gear
Warm jacket or tracksuit

Tool bag with:
Allen keys
Spanners (8, 10 and 15)
Phillips and flat screwdriver
Pliers
Cable cutter
Spoke spanner
Oil
Bottom bracket tools
Chain breaker
Spare tubular glue
Spare parts
Water bottle cage
Saddle pin bolt
Brake and gear cables
Tyres

Miscellaneous:
Racing licence
Proof of anti-tetanus injections
Personal medical details (allergies, blood group etc.)
Money
Embrocations/massage cream
Sun block cream
Nail-clippers
Spare shoelaces
Spare cleats and attaching tool
Cologne and small towel (useful for cleaning hands)
Chamois cream
Extra fuel — snacks, corn syrup
Towel, soap, shampoo
Safety pins

Longer events

To the above, add:
Spare chainrings and sprockets
Extra clothes and toiletries for the number of days you will be away.
Spare racing clothes. It may not be possible to launder clothes, so take a change for each day, plus an ample supply of spare socks and gloves.

'There is no better feeling than winning. All the hard work and suffering is forgotten. Coming second is great, but who remembers the runner-up?' *Gary Beneke, Rapport Tour winner and author of this chapter.*

There is another side to racing, as Hans Degenaar, veteran of three Rapport Tours and ex-Springbok cyclist says: 'Cycling has always rewarded me more than I can properly express to others. Because of some inborn attitude that leads me to depend little on supergadgets, cautious diets or fastidious training routines, I have simply got along without these. With respect to those who achieve results with the aid of these, though, I find no fault; we all achieve happiness in our own way. To those who know all about the joys of cycling, there is little to be said, as they know it already. To those who race to win, and only to win, I would say, "Caution, brother, caution. After all, it's only a game."'

CHAPTER FIFTEEN

TOURING

Bicycle touring can mean a weekend ride with your children and friends; it can also mean a solo Cape-to-Cairo trip, a leisurely meander through French vineyards, or it can mean a mountain-bike scramble across Lesotho along goat tracks. Bike touring combines most of the joys of hiking with the advantages of an easier way of carrying equipment and the ability to cover considerable distances if you want to.

Even the loveliest areas can, when you see them from a car, be a mediocre blur of half-felt and half-remembered beauty, but on a bike all your senses are exposed and alive to what's around you. The cycle tourist travels with scents and breezes flickering subtly over the skin and with farmyard stinks assaulting the lungs with a violence which the cocooned motorist will never know. If beautiful areas seem even more beautiful from a bike, the bad parts also seem worse — but always far, far more interesting than they would otherwise be. Once you've enjoyed bike touring in your own area, it seems the logical way to see other parts of the world too.

Another bonus of travelling by bike — and it's one that virtually all bike-tourists seem to comment on and value — is that so many strangers talk to you. Occasionally it's in four-letter words, but very often one's met with curiosity, friendliness and hospitality; the story is much the same all over the world.

Ways of touring

Most people's bike travels take the form of day trips, for which there's a minimum of organizing to do.

Longer trips fall into several main types. You may choose to be self-sufficient, and load camping equipment and other gear into panniers and on carriers; the obvious advantages are low cost (provided that you do enough camping trips to justify the initial expense of buying equipment) and independence, though the added weight will make greater demands on your legs. Or you may want to carry as little as possible and stop at hotels or nature-reserve huts for the night.

Another way of travelling — and it's a good way if you have children or novices on a long ride — is with a sag-wagon or support vehicle accompanying you. Apart from relieving cyclists of carrying heavy equipment, it also means that worn-out riders can have a break without holding the rest of the group up. And if it's fitted with a bike carrier, a sag-wagon can also transport riders over parts of the route that might be dull or dangerous to cover by bike.

You can also stretch the possibilities of a bike tour by covering some parts of a trip by plane, train or, less advisably, by bus.

A good way to start touring is by joining one of the rides organized by local Pedal Power Associations or by independent clubs; some are listed in the Appendix. The routes are usually well chosen, there's plenty of company and you can count on having experienced riders to turn to if you need help. Most of these rides cater well for new cyclists, and as long as you've done some preparation — a few rides of, say, 40 to 60 kilometres — you should be able to cope even if the tour is longer than anything you've done before.

Commercially organized cycle tours offer another way of getting started. Some are geared for keen cyclists; others expect to transport tour members up hills by lorry and the only cycling is on the level and down hills! At least two local tour operators supply good mountain bikes as part of their package. Addresses are given in the Appendix.

Planning a tour

One of the best things about bike touring is the freedom it gives from the plans and schedules and time-tables of our working lives; it's great to be able to make spontaneous choices about what fork in the road to take and where to spend the night. But successful touring does depend on thorough basic planning: choosing a bike that'll take the load of panniers without sending spokes pinging all over the road, for example, or selecting a route that doesn't have you fighting and weeping into head winds for every kilometre of the way.

Choosing a bicycle

Your best choices are between a standard touring bike and a mountain bike (more accurately known as an all-terrain bike). Both are described in Chapter 4.

If you plan to keep to tarred roads, a touring bike will, of course, be the swifter option. But, if speed is low on your list of priorities and adventure is high, mountain biking is the way to go. Mountain bikes are fine on tar but they're in their element on dirt: look at any large-scale map of our rural areas and you'll see that the network of gravel roads is far more extensive than our main roads, and that they open up vast areas of new and often unspoilt territory along our coasts, in our mountain ranges, in forest areas and in farming country.

Choosing routes

Traditionally, the most popular touring areas in this country are in the south-western Cape, the Garden Route (which stretches from Cape Town to Port Elizabeth) and the eastern Transvaal. They're popular for good reasons: all have a choice of minor roads with light traffic in most parts, there are campsites and hotels at conveniently spaced intervals, much of the countryside is interesting and some of it breathtaking, and all have a variety of places of historic and natural interest to see.

There are routes in many other areas too which are equally attractive but have been less explored. But many of these are becoming more widely used, particularly as mountain bikes increase in popularity and lead cyclists to areas like the mountainous Cedarberg (much of which has been proclaimed a wilderness area) in the south-western Cape, the Drakensberg and the forests and lakes of the Tsitsikamma area.

Choosing routes that have little traffic makes all the difference between enjoying a safe ride and bracing yourself for constant hazards. Southern Africa doesn't have the networks of quiet, tarred lanes that have made cycle touring in Europe and Britain so popular, and choosing roads therefore deserves careful thought. Obvious routes to avoid are those that lead to resorts, especially during holiday seasons (local calendars list school holiday dates for the different provinces). Horrors on these roads are cars pulling boats or caravans which are not only wide, but also sway — something the drivers seem unaware of. Avoid roads in or near industrial and agricultural areas that are used by heavy lorries, and the bus routes to the so-called homelands, especially during the peak months of December and January. One way of getting information about the condition and the busyness of roads is through the Automobile Association, if you are a member. Their information isn't gathered with cyclists in mind, but in the absence of any other other information sources, it can be useful.

In planning long tours, remember that southern Africa forms a giant plateau; if you ride from the coast inland to the Highveld, you'll be climbing to more than 1 220 metres above sea level; conversely, if your route takes you down to the coast, you'll have far more descents than climbs.

Maps

Though they are adequate for the cyclist who keeps to conventional routes, motorists' maps are limited when it comes to going off the beaten track. More illuminating are the large-scale maps available at specialist map shops and from the Directorate of Surveys and Mapping. The latter's 1:50 000-scale maps are excellent for areas where you want to do concentrated touring in one part, as you might in an area such as the Cape Peninsula, or particularly if you were mountainbiking somewhere wild like the Cedarberg. These maps show gradients, fences, water holes, different types of roads, including Class 5 tracks (jeeptracks), homesteads, hotels, police stations and so on. Their 1:250 000 maps are good for more spread-out tours, while still giving ample detail. See the Appendix for information on how to get copies.

Mountain bikers' routes

Mountain bikers who are planning to get away from main roads should check first that they are allowed in the areas they are heading for. Many gravel roads are public routes; however, those on private farms are not, though permission to use them is unlikely to be refused. The position in nature reserves varies; in many, cyclists may not use walkers' tracks, though good relations between some nature conservation authorities and cyclists do seem to be resulting in more areas being opened up to cyclists. Many authorities, however, are apprehensive, and the way in which the first waves of mountain bikers behave in reserves is critical to the future of off-road touring. A nature reserve planner (who is also a keen mountain biker) gives this advice:

- If you plan to ride in a reserve, contact the reserve manager before your trip and check what you may or may not do.
- Make it clear that a mountain bike is a bicycle, not a motor bike (many are confused about this).
- Understand that you can't ride where you will damage vegetation, or cause erosion, or disturb wildlife and walkers. Make it clear to the reserve manager that you are sensitive to these issues. There are plenty of places where you can do exciting off-road riding without wrecking future opportunities for cyclists.
- Several mountain bike clubs have forged constructive relationships with conservation authorities, and you may have a better chance of access if you are a member. Clubs are listed in the Appendix.
- If possible, contact the reserve manager again after your trip to give him or her feedback; information from mountain bikers will help them to form policies for the future and should help to reassure them that responsible cyclists are no more destructive than walkers.

Finding out whether a reserve is controlled by the National Parks Board, a provincial Department of Nature Conservation or the Forestry Department can be complicated, and a good hikers' guide can be a great help; an example is Jaynee Levy's *The Complete Guide to Walks and Trails in Southern Africa*, published by C. Struik. This book gives useful information on reserves (including addresses and phone numbers) and it mentions several which may be used by cyclists; those listed for cycling are few, as yet, but you can apply for access to others. You may also be able to get information from mountain bike clubs and from the main authorities in charge of nature reserves and forestry departments; addresses of authorities in several southern African countries are given in the Appendix.

Weather and climate

In general, the weather for cycle touring in southern Africa is good. Different regions do, however, have differing but more-or-less predictable weather patterns which you need to think about when planning a trip.

Wind

Most parts of the country have few very noteworthy patterns of prevailing winds. The exceptions are the Cape Peninsula and the southern Cape coasts. The Peninsula is notorious for strong south-easterly winds which prevail in summer, and for north-westers, which prevail in winter. Spring and autumn are the calmest times. The southern Cape coast, from about Port Elizabeth to Cape Agulhas, has south-westerly and north-easterly winds throughout the year, but particularly in summer.

Wind is probably the cyclist's cruellest opponent, especially if the frontal area of the bike is widened by laden panniers. No amount of route-planning will save you entirely from head winds. But knowing how to streamline yourself and your bike will help you to save effort; even more useful, if you are touring in a group, is a co-operative system of riding in one anothers' slipstreams. The basic principles of both are outlined in Chapter 7 and more detailed techniques are covered in Chapter 9.

Rain

Living with rain is part of cycle touring, though in this country, you can count on having far more sun than wet weather. If there's one place to avoid on account of rain, it's the south-western Cape in winter, where rain driven by cold winds often falls for days at a time. But even here, the periods in between are frequently sunny and crisp and perfect for cycling.

Other parts of the country are either drought-stricken, or have their rainy season in summer. Natal and the Highveld have summer-afternoon thunderstorms which tend to be short downpours accompanied by lightning.

Seasonal temperatures

Avoiding dehydration, heat exhaustion and hypothermia:

On average, summer temperatures in this country range between 20 and 35 degrees Celsius, and winter temperatures range between 10 and 20 degrees Celsius.

Summer heat can make cycle touring tough in summer, especially on the Highveld, and along the Natal coast where energy-sapping humidity can make it impossible to cover long distances.

Heat can be dangerous when it leads to dehydration and heat exhaustion (as it very easily can do). The causes and symptoms, and ways of dealing with the problem are dealt with briefly here; see also the section headed 'The regulation of body temperature during exercise' towards the end of Chapter 10.

Cyclists commonly make the mistake of under-estimating how much water they are losing through sweat. On a hot day a 75-kilogram person can lose as much as 2 litres in an hour and a half of exercise in heat. By the time you feel thirsty, you are already water-depleted and your blood volume is less than it should be. That means that the amount of blood flowing to your skin decreases, and that you stop sweating. As a result, you can't get rid of the heat that you are producing through exercise, and your body temperature rises. This can lead to heat stroke, and in extreme cases it has killed people. The warning signs of dehydration and heat build-up are weakness, dizziness, goose-bumps, a fast pulse and nausea. Danger signs are a hot, dry skin, confusion, a weak pulse which may be fast or slow, extreme weakness and paleness.

The risk of overheating is greatest in hot, windless weather, and especially on long, uphill rides when you don't have the cooling effect of air blowing over your skin.

To some extent you can protect yourself from overheating by acclimatizing yourself to exercising in hot weather (see 'Heat acclimatization' in Chapter 10). The best way of preventing dehydration is to drink before you set out and to keep drinking regularly as you ride. A victim of dehydration and overheating should be treated by cooling him as quickly as possible: get him into the shade, wet him with cold water, and see that he rehydrates himself by drinking water before setting off again. Unless you think ahead, it's quite easy, in this country, to find yourself without any water at all.

Cold is less of a problem for cyclists here — though the numbers of mountain climbers who die from it each year are a warning to any adventurers in isolated places.

Be prepared for extremes in temperature and scarce water supplies.

Touring equipment

There's a fine balance between taking enough for your needs and not overloading yourself with bulky or heavy gear that has to be lugged up every hill. The check-list in this chapter includes the basic equipment that most bike tourists find adequate, but it should be adapted, depending on the availability of supplies in the areas that are going to be ridden through.

Seasoned tourers estimate that for a self-sufficient camping trip your gear needn't (and shouldn't) weigh more than 16 to 19 kilograms; if it does, cycling will be very hard work. If you're planning to spend nights in hotels or at guest farms, your load shouldn't be more than 8 to 13 kilograms, depending on the time of year.

Keeping your load light depends partly on ruthless selection, and also on having the lightest equipment you can find. A down sleeping bag, for example, weighs about 400 grams less than a synthetic one offering the same warmth, and it can be squashed into a smaller space. (The catch is that it's more expensive.) Hikers' packs of dehydrated food weigh far less than tins, and aluminium cutlery is lighter than steel. If you weigh everything as you pack, it helps you to judge what you can do without. You'll find equipment that's designed for compactness and lightness in good campers' supply stores.

Plan to re-stock with food as you travel, if it's possible, instead of loading up heavy supplies at the start. And instead of carrying numerous changes of clothing, do laundry along the way, but bear in mind that chamois liners in shorts won't dry overnight unless you're in the desert.

Loading your equipment

Your equipment should be distributed over your bike in such a way that it doesn't unbalance it or affect steering; nor should it interfere with your movements. At the same time, it should be firmly attached but be easy to get at.

To ensure stability, it's important that weight doesn't shift and is kept low on the bike. The easiest way of doing this is by investing in purpose-designed panniers mounted on strongly made, rigid carriers. Guidelines to choosing and mounting panniers and carriers are given in Chapter 16. It is possible to make your own or to adapt rucksacks — but this must be done with due care for secure attachment and balanced weight. Don't be tempted to use a heavy backpack on a bicycle: not only is it uncomfortable, tiring and constricting but it also makes a cyclist dangerously top-heavy.

There are many designs of bag available, and a few are described here:

- **Saddle bag:** If you're only carrying enough for a night or two away, a saddle bag, supplemented perhaps by a handlebar bag, may be adequate. A saddle bag has the advantage of not requiring a carrier because it attaches to the seatpost and the underside of the saddle.
- **Handlebar bag:** This stores small items that you want quick access to such as money, sunglasses and lunch. Some types have a clear plastic envelope on the top flap for keeping a map where it'll be constantly visible, and a shoulder strap so that you can carry the bag with you when you're not riding. A handlebar bag should be mounted so that it can't, under any circumstances, interfere with braking or steering. If you carry sensitive equipment like a camera in it, the bag's mounting should be rigid and secure enough to minimize vibration.

- **Rear panniers:** A pair of these is basic equipment for most touring. Roomy and mounted low on the bicycle, they allow you to carry a fair amount of equipment without interfering with stability. They need to be secured to a specially-designed carrier that keeps them clear of the wheels. Heavily loaded rear panniers can cause a bike to tilt backwards, especially when you brake; in addition, they increase wear on the rear wheels, which are already bearing most of the burden of the rider's weight. Instead of overloading rear panniers, you should transfer some weight to front panniers.
- **Front panniers:** These are used in pairs and should be mounted fairly low on the front wheel, with weight as close to the axle as possible; this helps to keep steering stable. Take care not to unbalance your bike with heavily loaded front panniers: they could cause you to tip over in a somersault.

Balancing the load

Your heaviest equipment should be packed low in the panniers. In rear panniers it should be placed towards the centre of the bike (in other words, towards the front of the rear panniers). In front panniers, keep weight low and central. Your lightest things should be at the top of panniers.

If groups of items are packed in clear, strong plastic bags it'll be easier to find them when you need them and to slide them out without muddling up your other gear.

Longish items like tents and rolled-up sleeping mats can be strapped to the top of the rear carrier using elastic cords with hooks at their ends. Treat these cords with great respect: if they get loose and dangle into spokes, they can cause spectacular disaster.

Test-ride a loaded bike before you set off into the blue on it. Acceleration, braking and steering will probably feel unfamiliar. Rather than straining to propel your new load along, use lower than usual gears. Remember that on descents, the added weight slows braking speed and it tends to pull the bike towards the outside of corners. Your extra width will make it impossible to slip through narrow gaps and it will increase wind resistance. (It'll also improve the slipstream for anyone riding in your wake.) Announce your extra width by fixing panels of reflective material to your panniers — especially at the back. Finally, when you leave (and every time you re-mount your loaded bike) check that everything's secure and that nothing's flapping or dangling.

Well-positioned panniers and bags keep luggage organised and the bicycle balanced. Note the reflective tape on the sides of the bags.

Packing check-list

Camping and cooking

groundsheet	tent	cutlery	tin opener	matches/lighter
sleeping bag	pot	mug	fuel	cleaning things
sleeping mat	plate	kettle	stove	

Clothes

socks	spare cycling shorts
gloves	spare T-shirts or cycling tops
underwear	tracksuit or jersey and legwarmers
sandals/beach thongs	non-cycling clothes, if you'll need them

wind- and waterproof jacket (see Chapter 16)
swimming-costume (or, if you're male, multi-purpose shorts)
walking shoes, if your cycling shoes have cleats — but it's more sensible to have one pair of
    uncleated cyclist's touring shoes.

Miscellaneous

credit card/chequebook/money	small towel
identity documents	safety pins and/or needle and thread
passport	photography equipment
proof of advance bookings	small torch and spare battery
permits for nature reserves	soap powder
phone numbers/addresses	toiletries (use miniature sizes)
personal medical details	loo paper or kitchen paper
sunglasses	plastic bag for rubbish

Swiss army knife or other good multi-purpose penknife
maps/guide booklets (or copies of just the pages you'll need)
compass

Bike equipment

bike lock	long gear cable
puncture kit and tyre levers	spare spokes, nipples and spoke key
long brake cable	screwdriver and bike spanners
pump	spare chain links and chain breaker
nuts and bolts	light batteries and bulbs
fine wire	

water bottles (two or three large ones in hot, dry areas)
Allen keys to fit seatpin bolt, handlebar stem, derailleurs, pedals, etc.
maintenance and repair manual (see list in Appendix)
spare inner tube and spare tyre. (Rear tyres wear faster than front ones because they bear most
    of the rider's weight; this is aggravated by heavy rear panniers. Swopping front and rear tyres
    from time to time helps to even the wear and cut out the need to carry several spares.)

It's a long list, but it needn't take much space. For long-distance touring in isolated parts you
should also have the following:

spare brake blocks	transverse brake cable	hub cone spanners
freewheel-removing tool	crankset extractor	

First aid

bandage	antiseptic cream	anti-diarrhoea tablets (e.g. Lomotil)
sun block	adhesive plasters	corn plasters (mainly for nubbins on your rear)
painkillers	personal medicines	
insect repellent	water-purifying tablets	

Transporting bicycles by air or rail

It often makes sense to use other transport for parts of a tour when it's impractical or undesirable to cycle.

Planes: Taking a bike on a plane is usually a straightforward matter: you wheel it into the airport, and it goes off as part of your baggage allowance.

South African Airways handle expensive racing bikes regularly and reports of damage are rare. However, like many other airlines, they do make you sign a form which states that they won't accept liability for damage. Insuring the bike or protecting it in a box or bag is up to you. Before you hand a bike over, SAA expect you to remove the pedals and to turn the handlebars parallel to the frame before taping them securely in place. Both operations can be done in a couple of minutes using an Allen key. Your chain should be given a wipe so that oil isn't smudged over other people's luggage.

Some foreign airlines insist on bicycles being packed, and some even supply special boxes; it's important to know the rules before your departure day and to let the airline officials know that you're bringing a bike, especially if it's a tandem.

Zip-up bike bags made of strong material can be bought from some bike dealers. They're fairly expensive and too heavy to drag about on a tour with you, so are only practical if you have somewhere to store them on arrival. One advantage of a bag is that you can use it to sneak your bike onto other public transport; this is useful where railway officials discourage or bar bikes on trains. A disadvantage on airlines, however, is that other luggage may be dumped on top of it: make sure it's boldly marked 'FRAGILE'.

A cheap (sometimes free) alternative to a bag is a cardboard box of the kind manufacturers use to deliver bikes in; the bike, with pedals off and handlebars turned parallel to the frame, should be wedged in with the help of polystyrene offcuts, and like bike bags, the box should be plastered with FRAGILE signs.

Another cheap if bizarre-looking way of protecting a bike from scratches in transit is by sewing it into a casing made of foam-rubber offcuts. The casing can simply be thrown away on arrival.

Trains: The South African Transport Services allows bicycles onto suburban trains at a few stations, but, at the time of writing, the procedure is too complicated and expensive to be worth doing regularly. Bikes may be taken on long distance train journeys free as part of your baggage allowance if you are travelling as a passenger on the same train. Unaccompanied, they travel for the normal parcels rate. In transit, it's advisable to lock the bike if you can, and to remove your pump, lights, water bottles, etc. Railway officials warn that even when a bike is accompanied by a passenger you should label it clearly, not only with your name and destination, but also with the name or number of the train you are on.

The rules on trains in other countries vary. In America, Amtrak transports bikes for a low handling fee provided they are boxed (they supply containers); at many stations, passengers can get off but freight can't — so you need clear information before setting off, or you may find yourself on a bikeless tour. In Britain and Europe you can count on being able to move a bike to most destinations by train, but the rules are sometimes fiddly and changeable. On some lines bikes travel free, and on others there's a charge. It's best to enquire at tourist or rail offices there.

Touring with children

Children can be great company on a bike tour. But they can also burst into tears in the middle of the wilderness and bloody-mindedly refuse to pedal any further. If you're taking children on a long ride, you need to be flexible about goals, and to make realistic allowances for their mental and physical stamina. Keep to areas where there's a good choice of places to stop at, or have a sag-wagon accompanying you.

Judging when children are old enough for tours depends on individual maturity and on training. As a rough rule of thumb, children from ten onwards can usually manage longish rides. A few exceptional six- and seven-year-olds have ridden the 104-kilometre Argus Tour, and some well-prepared, fit, nine-year-olds have done the six-day 700-kilometre ride from Cape Town to Plettenberg Bay, occasionally taking a break in a sag-wagon but riding most of the route. At four, Bradley Pickering-Dunn did that ride as a stoker on his father's tandem.

You also need to check that they drink and eat before and during the ride or you may find them dangerously dehydrated and energy-depleted. Exercise often suppresses thirst and hunger sensations even when one's close to fluid and energy depletion, and you should never assume that children will judge for themselves what they need. A child should drink roughly 500 millilitres of fluid an hour in heat and have a good supply of high carbohydrate snacks. Salty snacks should be avoided. (Read the section 'Seasonal temperatures' in this chapter.)

Being pushed to go even marginally faster than one's natural speed is tiring over a long route; as far as possible, children should set the pace. You can help them conserve energy by teaching them to keep in a stronger rider's slipstream. Here are useful psychological tactics for keeping children going:

- Set short goals that can be achieved quickly; it's more encouraging to have the next stop in mind than the end of the day's ride.
- On wearisome stretches, a riding-and-resting system usually works well: you stop for two-minute breaks **before** a child starts flagging. Up hot hills this may be every eight minutes or so.
- Keep talking; this shrinks the dullest distances, and the conversations can lead to comradeship that you've never expected from children.

Choice of bicycles for children is limited; the main things to check are covered under 'Children's bikes' in Chapter 4. A tandem can be an excellent way of touring with a child. It can be built to take a short stoker, or you can get a standard tandem adapted by fixing a special bottom bracket on the rear seat tube. As the child grows, the bracket can be lowered. The latter method works with young children, but once they become strong pedallers the bottom bracket tends to get twisted out of alignment. If you do opt for a raised bottom bracket, test it thoroughly before setting off; the system is known to have teething troubles.

Seeing Africa on a bicycle

Foreigners cross oceans to cycle in 'real Africa', yet local riders have, on the whole, barely explored places such as Lesotho, KwaZulu, Ciskei and Transkei. As in any place where there's poverty, tourists sometimes have fears about security in these places, but all those I've spoken to who've been there on bicycles have come back with reports of safe trips with unexpectedly impressive scenery, and friendliness from local people, most of whom are hugely entertained by the sight of bike tourists. As Graham Phippen, who recently rode through parts of Transkei with a group of others on mountain bikes wrote afterwards:

Mountain biking through the Little Karoo.

To most of us, it seemed, before we left, to be a great unknown land full of fear and "what if ...". Would our trip work? Once we got there, it was clear that it would. We set off above a rural valley dotted with huts and fallow maize fields and threaded by a stream. Respecting that we had asked no one permission to cycle along the villagers' paths, this was not to be a whizzbang fling, but a chance to be at ease among the people — and an opportunity to test our mountain bikes in a setting no touring bike could endure for long ... Very soon we were surrounded by children and they wasted no time in calling more followers to witness. It took some bashful moments before any could pluck up the courage to come close, but soon we had a procession through the village. Kids rode on our crossbars and others ran alongside. We met elders too as they came to see what the stir might be ... Others in our group had made contact with one settlement explaining local customs and history and they were invited into a hut ...

This is simply one extract from a longer report of happy cycling in Transkei.

Picturesque and hospitable as these areas often are, they do also make you confront poverty and the signs of fractured family life head-on, as few other travellers can do. But seeing real life is what bike touring is about.

The following advice on bike touring comes from a nineteenth century British book, The Art and Passtime of Cycling by R. J. Mecredy. But anyone riding now in southern Africa's 'homelands', where livestock wanders freely, would be well served by it:

Pigs are a special source of disaster, and have a habit of running in front of the cyclist and then suddenly turning and rushing at him. For this reason do not attempt to race a pig, no matter how confident you may feel in your superior powers. Tethered goats should be regarded with great respect. By simply running across the cyclist's path they can bring him down with the smallest possible inconvenience to themselves, and they appear to be aware of the fact too.

Touring in local Third World areas demands self-reliance: often you will find no well-surfaced roads over a wide area, nor phones that work. Though there may be a thriving heavy-duty bike trade, rural shops are not the places to buy derailleurs or even spokes; you should have spares of the parts that are most likely to break as well as a basic repair kit, and a manual if you're unpractised at mending bikes. Accommodation needs to be thought about fairly carefully. Camping in the open isn't advisable, but there are some superb campsites in 'homeland' nature reserves, some with fully-equipped bungalows. They tend to be far apart, but make good bases for fixed-centre touring. Most of the towns have hotels. Information sources for accommodation are listed in the Appendix.

Protocol in some 'homelands' is fairly formal; take passports and/or identity documents, depending on where you go, and remember that a prior approach to the local Department of Tourism and the Police Chief are often appreciated.

Malawi: Breathtaking lake and mountain scenery and a hospitable and helpful population make Malawi excellent cycle-touring country.

There are good roads running the length of the country, but all-terrain bikes open up the best routes on rougher tracks. Large scale maps of Malawi are available from the Government Printer in Blantyre.

Malawi has few campsites as we know them, and camping in the open can only be done with the permission of local authorities. Government and privately-owned rest-houses, which range from clean, well-equipped buildings to rough mud huts, are numerous and very cheap.

It's easy to spend money in Malawi: there are good hotels and all imported goods — even basics like bread — are expensive. But if you eat locally-produced food and use rest-houses, you can have an excellent, cheap holiday: Eugene Parsons (who was a guest of the people seen above) had a 30-day cycling holiday for R300 in 1989.

The months of summer are usually too hot and wet for good cycling. The weather in mid-winter (June and July) is usually ideal, but that is when farmers burn their land, and much of the scenery is obliterated by a smoky haze. March to May are good months: the countryside is green then, following the rains.

Malaria is a danger: take preventative drugs, specifying that you are going to Malawi, as strains of the disease there are resistant to some more commonly-prescribed drugs.

Steve and Alastair Black (top), who have crossed the mountain kingdom of Lesotho several times on all-terrain bikes, in winter. Many tracks here can only be negotiated on a sure-footed pony or tough mountain bike. Basic supplies can be had from small stores along the way, but you are unlikely to find bike parts. Much of Lesotho is very thinly populated by friendly people living traditional rural lives. Between November and February summer rains make many of Lesotho's rivers impassable, and in winter frequent snowfalls make cycling difficult, but not impossible.

Touring in foreign countries

Travelling by bicycle is far and away one of the best ways of seeing French vineyards, New Zealand mountain ranges or the Malawian lakes, or wherever. In many foreign countries, cycle touring is well established and there are organizations which supply the type of detailed information that's required for planning.

Britain and Europe

Cycle touring has been popular for over a century here, and there are excellent organizations supplying information on routes and local facilities. The best known is the Cyclists' Touring Club, a British organization that was founded in the 1870s and that offers its members the most comprehensive information service of its kind in the world. The Club's mail-order service supplies maps, lists of cycle hirers, fact sheets on foreign cycling, and books. (The sort of book that's listed is *The CTC Route Guide to Cycling in Britain and Ireland* by Nicholas Crane and Christa Gausden: this contains 365 interlinking routes which have been tested by cyclists and which are through countryside chosen for its scenery and its quiet roads. Each route guide comes with much useful information.) Just some of the things listed in the pocket-sized CTC members' handbook are addresses of hundreds of bike repairers all over Britain, times and costs of ferry crossings, cycling organizations in other countries, and thousands of village and farmhouse bed-and-breakfast places where you won't be turned away on account of your bicycle or your smell. CTC members are entitled to special insurance facilities and to an international cycle-touring card which serves as an introduction to other touring clubs all over Europe. The Club's many District Associations organize day-rides and foreign tours. You will find the address of this and other organizations in the Appendix. (Many of these organizations are run by volunteers handling vast amounts of correspondence. They are sometimes understandably slow to respond to applications. Write early.)

Britain is justifiably one of the most popular countries for cycling through. It has tens of thousands of kilometres of superb minor routes — narrow, tarred lanes that tunnel their way through 500-year-old hedges before breaking out into wide open farmland, and which link a great diversity of towns and villages. Pubs offering robust but reasonably priced meals are plentiful and so is accommodation of every kind, except at the height of the tourist season. The cheapest accommodation is in Youth Hostels (which you can use even if you're old); there are hundreds of these, many in lovely parts of Britain and Europe. Local membership entitles you to use Youth Hostels anywhere; see the Appendix for information on how to join. Britain's sometimes foul weather can be largely overcome with good rainwear (see 'Rainwear' in Chapter 16), but it does make camping a dead loss for all but the hardiest.

Europe exposes the cyclist to a tremendous diversity of lifestyles and landscapes, all within relatively easy reach of one another. France is probably the country where cyclists have the happiest trips: the food — always uppermost in the cyclist's mind — is unparalleled, even if it's a simple picnic that you've bought at a market; there are thousands of kilometres of minor roads, many carrying very little traffic, even in the tourist season; and for scenery you can choose between mellow vineyards, the towering Alps, dramatic coastlines and a whole lot more.

For beginners to cycling, an easy place to start is the Netherlands: it's flat, compact and civilized, but picturesque. Moreover, it's literally designed for cyclists, with thousands of kilometres of bike-paths crossing its countryside and linking its towns. Then there are the Portuguese and Greek coasts, Scandinavian lakes and forests, and Swiss mountains — to mention just a few in a host of possibilities.

Of course, parts of Europe are unspeakably awful, and their awfulness is magnified if you're on a bike. It's important, therefore, to plan well. Several helpful books are listed in the Appendix; you should be able to purchase them through your local bookseller. Essential reading is Nicholas Crane's *Cycling in Europe* (published by The Oxford Illustrated Press). Crane gives an inspiring but realistic introduction to cycle-touring in sixteen countries and he packs his book with well-researched, practical information on routes, accommodation, weather, public transport, bike dealers, repairers and hirers, information sources and maps.

Other countries

Information is fairly easy to come by in countries where the local people tour on bikes; North America, Canada, Australia and New Zealand have well-researched routes and active organizations which share information, some of which are listed in the Appendix.

To see the wilder outposts of the world, you have to do most of your own research, unless you choose the more expensive option of joining a group and doing one of the many commercially organized tours available. A recent list drawn up by the League of American Wheelmen named about ninety operators running bike tours within the USA and as far afield as Inner Mongolia, Fiji, West and Central Africa, Peru and Papua New Guinea. For the really brave they list Beano Vegetarian Cycle Tours.

Bikecentennial in the USA and the Cylists' Touring Club in Britain also supply information on touring in foreign countries.

Novice Buddist monks try out a traveller's bike in Ladakh, Northern India.

Cycling through the stark Himalayan landscape, Ladakh.

CHAPTER SIXTEEN

ACCESSORIES
for cyclists

The boom in bicycles has been marked by a boom in additional equipment. Much of it is designed to make cycling safer, more comfortable and more convenient, and some — panniers, for example — can virtually double the usefulness of a bicycle. If you're creative enough, you can even transform a bicycle into a mobile business premises.

Helmets

A good helmet is the only item of cycling apparel that is really important to use. No one who values his or her brain should ride without one. Researchers have estimated that about 70 to 80 per cent of deaths in cycling accidents are caused by head injuries. Even more frightening is the thought of head injuries which don't kill but which can stunt mental ability for the rest of your life. Recent studies have shown that in the event of an accident the helmetless cyclist is more than eight times as likely to suffer brain injury as the rider who wears good head protection.

Helmet research and design have come a long way in recent years; there's a good choice of comfortable, effective, affordable models available. The main qualities needed are:

- A capacity to absorb shock and protect the brain.
- Secure fit.
- Light weight.
- Good ventilation.

A hardshell helmet.

It's impossible to judge effectiveness on appearances alone, and we strongly recommend that when you buy a helmet you rely on the stamp of approval given by one of the standards institutes that have made special studies of helmet design. The most respected are the American National Standards Institute (ANSI) and the Snell Foundation (also American). Both base their approval on the results of sophisticated laboratory and on-road tests of protection, comfort and convenience. Several makes of *hardshell* helmet that have been widely marketed have failed their tests dismally. The *hairnet* or *strip* helmets worn by many racers are useless against anything but minor bumps, and Snell were reportedly nervous of even testing these in case their laboratory equipment got damaged.

The key to a helmet's effectiveness is its energy-absorbing capacity. Put differently, its effectiveness depends on its ability to cushion and gradually decelerate the movement of the brain within the skull when the head hits a hard surface. To understand this, it's useful to look at how most brain injuries happen.

Most brain injures result from the brain's movement within the skull when the head crashes against a road or some other hard object. When this happens, the brain swings through the fluid surrounding it, and crashes against the bone of the skull. This lurching and crashing can result in the tearing and crushing of delicate tissues in the brain. The severity of injury is directly related to the speed of the brain's lurch and the consequent abrupt deceleration when it meets the skull. The abruptness of that deceleration depends on how far the head falls and on how fast the cyclist is moving. The violence is compounded if the cyclist crashes into a car or some object that's moving as well. A severe impact can cause brain damage, even when there's no visible external injury.

So the features of a helmet that protect the cyclist are:

- Most importantly, a firm but compressible *inner lining* that's got just enough give in it to decelerate the brain's lurch within the skull. Most are made from a fairly rigid polystyrene foam. It should have low resiliency; that is, once crushed, it should remain crushed. (Of course this means that once a helmet has been in an accident and the liner has been compacted, the helmet must be replaced. In fact, there are claims that the materials in liners age, and that helmets should be replaced about every five years.) Another function of the inner lining is to spread the force of impact.

- A hard *outer shell* — though this is no longer considered an indispensable feature. A hard shell prevents puncture, diminishes the force of impact by spreading it, and helps to protect the cyclist's face and head from the skinning that results from sliding along a road. Interestingly, several helmets without hard shells have recently received ANSI approval; they have the advantage of being lighter and often cheaper than others, and the fact that they have passed such uncompromising tests underlines the fact that the main cause of injury is the brain's movement in the skull.

While protection is obviously one's major concern, comfort and coolness aren't minor considerations: you'll be less likely to wear your helmet if it bothers you. This is specially true of children. They should help choose theirs, lest they resist wearing headgear on the grounds that it feels hot or looks funny. Improved

---

The ANSI and Snell tests

In recent years, two independent standards for comparing the relative value of different helmets have developed — the American National Standards Institute (ANSI) standard and the Snell Memorial Foundation standard. The theory on which these standards are based is that the brain can reasonably safely be exposed to a deceleration force of about 300 g. (A g, or a gravity, is a measure of acceleration due to gravity. A g is calculated as one metre per second squared — $g = m/sec^2$.)

Impacts of 150 g or less cause little or no injury, whereas impacts of 150–250 g may cause light concussion and temporary amnesia so that the injured cyclist remembers neither the accident nor the events leading to the accident. Deceleration forces of this magnitude carry little risk of long-term brain injury.

Impacts of 250–300 g cause more severe concussion and more prolonged amnesia, but the risk of persistent, long-term brain injury still remains low.

The crossover to more permanent brain injury seems to occur at forces of about 400 g. Impacts of over 400 g cause brain bruising and bleeding inside the brain; impact over 700 g will almost certainly cause permanent brain damage and may be life-threatening.

Both the ANSI and Snell standards specify that a safe helmet must reduce impact forces to less than 300 g. The testing methods used by both organizations are quite similar. They involve putting a weighted 'head' inside the helmet and dropping it from a specified height; when the helmet hits an anvil, the forces are measured with sophisticated devices contained in the 'head'.

The ANSI standard requires that the helmet be dropped four times from a height of one metre; twice onto a flat anvil and twice onto a rounded, hemispheric anvil; the latter tests the helmet's ability to distribute impact shocks when the head hits the type of rounded surface that you might find on a car.

In the Snell testing methods, the drop heights are higher: 1,2 metres for the hemispheric anvil and 2 metres for the flat anvil.

At present, whilst there is consensus that the ANSI standard is a minimum requirement for a cycling helmet, no one is certain whether the Snell standard is either better or possibly too demanding. The firmer polystyrene liner needed for helmets to pass the Snell test will protect the cyclist from major brain injury in a catastrophic situation where g forces are over 700, but it may be too rigid to reduce lesser forces, say 400 g, to safe levels in a less serious injury.

At present the best advice seems to be to:

- Use only ANSI- or Snell-certified helmets.
- Select helmets that produce the lowest g forces on both the ANSI and Snell tests. The information is not usually available on the helmet, but good dealers may be able to supply it.

design has made helmets far cooler to wear than they used to be, but you should be prepared to accept that your head may get sweaty in very hot weather. A squirt of water through the air-holes helps.

When choosing a helmet, check that it doesn't obstruct vision to the side and behind you; if you wear glasses when you ride, take them with you. No helmet's safe if it doesn't fit securely, so be prepared to spend time in choosing one or in moving on to other shops, if necessary, in your search. Adding a couple of foam-rubber sizing pads can help to improve fit, but don't overdo this.

Clothes

Cyclists' clothes have provoked mirth and ridicule for years, but are now considered so stylish that people who never cock a leg over a bicycle frame stand around looking athletic in slinky black racing shorts and leanly-cut tops. It's enough to make the territorial cyclist revert to khaki farmers' shorts, if it weren't for the fact that cycling gear is by the far the most comfortable and practical clothing to ride in.

Whatever clothes you ride in should allow free movement, have no seams cutting into you, and the fabric should 'breathe'; clothes shouldn't be able to flap and increase wind resistance or get tangled in the bike.

Cyclists' *shorts* are made of a stretchy, close-fitting fabric (usually lycra) with a cut that prevents them from wrinkling and causing chafing. Most have a partial lining of chamois leather and are designed without the seams which in conventional shorts can strangle you in the crotch. Some have triple lining sandwiching a layer of high-memory foam that recovers its shape well. Cycling shorts are meant to cling like a second skin and thus avoid the friction between cloth and the body which is a major cause of chafing. To get the best use from shorts, wear them without underpants as these to some extent stop them from clinging to you. Some

cyclists virtually glue their behinds to the lining of their pants by rubbing lanolin on the chamois. This also softens the leather. But some riders feel that the waterproofing effect of lanolin stops sweat escaping.

For cold weather, ankle-length cyclists' pants made much like the shorts are available. Alternatively, full-length legwarmers can be worn and then rolled off when you've warmed up.

Cycling pants should be washed very often; they provide a sweaty and warm environment in which germs can breed quickly and cause unpleasant infections. Make sure they're thoroughly rinsed; women in particular can be driven mad by detergent residue in shorts. A light rub with lanolin once the lining's dry will keep it soft.

Touring shorts which look like ordinary clothes but have a chamois or terry-cloth liner exist but are hard to come by locally.

Cycling *tops* are cut long, so when you ride your back remains covered; their close fit helps to keep wind-drag down, and the row of convenient pockets across the lower back holds puncture kits, money and snacks. A good cloth to go for is a cotton-polyester mix, woven to concentrate the cotton on the inside where it acts as a comfortable sweat absorber. The polyester keeps the shirt in shape, preventing downward sag, and, to a minute degree, its smoothness diminishes wind-drag.

Cyclists' *gloves* are padded at the palm to prevent chafing and numbing of the hands where they grip the bars; they also protect the specialized, hard-to-replace skin on the palms of your hands in the event of an accident. Gloves with a gel-filled padding give extra protection. Winter gloves as well as cool, open-backed gloves with cut-off fingers are available. Unfortunately gloves are soon irredeemably wrinkled and stiffened by sweat, and expensive ones seem to be as short-lived as cheap ones. Washing helps, but most are made from material that isn't made for the laundry.

Cyclists' training or racing *shoes* are so well adapted to their purpose that off your bike you can only hobble in a crippled fashion in them. They have light, soft uppers, no heels, and cleats which slot into the pedal and help to ensure firm grip. A reinforcing material makes the soles very rigid; this is an aid to efficient pedalling (enabling the foot to act as a lever on the pedal) and it also ensures greater comfort. Takkies or other soft-soled shoes tend to flex over the pedal, causing an uncomfortable and sometimes numbing line of pressure across the ball of the foot; a shoe with a rigid sole (and it doesn't have to be a proper cycling shoe) helps to disperse that pressure.

A racing shoe with cleats slotted into a Look pedal.

Depending on what sort of cleats they have, cycling shoes are made to be used with pedals that have toe-clips fixed to them, or to be used with the more recently developed clipless pedals (commonly known as Look pedals, though Look is simply one of several good makes).

The older style of cleat has a groove which slots over the ridge of the pedal; shoes with these attached to them need toe-straps to help keep the foot in place.

The cleats for clipless pedals are designed to slot so securely into the pedal that there's no need for a toe-strap to hold the foot in place.

Cyclists' touring shoes are also available; unlike racing shoes, these look like normal shoes. They have no cleats and are comfortable both for walking and cycling.

Rainwear

A cheap, lightweight rainjacket that can be stuffed into a back pocket is good enough protection against the occasional shower. But if you're likely to do much cycling in wet weather, it's worth investing in good rainwear that will also keep wind out.

If you expect to ride much in really hard rain — as you might have to on a tour — rainwear made from the expensive but very effective Goretex will be your best choice. This fabric has a remarkable ability to keep even heavy rain out while allowing sweat vapour to escape. Cape Union Mart in Cape Town have recently produced leanly-cut rainjackets with an elastic lower hem in a lightweight Goretex which is far softer than that often used for hikers' clothes. It comes with optional matching rainproof trousers. It's safest not to use the hood when cycling because it may block your vision when you turn to look behind you. This is specially true of heavier grades of Goretex.

Jackets made from Ventex — a less expensive rainproof fabric that also 'breathes' — are available in a cut specially designed for cycling.

However, even rainwear made from one of the high quality materials described may not be waterproof unless the seams are properly sealed. Check the insides of seams: they should have a strip of fabric bonded over them.

Remember that rainwear is worn when visibility is poor; motorists are far more likely to see you through fog and drizzle if you dazzle them in a bright, light colour such as yellow than if you choose discreet blues or greys.

Cyclists' glasses

Cyclists' glasses.

These offer protection against grit, insects and wind, all of which frequently reduce cyclists' vision of the road to a watery blur. Their other important use is to cut glare and to protect eyes from the slow but insidious and irreparable damage which the sun's ultraviolet (UV) rays can cause to the eyes of those who spend a lot of time out of doors. Prolonged exposure to UV radiation can destroy retinal cells; this is one of the main causes of blindness in the elderly. When choosing glasses, read the product information and buy those that absorb the most — almost 100 per cent — UV light.

It's better to use no dark glasses at all than to use a type that doesn't absorb UV light; the dark lenses cause pupils to dilate, allowing abnormally high levels of UV radiation to reach the retina and the lens of the eye. The younger you are, the more protection you need: the eyes of children under about ten have little or no built-in UV-filtering properties, while the eyes of the average 45-year-old filter about 90 per cent of UV rays.

Look for well-fitting glasses that can't easily be dislodged by jolts or by wind. It's safest to use proper cycling glasses; they're designed so that it's almost impossible for either the lenses or frame to cause injury if you crash, and the wrap-around design allows unobstructed vision.

Reflectors and lights

Riding at night and use of lights and reflectors is covered in the section 'Not being seen' in Chapter 8. This information should be read in conjunction with that section.

Common sense and the law require cyclists to have a red retro-reflector on the back of the bike and a white one in front at all times; after dusk, it's compulsory to have a front-mounted white light and optional but advisable to have a rear-mounted red light.

Reflectors should, ideally, be able to be spotted and recognized at about 200 metres against the glare of an oncoming vehicle's dipped headlights; 200 metres is the safe stopping distance for almost all vehicles on the road. In practice, very few reflectors meet this requirement; even those complying with the SA Bureau of Standard's specifications fall far short of it. But for most urban riding, reflectors with SABS or BS (British Standards) approval have adequate retroreflective power and are waterproof — an important factor in performance. Many reflectors on the market fall hopelessly short of any standard, so you should check that yours have the SABS or BS stamp on them. The larger they are, the more visible they'll be.

There are two main types of lights: those that are battery operated and those that work off a dynamo.

Battery lights are more convenient for cyclists who occasionally need lights. Mounting is usually quick and simple. Most types have a bracket which clamps to the bike; the light unit can be slipped in for use when riding or removed to be used as a torch or to keep it out of pilferers' hands when you park. Their disadvantages are that most are less bright than dynamo lights, and they obviously cost more to run.

As batteries start to run down, the beam fades, and there's a risk of the rider not noticing until it's a dangerously weak glimmer. On lights fitted with cheap bulbs, this can be made worse by the fact that the bulbs themselves also lose brightness after a while, and need to be replaced. It's worth having the more expensive krypton or halogen-gas filled bulbs as they start off brighter and remain bright.

Buying a battery-charger and rechargeable batteries is one way of saving money on bike lighting. If you do use recharged batteries in lights, you should remember that after a recharging the battery will work for about three hours before abruptly conking out and leaving you in the dark; lights running on recharged batteries don't fade out slowly as other types of battery lights do. With any battery-powered light, and particularly when you are using recharged batteries, you should always carry spare, charged batteries.

It's important to have rainproof light units; if water seeps through to the batteries, it not only destroys them but also damages the light unit itself.

A *dynamo system* will probably be your best choice if you regularly need lights when you ride. However, for reasons that will be explained, you'll have to back it up with other lighting. Most dynamo lights are brighter than battery-powered lights and, though they are initially more expensive to buy, they're cheaper to run. But fitting them on the bike is more complicated; they need careful adjustment and their more complex mechanism makes them more likely to fail than battery lights are. However, regular checking to see that the bulbs are in good condition and that all the wires and other connections are secure will help to prevent failure. Once mounted, dynamo lights are usually left in place — at least for the winter, or the period when you need lighting. (For this reason, many riders who want to use their bikes for daylight training as well, and who don't want to carry extra weight, find dynamos an impractical option.)

The energy powering these lights is generated by a roller lying against one of the tyres of the bike while it's rotating. The faster you're going, the more power is generated; at high speeds this can be enough to blow the bulb, unless the system you choose is fitted with a voltage regulator. Unfortunately, no one's come up with a dynamo that stores surplus power for use when the wheels aren't rotating: when you stop the bike, the light cuts out. Many cyclists wrongly think that their stops are too brief to be dangerous: but most stops are at intersections, which is where a high proportion of accidents happen. Intersections aside — if you stop, it's usually because something's gone wrong and the chances are that you'll need a light to see by, and so that others can see you. So it's essential to have good reflectors and other lights to fall back on. The better types of dynamo lights have a built-in battery-powered back-up.

Battery lights

Water on the tyre can also be a cause of failure; it can reduce the friction on the roller and stop the lights from working, though the better makes of dynamo have managed to overcome this problem.

As with battery-operated lights, the bulbs that light up the most brightly are the krypton or halogen gas-filled type.

Some dynamo systems get their power from a roller lying against the sidewall of the tyre; others operate off the centre of the tyre tread. The latter type is reported to be better: it causes less wear to the tyre and less resistance, and so slows your ride down less.

When mounting lights, the main thing to bear in mind is that lights are chiefly to make **you** visible to motorists; their ability to light up the road ahead is an important but secondary consideration. Front and rear lights should be mounted high with the beam parallel to the road surface; see that they're visible from as wide a range of vantage points as possible.

Small lights that attach to wrists and ankles are eyecatching. Seeing that all their batteries are fresh takes some organizing, but the trouble's worth it. Battery-powered flashing lights that attach to Sam Browne belts or to the back of a bicycle can be dazzlingly effective at slowing motorists down, partly because people associate them with danger signals.

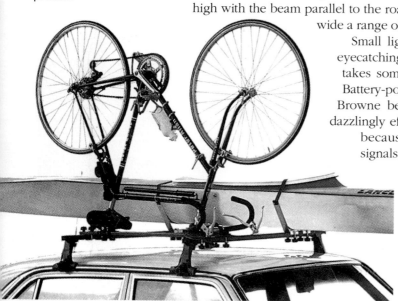

A roof rack: this one is designed to support bikes in the inverted position.

Car racks

Bumper racks (rear racks) are the cheapest and the simplest to use. But they expose bikes to the obvious danger of being crunched by other cars, and they obstruct the car boot. At most, they take three bikes. Positioning should be carefully done to avoid knocking the bikes' wheels if you drive through a dip and to prevent heat from the exhaust pipe from damaging the tyres. There's also a risk of blocking the visibility of your car's rear signals. Use protective pads to prevent your bike and the paintwork of your car from being scratched.

Some *roof-mounted racks* take up to six bikes, though most locally available models take up to four. Most have fittings to take canoes, skis, surfboards, whatever. The main risk with this type of rack is of writing off several bikes at once by absent-mindedly ploughing through an arched gateway with them on the roof.

Tests have shown that the most stable position for roof-mounted bikes is upright, with the rear wheel and front fork resting on the rack. (The front wheel is removed.) However, this mounting requires a car with a fairly long roof. On most roof racks the bike rests on the handlebars and saddle.

Though you are unlikely to find more than one brand to choose from locally, the following are features to look for if you do have a choice:

- Lightness and ease of operation.
- Resistance to rust.
- Smooth, protective finish where the rack clamps to the car.
- Versatility: If you're likely to need a rack for other sport equipment, find out what fittings are available for different makes of rack. If you intend using the rack on cars of different widths, check that the bars of the rack are adjustable.

A roof rack.

If you plan to load bikes of very different lengths, for example a child's bike and an adult's, check that the make you choose will accommodate this. Locks: Some racks can be locked onto the car, and their fittings that hold bikes in place are also individually lockable. Apart from making theft difficult, this is important if you want insurance cover to hold.

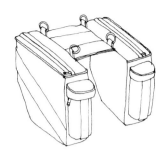

Rear wheel pannier

Bike computers

If you're training, or even touring, where signposts are few, a cycle computer gives you an easy way of measuring progress accurately. Some types are battery-operated; others have a solar cell with a battery back-up. Some 'remember' data while the power's off and while batteries are being changed; cheaper ones don't. Most people find that those that are mounted on handlebars are easier to read than fork-mounted models. The simplest ones tell you your speed, trip distance and time elapsed. As they get more complex and more expensive, they may record the following: highest speed, average speed, total distance covered as well as the distance of the ride you're on, cadence and heart rate. Some can be used as clocks and stop-watches. It's useful to have one that can easily be slipped out of its mounting and carried; left on a parked bike, a computer's likely to be wrenched off by some passer-by. If you ride more than one bike you may want a computer that can conveniently be moved from one to another; some can be bought with additional sets of the cable-and-sensor apparatus for each bike, while the expensive bit — the computer — gets moved about to different bikes.

Front wheel pannier

Rear wheel backpack (can be secured on top of rear carrier, or used as backpack).

Bags, baskets, panniers and racks

Rucksacks, baskets and shoulder bags will do for light loads. Heavy or bulky loads carried on the rider or high on the bike are destabilizing. Compact but fairly heavy loads like school bags can be safely carried on inexpensive, rear-mounted racks with sprung clips.

If you plan to tour and carry your own baggage, there's a variety of equipment to choose from. Some of the panniers and other travelling bags available have been described in Chapter 14 in the section 'Loading your equipment'. As that section points out, a fundamental thing to bear in mind when you load up for a tour is your bike's stability and the way the arrangement of your baggage affects it. It follows that an important determinant in your choice of panniers and the racks that support them should be their potential for stable loading.

Front and rear panniers all require metal racks for support. The qualities to look for in racks are:

- **Strength:** Strong steel racks are reasonably inexpensive but heavy. Strength and light weight can be had at a price if you buy good aluminium racks.
- **Rigidity:** Racks must be rigid enough to hold bags steadily in place and to minimize shifts of weight

Saddle/toolbag

Handlebar/shoulderbag

when you change direction or go up or down steep gradients. Shifting or vibrating of heavy baggage destabilizes steering and after a time contributes to metal fatigue on the bike as a whole. (Metal breaks if it's subjected to continual fatigue.) Look for racks that are well braced vertically and laterally and that fix to four or more sturdy points on the bike. The bracing should help bags to hold their shape and ensure that they keep clear of wheels.

- **Design:** The design should allow for well-balanced positioning of panniers. Front panniers should be low with weight as close to the wheel axle as possible. Rear carriers should hold panniers forward towards the centre of the bike and they should have a horizontal section strong enough to carry a tent or other fairly heavy equipment over the back wheel without sagging.

Features to look for in panniers are:

- **Packing space:** Try to get bags close to the size you're likely to fill. Baggage in half-empty bags lurches about.
- **Secure attachment points:** Panniers should attach to the rack at two places at the top and at a third place on the dropouts or fork ends.
- **Firmly reinforced back panels:** The inner side, next to the wheel, is usually braced with a board to keep the pannier flat and away from the wheel. Large panniers need reinforcing at the base as well.
- **Reinforced seams at corners, and good finish:** The stresses of carrying loads will soon reduce a poorly-made pannier to frayed shreds.
- **Water resistance:** The product information tag may tell you how waterproof a pannier is. Check to see if the stitch holes at seams look leakproof. Closures need a good degree of overlap to keep rain out. You can improve on waterproofing by applying one of the sealing compounds available at camping shops.
- **Easy access** to the bags through uncramped openings.
- **Straps and buckles** that allow you to squash the pannier up compactly if it's only partly full.
- **Retro-reflective panels** stitched to the panniers.

Pumps

Having tyres at the right air pressure makes a critical difference to performance and to tyre wear, so it's worth having the wherewithal to make pumping easy and accurate.

Stand pumps (workshop pumps) deliver powerful blasts of air and have their own pressure gauges.

If you use narrow tyres or tubulars but don't have a stand pump, it's a good idea to have a separate pressure gauge.

For carrying with you on rides, you'll need an ordinary pump; most clamp parallel to the top tube or the seat tube. Check that the pump you buy is designed to deliver the pressure needed for your tyres (it's marked on the sidewalls) and that its connection will fit the valves.

Stand pump

Maintenance stands

A maintenance stand has a tripod base and an adjustable arm that holds a bike at working level with its wheels off the ground. Moving parts are all free and easy to get at. Most have a handy tray to hold tools.

Apart from making the job of servicing or fixing a bike very much easier, the stand means you can move your work from the garden into the house or garage with a minimum of disturbance to the job being done.

Locks

In 1988, over 26 000 bicycles were reported stolen in South Africa. Many were locked at the time. Though bike theft is nowhere near to being the sophisticated operation that it is in Britain and Europe, where thieves sweep up lorryloads of bikes and ship them to Third World countries, it is extremely common.

Most bike locks made of chains or cables can be broken easily with a pair of bolt cutters. Many combinations are apparently simple to crack. If the lock can be got down on the ground, it can be smashed with a hammer or brick. If you regularly park at the same spot, you could leave a heavy hardened chain fitted with a really good lock there; you'll probably have to assemble it yourself, as bike shops don't carry rugged enough chains. Sheath it in an old inner tube to protect the bike's paint.

Far and away the best locks are the U-shaped hardened steel types. The best known are Citadel and Kryptonite. Though heavy (about a kilogram), they are easy to carry with you if you have attachment clips specially made for them. They're impervious to attack by hacksaws, boltcutters, acids, crowbars and lockpicks. But, if you lock your bike to a lamp post with one of these and then lose your key, it's almost easier to carry the lamp post home than it is to remove the bike from it. (We once had to bring a two-metre school bike-rack home for the holidays because one of our children had shackled her bike to it and lost the keys.) If you buy a U-lock, keep spare keys somewhere safe and record key numbers. Replacements can be got from the manufacturers overseas.

Maintenance stand

This photograph was used for an advertisement for WOLBER wheels.

Children's seats

There's very little local choice in carriers for children; the most widely used are plastic rear-mounted seats which take children weighing up to about 18 kilograms. Points to look for are:

- **Secure fit and stability:** Test it when mounted and loaded by shaking and swaying the bike to see whether it shifts and how it will affect handling. On a bike with no top tube (a 'woman's' frame) the extra weight of a child and carrier is likely to cause instability. With a top tube, getting on the bike is a clownish operation unless you're long-limbed, but it's far preferable to being wobbly.
- **Easy mounting:** It usually takes a fair amount of manipulating to get a seat fitted the first time; after that, you will probably want one that comes on and off quickly.
- **Supportiveness and comfort:** See that there's a good safety strap and that there's no way feet can get into spokes.

If you carry a child and loads of shopping as well, see that weight is well distributed. Front panniers for the shopping will counter-balance the extra load on the back.

If the bike falls, it's almost inevitable that the child's head will hit the road. Children in carriers should always wear helmets. If you can't get one that fits, make do with one that has extra foam liners in it.

A word about riding with a baby in a backpack: this makes the rider top-heavy and it inhibits movement, making it difficult to look about, or to react quickly. And having an infant pulling your hair and doing God-knows-what-else on your back is dangerously distracting.

Rear-view mirrors

A good mirror is a great ally in traffic. Most good locally-available models fit into the ends of handlebars. Points to look for in a mirror are a wide field of vision and firm adjustability.

Wind-trainers and rollers

A wind-trainer provides a stable way of training indoors with your bike clamped to it. A roller under the rear wheel generates wind resistance.

Training on rollers takes skilful balancing and demands a high level of pedalling effort simply to stay upright. Like a wind-trainer, it's a boring but effective way of keeping fit. However, on both, the amount of riding you can do is limited because you tend to overheat unless there is wind blowing over you.

APPENDIX

Pedal Power Associations

Pedal Power Foundation of Southern Africa
P. O. Box 6503, Roggebaai, Cape Town 8012.

The PPF was formed in 1978 with the aim of popularizing cycling, and protecting and furthering the commuting and recreational cyclists' rights to better facilities. Council members represent cyclists at municipal, provincial and government level. The PPF's main purpose is to loosely connect the regional Pedal Power Associations (PPAs) and offer advice where warranted. The PPF AGM is usually held in Cape Town, usually on the day following the Argus/M-Net Cycle Tour. Conferences on bicycling issues have been organized (roughly a year apart) by the PPF. The PPF councillors include bicycle planners, road engineers and the chairperson of each PPA.

Regional Pedal Power Associations

Regional PPAs are by far the most active motivators of organized recreational bicycling in this country. Though connected to one another through the PPF, they are free to run their organizations and their events as they wish. Their main activities are to organize bike events (for example weekends away, film shows, talks, and sales of used bike equipment). They also play a valuable role in advising other planners of mass bike rides on organization and safety; through these events they have successfully encouraged the use of protective helmets among cyclists. Bike events that are advertised as having PPA backing are widely regarded as being safer and better run than those that don't.

Membership benefits include reduced entry fees for fun rides, discounts at some bike shops and newsletters with information about forthcoming events.

The following is a list of regional associations. In some cases sponsors and outside organizers have taken over much of the running of the main events listed under individual PPAs; in all cases, however, the PPA originated and helps to run the event.

Border Pedal Power Association

P. O. Box 8130, Nahoon (East London) 5210.
(or 8 Edge Road, Beacon Bay, 5241.)

Weekend rides with an emphasis on family touring are organized throughout the year. Their main events are the Daily Despatch Tour in autumn and Lions Club events throughout the year.

Eastern Province Pedal Power Association

P. O. Box 14005, Sidwell (Port Elizabeth) 6061.

The EPPPA produces a newsletter and helps other organizations run cycling events. Their annual family rides to The Islands State Forest and to the Kabeljou's River are popular. Their main event is the Herald Cycle Tour, which is over about 104 kilometres and takes place in autumn.

Griqualand West Pedal Power Association

P. O. Box 33, Kimberley 8300.

Natal Pedal Power Association

P. O. Box 1049, Durban 4000.
(or 413 Volkskas Building, Gardiner Street, Durban 4001.)

The NPPA has a busy diary that satisfies its fit and competitive members as well as its less ambitious tourers. A well-produced newsletter keeps members informed of NPPA events, local mountain bike activities and wider cycling issues.

Main events are:
- Tour across Southern Africa (TASA): a two-week, 2 000-kilometre ride from Port Natal (Durban) to Port Nolloth in Namibia; the first one was ridden in the winter of 1989, and it's hoped to make it an annual event and to establish the route as one of several South African cycle trails.
- Tour of Natal: a week-long coastal and midlands tour in winter.
- The Great Bike Ride Across Natal (GABRAN): an autumn tour over several days, from the Drakensberg to Durban.

Southern Transvaal Pedal Power Association

P. O. Box 3521, Randburg, (Johannesburg) 2125.

The STPPA has several thousand members, many of whom join one of its 27 affiliated clubs. These are based in different areas and cater for riders with differing ambitions. The well-produced quarterly magazine *Pedal Power* (published jointly by the NTPPA and the STPPA) covers a range of cycling topics and lists forthcoming rides.

Main events are:
- The Cresta Century ride in February.
- The Selwyn Segal 95/40-kilometre ride in May or June.
- The Star 100 in August or September.

Northern Transvaal Pedal Power Association

P. O. Box 40136, Arcadia (Pretoria) 0007. Phone 012-714664.

The NTPPA has seven affiliated clubs in and around Pretoria with a club as far afield as Barberton. Membership is about 1 500 and the NTPPA organizes fun rides, tours and classic events such as the Magalies 108, the 145-kilometre Jock Tour in the Eastern Transvaal and the 165-kilometre Vasbyt.

Western Province Pedal Power Association

P. O. Box 23190, Claremont (Cape Town) 7735.

The WPPPA is the oldest regional association, and at the time of writing, its membership of 8 000 makes it the largest. Its calendar lists events almost every weekend except in the winter.
Main events are:
- Argus/M-Net Cycle Tour: a 105-kilometre ride in autumn around the Cape Peninsula, that has drawn as many as 12 000 cyclists.
- Burger/Sanlam 100: usually ridden in October with 3 000 to 5 000 entrants.
- Apple Tour: a weekend ride to Villiersdorp in autumn.
- Tulbagh Tour: a weekend ride from Cape Town in the spring.

Windhoek Pedal Power Association
P. O. Box 726 Windhoek 9000, Namibia. Phone 061-34131.

The WPP has a fun ride on the first Sunday of every month. They do unusual things with bikes in this club: their newsletter recently published a request for surplus dynamos, spokes and bike wheels for someone who was building wind-chargers to generate power to keep elephants away from water cisterns.

Main events are:
- Swabank Cycle Tour in autumn.
- Cymot Biathlon and M+2 Namib Tour in winter.
- Old Mutual Namib Triathlon in Swakopmund, just before Christmas.

Mountain bike clubs

The following is an incomplete list of local clubs; for the most up to date information, contact your mountain bike dealer or your local Pedal Power Association.

Mountain Bicycle Club of Johannesburg
P. O. Box 32668, Braamfontein 2017.

Dirtwheels Mountain Bike Club
P. O. Box 905-1102, Garsfontein 0042.

Durban Off-Road Cyclists (DORC)
P. O. Box 11463, Marine Parade 4056.

Hilton Mountain Bike Club
P. O. Box 830, Hilton 3245.

Drakensberg Mountain Bike Club
Inkosana Lodge
P. O. Box 60, Winterton 3340. Phone 03682
(ask for 3520)

Responsible Organised Mountain Pedalers (ROMP)
P. O. Box 1509, Cape Town 8000.
Phone 021-496740
Fax 021-448176

Mountain Bike Hard Ride
P. O. Box 527, Lonehill 2062. Phone 011-4651245.

The USA

In America, the **National Off-Road Bicycle Association (NORBA)** sets rules for competition, and has drawn up a code of off-road behaviour in a determined effort to prevent rifts between mountain bike riders and environmentalists. The address is:

750 East Boulder, Colorado Springs, Colorado. Phone 719-578-4717.

Britain

Britain's national organization, **The Mountain Bike Club** (which used to be called NORBA) is appropriately based at:

3 The Shrubbery, Albert Street, St. Georges, Telford, Shropshire TF2 9AS.

Touring organizations

South Africa

Apply to Pedal Power Associations for information on touring. All work is done by volunteers, so in some cases you may have to allow a few weeks for a reply.

Britain

The Cyclists' Touring Club (CTC)
Cotterell House, 69 Meadrow, Godalming, Surrey GU7 3HS, England. Phone 048686-7217.

This is the world's oldest and largest cyclists' organization. Its paid-up members have access to the most comprehensive bike touring information service in existence. This includes information on touring in Britain and abroad, lists of bike hirers, repair shops, low-cost accommodation and a great deal more. CTC district associations organize weekend rides and longer tours in Britain and other parts of the world. Members enjoy insurance benefits and are entitled to camping carnets — documents giving the holders access to the facilities of touring clubs in most countries.

If you write to the CTC, allow a few weeks for them to reply and enclose a self-addressed envelope; they ask for international reply coupons (in lieu of stamps), but you'll have to explain that our post offices don't supply them.

The USA

America has a great number of bike touring organizations. Here are the two main ones:

League of American Wheelmen

Suite 209, 6707 Whitestone Road, Baltimore, MD 21207, USA. Phone 301-944-3399.

The League of American Wheelmen (LAW), a national organization of bicyclists was founded in 1880. It protects the rights and promotes the interests of cyclists, provides information for its members and others, serves a nationwide network of affiliated bicycling clubs and sponsors bicycling activities. The League's *Bicycle USA Almanac* issue is packed with information on routes, climate, accommodation and more, and includes a calendar of forthcoming recreational events.

Bikecentennial

P. O. Box 8308, Missoula, MT 59807, USA.

Bikecentennial has developed a nationwide network of well researched routes and mapped about 25 600 kilometres of touring routes in the USA. Members get discounts on equipment and accommodation, and a wealth of touring information, not only in the USA but in many other countries all over the world, much of it in *The Cyclists' Yellow Pages*. Bikecentennial helps cyclists find touring companions. They publish a magazine, *Bike Report*, nine times a year.

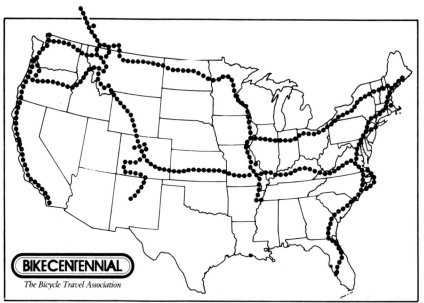

BIKECENTENNIAL'S NATIONAL BICYCLE TRAIL NETWORK

The Touring Cyclists' Hospitality Directory

13623 Sylvan, Van Nuys, California 91401, USA.

In return for making their own homes or lawns available to touring cyclists wanting a bed or place to camp, applicants are given a list of people who'll provide hospitality to cycle tourists (in the USA and Canada).

Canada

Canadian Cycling Association

1600 James Naismith Drive, Suite 810, Gloucester, Ontario, K1B 5N4, Canada. Phone 613-7485629.

The CCA is the largest distributor of bicycle touring information for all Canadian provinces.

Australia

Australian Cycle Trails
P. O. Box 57, Broadway, NSW 20007, Australia.

Bicycle Institute of Victoria
50 Stirling Street, Footscray, Victoria 3011.

The BIV's touring information service is one of its many activities. It's affiliated to several cycling clubs.

Pedal Power (ACT) Inc.
P. O. Box E 305, Canberra City, ACT 2600.

This is an active cyclists' pressure group which has a touring section and a magazine with a comprehensive touring calendar.

New Zealand

Dunedin Cyclists' Coalition
20 Gillespie Street, Dunedin, New Zealand.

Europe

Most of the organizations in Europe publish their information in their own languages. We recommend that you use Nicholas Crane's book, *Cycling in Europe*, which gives detailed information on riding in 16 countries. See the list of books in this Appendix.

Countries not listed here

The **Cyclists' Touring Club** helps members with information on most countries in the world. (It's listed under the heading 'Britain'.)

Commercial bike tours

Abracadabra Tours
Pickering's Cycles, Shop 10, The Link Centre, Main Road, Claremont (Cape Town) 7700.
Phone 021-616102 (office hours), or 616368 after business hours.

Run by Bruce Pickering-Dunn, who in his years as leader of the popular Newlands Pool Sunday Morning Rides shepherded countless novices into confident touring, Abracadabra Tours are known for good routes, good food, good humour. A support vehicle accompanies tours. Regular tours include the following:

- Cape Town to Plettenberg Bay. Six days' riding, three days' camping at the sea. December/January.
- Winelands Tour. Six days. March, after Argus Tour.
- Langkloof/Garden Route. Six days, late summer.
- Eastern Transvaal. Nine days in spring.
- Spring Tour, southern Cape coast.

Other trips are organized on request.

The River Rafters
P. O. Box 14, Diep River (Cape Town) 7856. Phone 021-725094/5.

Tours combine rafting and mountain biking in the Cedarberg area in winter; mountain bike tours are organized in the Knysna forest area in summer. Cannondale bikes, all food and equipment and support vehicles are supplied.

Breede River Adventures
24 Roslyn Road, or P. O. Box 80, Rondebosch 7700. Phone 021-6898728/9.

Two and three-day mountain bike tours, some combining canoeing in the southern Cape. Cannondale bikes are provided.

Maps

The Chief Directorate of Surveys and Mapping supplies 1:50 000, 1:250 000, 1:500 000, and smaller scale maps; the medium-scale maps show fences, tracks, waterholes and other details that mountain bikers in particular will find valuable. A free index map shows the full range published. The maps are available from:

The Government Printer
Bosman Street, (or Private Bag X85), Pretoria. Phone 012-3239731.

The Chief Directorate: Surveys and Mapping
Rhodes Avenue, (or Private Bag 7705) Mowbray 7700. Phone 021-6854070.

Selected maps are available from The Surveyor-General, Aliwal Street, Private Bag X20634, Bloemfontein, phone 051-479181, and from The Surveyor-General, 300 Pietermaritz Street, P. O. Box 396, Pietermaritzburg, phone 0331-51215.

Maps of **Transkei** are available from The Surveyor-General, Private Bag X5031, Umtata 5100, Transkei.

In **Britain**, Ordnance Survey and Bartholomew's maps are widely available in book shops; these come in a good range of scales. If you want them for advance planning, the addresses are:

Ordnance Survey, Romsey Road, Maybush, Southampton SO9 4DH, England and J. Bartholomew and Son Ltd, 12 Duncan Street, Edinburgh EH9 1TA, Scotland.

In **Europe** the excellent Michelin maps are available in a range of scales.

Map Studio, Dumbarton House, 1 Church Street, Cape Town 8000 stock a range of local and foreign maps, including the maps that have been mentioned.

Nature Conservation Authorities, Forestry Departments, etc.

Hikers' guides are good sources of information on what areas are suitable for touring on mountain bikes. (Few mention cycling, but they give you an idea of what the area is like and they tell you who to contact for permission to go into it.) You should also be able to get information from your local Nature Conservation Department, National Parks Board office or Forestry Department. Their addresses and phone numbers are listed under Environment Affairs in the Government Departments section at the back of phone directories. The addresses of main offices are listed here.

South Africa

The National Parks Board
P. O. Box 787, Pretoria 0001.

Chief Directorate: Nature and Environmental Conservation
Cape Provincial Administration, Private Bag 9086, Cape Town 8000.

Division of Nature and Environmental Conservation
Transvaal Provincial Administration, Private Bag X209, Pretoria 0001.

Natal Parks Board
P. O. Box 662, Pietermaritzburg 3200. Phone 0331-471961.

Director-General, Environment Affairs
Private Bag X447, Pretoria 0001.

Ciskei

Department of Tourism, Private Bag 0026, Bisho.

Bophuthatswana

National Parks and Wildlife Management Board, Private Bag X2078, Mafikeng 8670. Phone 01401-24114/5/6/7.

Lebowa

Department of Environmental Conservation, Private Bag X01, Chuniespoort 0745.

Malawi

Department of Tourism, P. O. Box 402, Blantyre.
Ministry of Forestry and Natural Resources, Mulanje Mountain, P. O. Box 50, Mulanje.

Department of National Parks and Wildlife, P. O. Box 30131, Lilongwe 3.

Namibia

Directorate of Nature Conservation and Recreation Resorts, Private Bag 13306, Windhoek 9000.

Transkei

Department of Forestry and Agriculture, Private Bag X50002, Umtata.

Zimbabwe

Zimbabwe Tourist Development Corporation, P. O. Box 8052, Causeway, Zimbabwe.
Phone 793666/7/8/9.

(or Tourism House, corner Stanley Avenue/Fourth Street, Harare.)

Accommodation

Struik Publishers in Cape Town publish the following useful guides in English and Afrikaans:

Guide to Holiday Houses in Southern Africa
This includes a variety that ranges from huts in nature reserves to plush private homes.

Guide to Caravan Parks in Southern Africa
Many of the camp sites listed offer accommodation in simple but well-equipped huts.

Guide to Hotels in Southern Africa.

The Youth Hostels Association

606 Boston House, Strand Street, Cape Town 8001. Phone 021-4191853.

South Africa has only about five Youth Hostels. They are in built-up areas and therefore less useful to bike tourers than those in many other countries. But they are comfortable and good value. Membership of the Association here entitles you to use Youth Hostels all over the world. There are hundreds in Britain, Europe, the USA and other countries. Many are in lovely rural areas, and after camping, offer the least expensive accommodation you can get. Regulations vary; most take people of any age but expect them to bring sheet sleep sacks and to do their own cooking and cleaning.

Here are the addresses of the American and British Youth Hostels Associations:

American Youth Hostels Inc.
P. O. Box 37613, Washington DC 20013-7613, USA. Phone 202-783-6161.

The Youth Hostels Association (Britain)
Trevelyan House, 8 St. Stephen's Hill, St. Alban's, Herts AL1 2DY England. Phone 0727-55215.
Their Travel and Services Department is at 14 Southampton Street, London, WC2.

Racing

The South African Cycling Federation
P. O. Box 4843, Cape Town 8000.

The SACF is affiliated to the SA Olympic and National Games Association and to the SA Confederation of Sport. It is the governing body for local cycle racing. Their mouthpiece is the monthly journal, *Tri-Cycling*. The following regional associations are affiliated to the SACF:

Border Cycling Association
P. O. Box 1343, East London 5200.

Eastern Province Cycling Association
P. O. Box 2362, North End 6056.

Griqualand West Cycling Federation
33 Drakensberg Street, Carters Glen, Kimberley 8301.

Natal Cycling Union
P. O. Box 596, Pietermaritzburg 3200.

Northern Natal Cycling Union
P. O. Box 9043, Newcastle 2940.

Northern OFS Cycling Association
P. O. Box 1197, Welkom 9460.

Orange Free State Cycling Association
60 De Bruyn Street, Universitas, Bloemfontein 9322.

Northern Transvaal Cycling Union
5 Eileen Street, Kilner Park, Pretoria 0186.

SA Defence Force Cycling Association
P. O. Box 913316, Voortrekkerhoogte 0143.

Southern Transvaal Cycling Union
P. O. Box 10636, Johannesburg 2000.

Western Province Cycling Association
P. O. Box 202, Table View 7439.

Western Transvaal Cycling Union
37 Henry Street, Risiville, Vereeniging 1939.

National BMX
4 Datchet Place, New Germany 3610.

Off-Road Mountain Bike Association
P. O. Box 1511, Parklands 2121, Fax 011-4042129

Planning for bicycles

Friends of the Earth
26 Underwood Street, London N1 7JQ, England.

This environmental pressure group is part of a world-wide federation. Bicycling issues are high on its agenda and its energetic campaigns have done much to bring cyclists' needs to the attention of authorities, often with positive results. Their *Bicycle Planning Book* by Mike Hudson sets out useful guidelines.

Cycle Campaign Network
London Cycling Campaign, Tress House, 3 Stamford Street, London SE1.

The LCC's determined and intelligently-fought campaigns for better facilities have made some impressive headway against conservative planners.

National Transport Commission, South Africa.
Guidelines for the Planning and Design of Bicycle Facilities in Urban Areas, 2nd edition. J.C. Vorster.

Books

The books listed here were available locally at the time of going to press. If your local bookseller can't supply or order titles that you want, **Technical Books** has a mail order service and will import individual copies of books. The address is P. O. Box 2866, Cape Town 8000. Phone 021-216540.

The first two books listed are bicyclists' bibles, and are sufficiently different from each other to make it worth owning both:

Richard's Bicycle Book
by Richard Ballantine
published by Pan

Entertaining and practical, this paperback is packed with useful information on a vast range of topics. Ballantine's views on the bikes's social and ecological value are nearly always convincing, sometimes controversial but never dull. His well-organized maintenance and repair section is thorough and clearly illustrated.

The Penguin Bicycle Handbook
by Rob van der Plas
published by Penguin

One of the most comprehensive bike books around, this concise and authoritative paperback lives up to its claim of being a 'definitive manual on how to use your bicycle to its greatest advantage'. The author, an engineer, writes with level-headed clarity about a wide range of cycling topics but concentrates on the mechanics of bikes and gives well-illustrated step-by-step guidelines to doing simple and advanced maintenance and repair jobs.

Richard's New Bicycle Book
by Richard Ballantine
published by The Oxford Illustrated Press, UK

A hardback, de-luxe revised edition of the paperback. The witty selection of illustrations looks great in this version.

The Penguin Book of the Bicycle
by Roderick Watson and Martin Gray
published by Penguin, UK

This is a fascinating overview of the bicycle revival, with emphasis on the bike in social, historical and environmental contexts.

The Complete Book of Bicycling
by Eugene A. Sloane
published by Simon & Schuster Inc., New York

Popular and very comprehensive, this gives up-to-date information on technology, cycling and health, and a lot more.

Roadside Bicycle Repairs
by Rob van der Plas
published by Bicycle Books, San Francisco

Step by step instructions are contained in a slim, light, pocket-sized book.

Anybody's Bike Book (Third edition)
by Tom Cuthbertson
published by Ten Speed Press, USA

This is a jokey, down-to-earth, popular repair manual.

Mountain Biking
by Max Glaskin and Jeremy Torr
published by Pelham Books (Published by Penguin), Britain

This is a practical and motivating introduction to a new sport, but quite a lot of the information applies specifically to Britain.

Eugene A. Sloane's Complete Book of All-Terrain Bicycles
by Eugene A. Sloane
published by Simon & Schuster Inc., USA

The book features road-tested research and statistics on choosing, riding and maintaining all-terrain bikes.

Richard's Mountain Bike Book
by Nicholas Crane
published by Oxford Ilustrated Press, UK

We haven't seen it, but both the author and publisher are known for their outstanding bike books.

On Your Bicycle: An Illustrated History of Cycling
by James McGurn
published by John Murray, UK

This is a superbly researched, well-illustrated and witty history of bikes and the people who have made and ridden them.

The CTC Route Guide to Cycling in Britain and Ireland
by Nicholas Crane and Christa Gausden
published by Penguin, UK

This is the Cyclists' Touring Club's official guide. It contains 365 interlinking routes chosen for beauty, interest and safe roads.

Cycling in Europe
by Nicholas Crane
published by The Oxford Illustrated Press, UK

A meticulously researched and very readable guide to touring in 16 countries, packed with information on routes, accommodation, weather, repair shops and a lot more.

Cycle Racing: Training to Win (Revised edition)
by Les Woodland
Pelham Books (published by Penguin), UK

Woodland describes himself as a failed racer who's tried more crackpot schedules than anybody. He is, in fact, a respected British Cycling Federation coach and his book is a mine of well-tested and valuable information delivered in forthright, easy language.

Cycle Racing
by Frank Westell and Ken Evans
published by Springfield Books UK

A definitive book on racing.

Magazines and other publications

Most of the magazines on this list can be ordered through your local newsagent. We've given addresses in case you prefer to subscribe.

Pedal Power
68 Waterfall Avenue, Craighall 2196.

The lively and friendly quarterly journal of the Southern and Northern Transvaal Pedal Power Associations; its general articles make it of interest to a wider readership.

Tri-Cycling
P O Box 32083, Braamfontein 2017. Phone 011-887650

Launched on 1 September 1989, this full colour magazine is published monthly and is the new mouthpiece of the S.A Cycling Federation. Triathlon sports are included, but the emphasis is on cycling.

Cycle S A
P O Box 14461, Kenwyn 7790. Phone 021-222037
A bi-monthly magazine concentrating on the fun side of cycling and covering racing as well.

Cycling Science
P. O. Box 1510, Mount Shasta, California 96067, USA.
A new magazine edited by Chester Kyle and Edmund Burke and written by engineers, designers, industrialists, coaches, trainers and inventors who originate the cutting edge of cycling technology.

Bicycling
33 E. Minor Street, Emmaus, PA 18049 USA.
Aimed mainly at a youngish readership of fast recreational cyclists with dollars. Articles on fitness, technical matters, technique, and buyers' guides predominate.

Mountain Bike
P. O. Box 989, Crested Bute, Colorado 81224, USA.
Mountain bike equipment, technique, touring and competition.

Bicycle
Bicycle Subscriptions Department, Competition House, Farndon Road, Market Harborough, Leics., LE16 9NR, England.
This attractive, witty and useful magazine is aimed at commuters, tourers, mountain bikers and racers.

Winning
1524 Linden Street, Allentown, PA 18102, USA.
Bursting with exciting colour photographs, *Winning* covers road racing and competitive mountain biking in the US and abroad. Mainly news value.

Frame builders

Francois du Toit
Lejeune Cycle Manufacturers, P.O. Box 772, Bellville 7535. Phone 021-941 266.
Trained by Lejeune in France, du Toit specializes in hand-built racing and touring bikes. He repairs, renovates and modifies existing frames and builds bicycle and tandem frames to customers' specifications. He carries a full range of Reynolds, Oria and Columbus tubing. Orders for his bicycles are usually placed through dealers.

Gotty Hansen
Hansom Cycles, P. O. Box 564, Hammanskraal, Bophutatswana. Phone 01464-2554 or 3671.
Gotty Hansen trained at Peugeot Cycles in France. He specializes in the middle to upper range of bicycles but has been versatile enough to make a tricycle for a paraplegic, a racing wheelchair and a cycle for six riders. He builds frames to customers' specifications and stocks a range of tubing. Orders are usually placed through dealers.

Appropriate technology

Institute for Transport and Development Technology
Box 56538, Washington DC 20011, USA.

One of the ITDP's concerns is with developing transport technologies that are ecologically sound as well as practical in First and Third World conditions. Bicycles and other pedal-powered technologies feature high on their list of priorities. Their Board of Directors has an excitingly broad range of people from all over the world and includes David Gordon Wilson of the Massachusetts Institute of Technology and James McCullagh, editor of *Bicycling* magazine. Their 'Bikes for Africa' project is providing bicycles and technical assistance to development groups in Mozambique.

A pedal-powered washing machine and/or grape press.
Illustration by Gus Ferguson.

Gear table (metric)

Number of teeth on front chainwheel	Number of teeth on rear sprocket																				
	12	13	14	15	16	17	18	19	20	21	22	23	24	25	26	27	28	29	30	31	32
35	6,23	5,75	5,34	4,98	4,67	4,39	4,15	3,83	3,73	3,56	3,39	3,25	3,11	2,99	2,87	2,76	2,67	2,57	2,49	2,41	2,33
36	6,40	5,91	5,49	5,12	4,80	4,52	4,27	4,04	3,84	3,66	3,49	3,34	3,20	3,07	2,95	2,84	2,74	2,65	2,56	2,48	2,40
37	6,58	6,07	5,64	5,26	4,93	4,64	4,39	4,15	3,95	3,76	3,59	3,43	3,29	3,16	3,03	2,92	2,82	2,72	2,63	2,54	2,46
38	6,76	6,24	5,79	5,41	5,07	4,77	4,50	4,27	4,05	3,84	3,68	3,52	3,38	3,24	3,12	3,00	2,89	2,79	2,70	2,61	2,53
39	6,94	6,40	5,94	5,55	5,20	4,90	4,62	4,38	4,16	3,96	3,78	3,62	3,47	3,33	3,20	3,08	2,97	2,81	2,77	2,68	2,60
40	7,12	6,57	6,10	5,69	5,34	5,02	4,74	4,50	4,27	4,07	3,88	3,71	3,56	3,42	3,28	3,16	3,05	2,94	2,83	2,75	2,66
41	7,30	6,73	6,25	5,84	5,47	5,15	4,86	4,60	4,37	4,17	3,98	3,80	3,64	3,50	3,36	3,24	3,11	3,01	2,92	2,81	2,75
42	7,47	6,90	6,40	5,98	5,60	5,27	4,98	4,72	4,48	4,27	4,07	3,90	3,73	3,58	3,45	3,33	3,20	3,09	2,98	2,88	2,79
43	7,65	7,06	6,56	6,12	5,74	5,40	5,10	4,83	4,59	4,37	4,17	3,99	3,82	3,67	3,53	3,39	3,28	3,16	3,05	2,96	2,86
44	7,83	7,23	6,71	6,26	5,87	5,52	5,22	4,94	4,70	4,47	4,27	4,08	3,91	3,76	3,61	3,48	3,35	3,24	3,13	3,03	2,92
45	8,01	7,39	6,68	6,40	6,00	5,65	5,34	5,05	4,80	4,57	4,37	4,18	4,00	3,84	3,69	3,56	3,43	3,30	3,20	3,09	3,01
46	8,18	7,55	7,01	6,55	6,14	5,78	5,45	5,17	4,91	4,67	4,46	4,27	4,09	3,93	3,78	3,62	3,50	3,39	3,26	3,16	3,07
47	8,36	7,72	7,17	6,69	6,27	5,90	5,57	5,28	5,02	4,78	4,56	4,36	4,18	4,01	3,86	3,71	3,58	3,45	3,35	3,24	3,13
48	8,54	7,88	7,32	6,83	6,40	6,03	5,69	5,39	5,12	4,88	4,66	4,45	4,27	4,10	3,94	3,80	3,65	3,54	3,41	3,28	3,20
49	8,72	8,05	7,47	6,97	6,54	6,15	5,81	5,50	5,23	4,98	4,75	4,55	4,36	4,18	4,02	3,86	3,73	3,60	3,48	3,37	3,26
50	8,90	8,21	7,63	7,12	6,67	6,28	5,93	5,62	5,34	5,08	4,85	4,64	4,45	4,27	4,10	3,94	3,80	3,67	3,56	3,43	3,33
51	9,07	8,38	7,78	7,26	6,81	6,40	6,05	5,73	5,44	5,18	4,95	4,73	4,54	4,35	4,19	4,03	3,88	3,75	3,62	3,52	3,39
52	9,25	8,54	7,93	7,40	6,94	6,53	6,17	5,84	5,55	5,29	5,04	4,83	4,62	4,44	4,27	4,12	3,92	3,82	3,69	3,58	3,45
53	9,43	8,70	8,08	7,54	7,07	6,66	6,29	5,95	5,66	5,39	5,14	4,92	4,71	4,52	4,35	4,18	4,03	3,90	3,77	3,65	3,51
54	9,61	8,87	8,23	7,69	7,20	6,78	6,40	6,07	5,76	5,49	5,24	5,01	4,80	4,61	4,43	4,27	4,12	3,97	3,84	3,71	3,60
55	9,78	9,03	8,39	7,83	7,34	6,91	6,52	6,10	5,87	5,59	5,34	5,10	4,89	4,69	4,51	4,34	4,19	4,05	3,91	3,79	3,66
56	9,97	9,20	8,54	7,97	7,47	7,03	6,64	6,29	5,98	5,69	5,43	5,20	4,98	4,78	4,60	4,41	4,27	4,12	3,99	3,86	3,73
57	10,14	9,35	8,68	8,11	7,62	7,15	6,76	6,40	6,08	5,78	5,53	5,29	5,06	4,86	4,67	4,50	4,33	4,20	4,05	3,92	3,80
58	10,31	9,52	8,83	8,26	7,286	7,72	6,87	6,51	6,19	5,89	5,63	5,38	5,16	4,95	4,76	4,59	4,41	4,27	4,12	3,99	3,86
59	10,50	9,69	8,98	8,39	7,87	7,40	7,00	6,64	6,29	5,99	5,72	5,48	5,25	5,03	4,84	4,67	4,50	4,33	4,20	4,05	3,92
60	10,67	9,86	9,15	8,54	8,01	7,53	7,11	6,74	6,40	6,10	5,82	5,57	5,33	5,12	4,93	4,73	4,56	4,41	4,27	4,12	3,99

The table above is for 27-inch (700 mm) wheels. The figures in the boxes tell you how far a bike goes for each turn of the pedals. To calculate gear ratios in inches, multiply the number of teeth on the front chainwheel by the wheel diameter (measured in inches), and divide your answer by the number of teeth on the rear sprocket.

Aerodynamics: measuring drag coefficients

When trying to reduce air drag it is useful to be able to measure the drag force. This is best done in a properly equipped wind tunnel — which is expensive and a remote option for most of us. However, some inexpensive methods have been devised, which may possibly give better results!

The coefficient of drag, C_d, is simply a ratio which shows how the drag of a particular shape compares to that of a flat plate of equal area, A, held at right angles to the airstream. Consider three concepts of the same idea:

C_d concept 1: Ping-pong bat

Suppose that you have a thin, circular ping-pong bat with a very thin handle. As you make a forearm stroke you will feel the air resistance. Call that retarding force *one unit*. Now make a scale model of your machine so that its frontal area is the same as the bat, and move it through the air at the same speed. Suppose that the drag force is now half: the drag coefficient of your machine is 0,5.

C_d concept 2: Disturbed wake

Suppose that you could measure the cross-sectional area of the disturbed wake behind your machine, about a third of the machine length behind. And suppose that the cross-sectional area of the disturbed wake is half the frontal area: the drag coefficient of your machine is 0,5.

C_d concept 3: Scientific definition.

Below 150 kilometres an hour the drag coefficient of the body is proportional to the drag force divided by the product of the frontal area and the dynamic pressure of air.

$$C_d = \frac{D}{A \times \text{dynamic pressure}} \qquad \text{where dynamic pressure} = \frac{\text{air density}(\rho) \times \text{air speed}^2\ (v^2)}{2}$$

By juggling these equations around a little one can show that $\qquad D = A \times C_d \times v^2 \times \dfrac{\rho}{2}$

D is the total drag force in newtons.
A is the frontal area in square metres
C_d is the coefficient of drag — a number.
ρ is the density of air in kilograms per cubic metre.
v is the air speed in metres per second.

The two factors which determine the performance of a shape are frontal area, A, and drag coefficient, C_d. Since some shapes are more streamlined, while others are smaller, the product of these two values, C_dA, is often used for comparing shapes and is called the *effective frontal area*.

x (per cent c)	y (per cent c)
0	0
0,5	1,525
0,75	1,804
1,25	2,240
2,5	3,045
5,0	4,269
7,5	5,233
10	6,052
15	7,369
20	8,376
25	9,153
30	9,738
35	0,154
40	10,407
45	10,500
50	10,434
55	10,186
60	9,692
65	8,793
70	7,610
75	6,251
80	4,796
85	3,324
90	1,924
95	0,717
100	0

L.E. radius: 2,550 per cent c

NACA 66₁-021 Basic Thickness Form

Left: Co-ordinates for symmetrical airfoils. The shape can be scaled thicker or thinner by multiplying the y values by a constant.

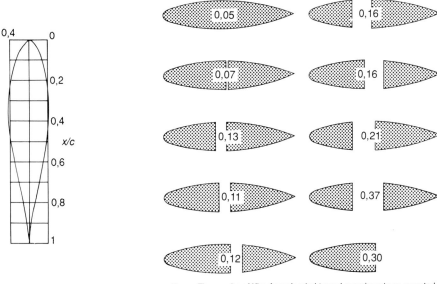

Above: The results of Kim Aaron's wind tunnel experiments as reported in the *First HPV Scientific Symposium*, 1981. Notice the high penalty for interrupting the surface: the complete shape has one-sixth the drag of the front half alone. Openings for wheels, feet, head or ventilation result in drag penalties of such magnitudes.

What do low-drag shapes look like?

Photos of streamlined HPVs can be found in Chapter 9. In this section the aerodynamic drag of ordinary bicycles, theoretical shapes and record-breaking streamliners are illustrated.

AERODYNAMIC DRAG

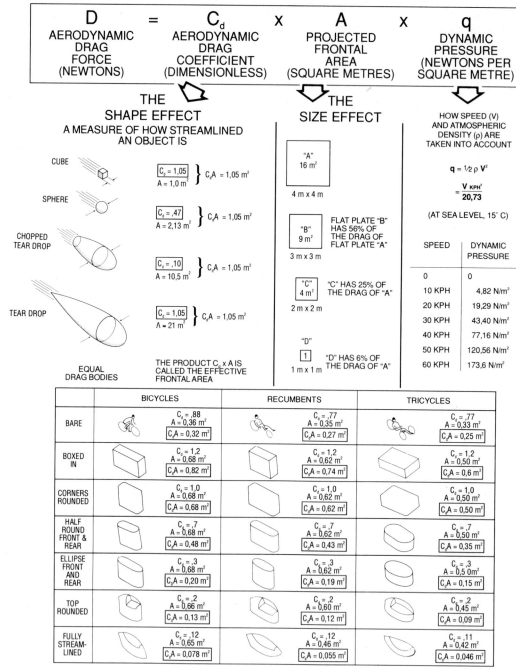

© 1983 Douglas Malewicki

Some simple geometric shapes, their drag coefficients and the idea of *effective frontal area* are shown here. Simple shapes for complete fairings for standard bicycles, supine recumbent bicycles and supine recumbent tricycles are tabulated to show how their C_dA values compare.

HUMAN POWERED VEHICLE PERFORMANCE

DESCRIPTION	AERODYNAMIC DATA				ROLLING RESISTANCE CO-EFFICIENT C_r	GROUND LEVEL, NO WINDS			EFFECT OF HILLS	
AIR	FORCES AT 32 KPH NEWTONS AIR (SEA LEVEL) ROLLING	DRAG COEFFICIENT C_d	FRONTAL AREA (M²) A	EFFECTIVE FRONTAL AREA (M²) C_dA		POWER REQUIRED AT 32 KPH AS A PERCENTAGE OF THE TOURING (ARMS STRAIGHT) BICYCLIST	ALL DAY TOURING SPEED AT 75 WATTS POWER OUTPUT (KPH)	MAXIMUM SPEED WITH 750 WATTS POWER OUTPUT (KPH)	STEADY SPEED UP A 5% GRADE AT 300 WATTS POWER OUTPUT (KPH)	STEADY SPEED COASTING DOWN A 5% GRADE (KPH)
STANDARD BICYCLES										
BMX (YOUTH OFF ROAD RACER) 13,7 KG BIKE 55 KG RIDER 51 cm DIA, 40PSI KNOBBY TYRES	24,55 / 9,34	1,1	0,45	0,50	0,014	146%	16,3	44,7	19,6	31,7
EUROPEAN UPRIGHT COMMUTER 18 KG BIKE 73 KG RIDER 69 cm DIA, 40PSI TYRES	27,31 / 5,34	1,1	0,51	0,55	0,006	140%	18,2	44,4	17,5	38,6
TOURING (ARMS STRAIGHT) 11 KG BIKE 73 KG RIDER 69 cm DIA, 90PSI CLINCHER TYRES	19,57 / 3,69	1,0	0,40	0,40	0,0045	100%	21,1	50,0	19,6	44,6
RACING (FULLY CROUCHED) 9 KG BIKE 73 KG RIDER 69 cm DIA, 105PSI SEWUP TYRES	15,48 / 2,40	0,88	0,36	0,31	0,003	77%	23,6	54,5	20,9	50,2
IMPROVED PRODUCTION										
AEROCOMPONENT (FULLY CROUCHED) 9 KG BIKE 73 KG RIDER 69 cm DIA, 105PSI SEWUP TYRES	14,55 / 2,40	0,83	0,36	0,30	0,003	73%	24,1	55,7	20,9	51,8
PARTIAL FAIRING (ZZIPPER CROUCHED) 9,5 KG BIKE 73 KG RIDER 69 cm DIA, 105PSI SEWUP TYRES	13,21 / 2,40	0,70	0,38	0,27	0,003	67%	24,8	57,4	21,1	54,5
RECUMBENT (EASY RACER) 12 KG BIKE 73 KG RIDER 69 cm REAR 51 cm FRONT SEWUP TYRES	13,21 / 4,18	0,77	0,35	0,29	0,005	75%	23,2	56,6	20,1	54,2
TANDEM 19 KG BIKE TWO 146 KG RIDERS 69 cm DIA, 90PSI CLINCHERS (83 KG PER PERSON)	23,66 / 7,21	1,0	0,48	0,48 (2,4 PER PERSON)	0,0045	66%	24,5	58,9	20,9	56,6
DRAFTING CLOSELY FOLLOWING ANOTHER BICYCLIST 9 KG BIKE 73 KG RIDER 69 cm DIA, 105PSI SEWUP TYRES	8,63 / 2,40	0,50	0,36	0,18	0,003	47%	28,2	70,0	21,9	67,1
RECORD HPVs										
BLUE BELL 2 WHEELED SINGLE RIDER 18 KG BIKE 73 KG RIDER 69 cm REAR 51 cm FRONT 105 PSI SEWUPS	2,71 / 3,56	0,12	0,46	0,055	0,004	27%	36,2	94,3	20,8	124,5
KYLE 2 WHEELED 2 RIDERS 24 KG BIKE TWO 73 + 73 KG RIDERS 105 psi SEWUPS (83 KG PER PERSON)	6,41 / 4,98	0,2	0,65	0,13 (0,065 PER PERSON)	0,003	24%	37,5	91,1	22,5	112,5
VECTOR SINGLE TRIKE 31 KG BIKE 73 KG RIDER SEWUPS 69 cm REAR 51 cm FRONT	2,27 / 4,54	0,11	0,42	0,046	0,0045	29%	35,1	98,5	18,2	145,0
VECTOR TANDEM TRIKE 34 KG BIKE TWO RIDERS 73 + 73 KGS 61 cm SEWUPS (90 KG PER PERSON)	2,76 / 7,92	0,13	0,43	0,055 (0,028 PER PERSON)	0,0045	23%	41,2	116,7	20,9	174,4
THEORETICAL LIMITS										
PERFECT BIKE NO ROLLING RESISTANCE ZERO DRAG ON ENTIRE BIKE DRAG OF HUMAN ONLY IN TOURING POSITION.	13,66 / 0	0,8	0,35	0,28	0	59%	26,9	57,8	21,6	55,8
DRAGLESS HUMAN ZERO DRAG ON HUMAN DRAG OF BIKE ONLY ROLLING RESISTANCE INCLUDES HUMAN'S WEIGHT	5,92 / 3,60	1,1	0,11	0,12	0,0045	41%	29,6	73,7	21,4	80,9
PERFECT RECUMBENT DRAG ON FLAT ON BACK HUMAN ONLY.	3,20 / 0	0,6	0,11	0,065	0	14%	43,6	93,8	27,0	107,6
PERFECT PRONE BIKE DRAG ON 50 KG SMALL BUT POWERFUL HUMAN ONLY	2,27 / 0	0,6	0,074	0,046	0	10%	48,9	105,1	37,3	105,1
PERFECT PRONE STREAMLINER	0,21 / 0	0,05	0,13	0,0065	0	1%	93,8	202,6	41,2	280,8
MOTOR PACED 19 KG 73 KG (VEHICLE BREAKS AIR FOR RIDER) 70 PSI MOTORCYCLE ROAD RACING TYRES	0 / 5,38	—	—	VARIES WITH SPEED NEGATIVE OVER 160 KPH	0,006	23%	47,3	473,0	20,3	∞
MOON BIKE 1/6 g ENVIRONMENT 11 KG 73 KG 6,8 kg SPACE SUIT 69 cm DIA 90 PSI CLINCHERS	0 / 0,67	—	—	0	0,0045	3%	382,1	3820	126,1	∞

© Douglas Malewicki

A table of human powered vehicle performance, showing ordinary bicycles, record-breaking streamliners, theoretical shapes and their theoretical performance in still air over level ground, as well as up and down a 5 per cent gradient, on earth, on the moon and in space!

Three methods of measuring drag coefficient

Method A: Balance bar (for scale models of full fairings)

Make a 1/5-scale model of your machine out of EPS (expanded polystyrene). Measure the frontal area and cut a square (or circle) of stiff cardboard with the same area. Make a cardboard sleeve and glue it to the centre back of the cardboard square. Mark the middle of a 3-millimetre diameter dowel stick. Slide the square onto one end of the dowel. Push the other end of the dowel through the polystyrene model at right angles to the direction of travel. Stand up on the back of a bakkie or through the sliding roof of a car and try to balance the model and square about the center of the dowel. The air speed need not be more than 20 kilometres an hour. If the distance from the center of the dowel (pivot point) to the center of the model is half the distance from the pivot to the center of the square, then the drag coefficient is 0,5.

This method depends upon model accuracy, but the model should **not** be made smoother than the finish obtained with medium-fine sandpaper. You may be able to hold it close to the roof of the car and get the effect of the road plane, but, really, the method is far too rough for that.

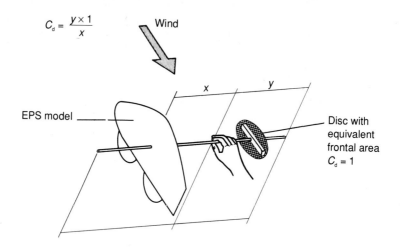

$$C_d = \frac{y \times 1}{x}$$

Method A: Balance Bar

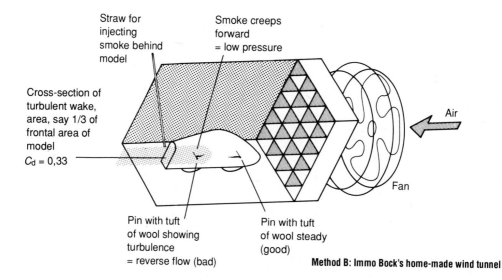

Method B: Immo Bock's home-made wind tunnel

Method B: Immo Bock's home-made wind tunnel (for scale models of full fairings)

Make a cardboard egg-crate about 0,5 m x 0,5 m x 0,1 m with about five dividers either way (see sketch). Make a floor panel and back panel, each about 0,75 m x 0,5 m and paint them black (or any dark colour). Set up a household fan to blow through the egg-crate and past the panels. Place your 1/5-scale EPS model in the airstream. Use a long straw to inject a puff of smoke in the wake behind the model to show the extent of turbulence. Observe the cross-sectional area of the turbulent wake one third of a length behind the model. This will give you an indication of the drag coefficient.

This method is useful because the model can be tested in oblique airstreams. Usually the flow around the vehicle is pretty much the same for headings up to 5 degrees left or right, and then it breaks away on the lee side, causing a rapid increase in drag. Note that when the smoke creeps up the sides of the vehicle it means that all of the surface of the vehicle in contact with the smoke is in a low pressure zone and therefore creating drag. Some shapes are better than others in their ability to work effectively in oblique winds, and devices can be used to improve the flow. This is an important aspect for a road vehicle where winds are seldom near to the direction of travel. Dr Immo Bock devised this method to test his patented *Trapezium Wings* which are fitted to caravans to reduce air drag and improve cross-wind stability.

The apparatus can also be used to detect turbulent flow by means of tufts. Glue a 50 millimetre length of cotton onto the head of a pin and stick the pin into the model so that the cotton is about 15 to 20 millimetres off the surface. The flow is excellent when the cotton is steady in the flow, and disastrous when it shows reverse flow or swirls around wildly.

Method C: Terminal speed on a constant slope (actual vehicle with rider; calm weather)

This method requires a straight length of road with a smooth surface and a constant gradient where terminal velocity can be achieved. You will need the following measurements:

- The *total weight* (newtons) of machine with rider:
  Use a bathroom scale — 11 kg + 80 kg = 91 kg × 9,8 = 891,8 N.
- The *maximum frontal area*, A, in square metres:
  See the section 'Body size' in Chapter 9 — 0,56 m^2.
- The *slope of the road* measured in per cent:
  Place a one-metre-long spirit level on the road and wedge up until level; mark off 10 metres down the road and measure the drop by sighting the spirit level — 600 mm in 10 m = 6%.
- Air temperature and *barometric pressure* for ρ in kilograms per cubic metre:
  See the section 'Air density' in Chapter 9 — 15° C and 1 017 millibars.
  1 017 millibars @ 15° C = 1 017 x 0,00129 = 1,23 kg/m^3.
- Velocity in metres per second:
  Use an on-board electronic speedometer — 54 km/h ÷ 3,6 = 15 m/sec.

We now have values for A (frontal area), ρ (air density) and v, (speed). In order to find C_d from the formula, all we need is a value for D (drag force). The total drag force, D, will be air drag plus rolling drag, which together must be equal to the driving force, F, because the speed is stable. $D = D_a + D_r = F$. The driving force is gravity acting on the mass in the direction of the slope:

$F = ma \times$ slope $F = 91$ kg $\times 9,8$ N $\times 6\%$ $F = 891,8$ N x 6% = 3,5 N = D

Since D is composed of air drag, D_a, and rolling drag, D_r, we must eliminate rolling drag:

$D_r = ma(C_r + 0,0002 V)$ where C_r is about 0,005 for high pressure tyres. (See the diagram on page 271.)

$D_r = 891,8(0,005 + 0,0002 x 15) = 891,8 x 0,008 = 7,13$ N.

Air drag **only** is therefore: $D_a = F - D_r = 53,5 - 7,13 = 46,37$ N.

We now have all the values needed to complete the calculation:

$$C_d = \frac{2 \times D_a}{A \times \rho \times v^2} = \frac{2 \times 46,37}{0,56 \times 1,23 \times 15^2} = \frac{92,74}{154,98} = 0,598$$

This method is quite popular but requires great patience waiting for calm weather and pedalling back to the top of the hill to get a number of readings. In some respects these on-road full-size rolling tests get real world results unobtainable in wind tunnels. However, wind tunnels provide controlled and repeatable tests and therefore a combination of both will always be best.

SELECT BIBLIOGRAPHY

General:

Ballantyne, Richard, *Richard's New Bicycle Book,* The Oxford Illustrated Press, 1988.
Crane, Nicholas, *Cycling in Europe,* The Oxford Illustrated Press, 1984.
Max Glaskin and Jeremy Torr, *Mountain Biking,* Pelham Books, 1988.
Sloane, Eugene A, *Complete Book of All-terrain Bicycles,* Simon and Schuster Inc., 1985.
van der Plas, Rob, *The Penguin Bicycle Handbook,* Penguin Books, 1983.
van der Plas, Rob, *The Bicycle Touring Manual,* Bicycle Books, 1987.
Watson, Roderick and Gray, Martin, *The Penguin Book of the Bicycle,* Penguin Books, 1978.

Chapter 2

The Cape Chronicle, October 1860.
Caunter, C. F., *The History and Development of Cycles,* Her Majesty's Stationery Office in conjunction with the Science Museum, London, 1955.
Gutsche, Thelma, *The History of the Wanderers Club,* Howard Timmins, Cape Town, 1966.
Hattersley, A F, An Illustrated Social History of South Africa, Balkema, Cape Town, 1969.
The Hub, 1896 -1897.
Jowett, W, *Centenary, 100 Years of Organised Cycle Racing,* S.A. Cycling Federation.
Maree, D R, *Bicycles in the Anglo-Boer War of 1899-1902,* S.A. National Museum of Military History.
McGonagle, Seamus, *The Bicycle in Love, Life, War and Literature,* Pelham Books, London, 1968.
Mecredy, R J, *The Art and Passtime of Cycling,* Mecredy and Kyle, Dublin, 1893.
Wilkinson-Latham, R, *Cycles in Colour,* Blandford Press, 1978.
Woodforde, J, *The Story of the Bicycle,* Routledge and Kegan Paul, London, 1970.

Chapter 9

Abbott, I H and von Doenhoff, A E, *Theory of Wing Sections,* Dover Publication, 1959.
International Human Powered Vehicle Association publications.
Sharp, A, *Bicycles and Tricycles,* MIT Press, 1986.
Whitt, F R and Wilson, D G, *Bicycling Science* (second Ed), MIT Press, 1982.

Chapters 10 and 11

Burke, E R (Editor), *Science of Cycling,* Human Kinetics Publishers, 1986.
Burke, E R (Editor) *Medical and Scientific Aspects of Cycling,* Human Kinetics Publishers, 1988.
Sjogaard, G, Nielsen B, Mikkelsen F, Saltin B, Burke E R, *Physiology in Bicycling,* Movement Publications, Inc.

INDEX